Voices from the Rainbow

Traci Leigh Taylor

Mother Warrior Press
Hillsboro, Oregon

Mother Warrior Press
PO Box 2953
Hillsboro, OR 97123

http://www.mommatraci.com/

Voices from the Rainbow/ Traci Leigh Taylor. -- 1st ed.
ISBN 978-0-692-26227-6

For Daniel and all who have shared their hearts with me.

Table of Contents

Poem
Introduction: Learning to Sing - Momma Traci

Part One: It takes a village
1. The path that got me here — Momma Traci 1
2. Coming to terms with who I was — Daniel Robinson 10
3. Finding each other again — Mrs. Carpenter 15
4. A place of acceptance and discovery — Kim Sandstrom . 19
5. Why couldn't I — Dawn Montgomery Ed.D................... 22

Part Two: Branches
6. Sexuality on a sliding scale — Jeremy 28
7. The Sound of High Heels — Danny 37
8. Just wish I'd done it sooner—Ryan 47

Part Three: Metamorphous
9. A family evolving — Marisa, Anthony, and Rita 54
   Singing her heart out —Marisa (Part 1) 55
   "It's Show Time!" — Anthony 62
   Supposed to feel like — Marisa (Part 2) 68
   God made them that way — Rita 73
10. I finally understood — Momma Traci 79
11. From a caterpillar to a butterfly — T.J. / Jaia 81

Part Four: Yellow Brick Road
12. Bringing Me Closer — Chad Allen 88
13. Friend of Kenny — Kevin 93
14. The Big Gay Musical — Fred M. Caruso 102
15. Back to Church — Rev Matthew 108

Part Five: Reaching Out
16. LGBTQ homeless youth center NY, Carl Siciliano 120
   I will take your acceptance—Raciel 121
   Learning to love himself—Michael 124
17. The Sexual & Gender Minority Youth Resource Center in Portland, Oregon — Momma Traci 127
   A chosen name—David 128

He could trust me—Suzie, David's mother *131*
I am me, no one else—Leo *132*
Going beyond differences—Belinda *136*

Part Six: Friendships
18. Mother and Daughter — Rochelle and Jennifer 142
    Not everyone will accept you —Rochelle *142*
    That moment was heaven—Jennifer *150*
19. Dear Abby — Durwood 154
20. Just One Tweet — Momma Traci 159
21. Am I Better Off Dead? — Paul 160
22. Finding Peace — Leo and Mario 165
    Will they ever leave me alone? — Leo *165*
    Fear of being deported—Mario *173*

Part Seven: Dear Momma Traci
23. Freedom to be me — Lee 178
24. Close your eyes and open your heart —Bridget 183
25. Not a choice — Keith 187
26. Learn and move on — Kieran 193
27. Jesus loves the Little children — Matt 196
28. I'd been lying to myself — Anthony 199
29. How things should be — Luca, Italy 205
30. Twin brothers — The Netherlands 210
    Coming out on my 18th birthday —Samuel *210*
    We never spoke about being gay —Adrian *214*

Part Eight: Unspoken Words
31. Unspoken Words — Momma Traci 220
32. Don't want to hide the truth — Wilfredo, Venezuela 221
33. Feel like a caged bird — M.C., London 226
34. Remaining closeted — Stan 230
35. Felt like a coward—Jeff 232
36. The way God made me — Gregory 235
37. Hoping not to disappoint—Trevor 245
38. So many lost years — Bear, Canada 248

Part Nine: Now I'm Really Confused

  39. Now I'm really confused — Lee and Marie 254

     In touch with feminine and masculine side —Lee 255

     What would that mean for our family? —Marie 261

  40. Didn't have a name for it — Kim Pearson,

     Trans Youth Allies 265

  41. Crawling under bus seats — Rev. David Weekley 276

  42. Making holes in fences—Darcelle XV 288

Part Ten: Over the Rainbow

  43. The bully and steps to respect—Jennifer, Elementary

     School Counselor 296

  44. Making it better for the next generation — Aaron Ridings

     Oregon Safe Schools and Communities Coallition 301

  45. The Indian way — mother and son 310

     Telling the story that would keep my secret —Raven

     Heavy Runner 310

     Toxic faith—Prairie Woman 321

  46. The funeral and miracles—Momma Traci 325

  47. The Rainbow — Momma Traci 326

Acknowledgements 327

Resource List 328

About the Author 333

The Voice

The voice pursued me all
of my life with guilt
that tightened around my throat.

Its hollow eyes haunt my
thoughts and steal my dreams.
It puts me on trial and

condemns me. I'm no good.
I'm not accepted. I'm
a disappointment. Now

that voice has become my
own and I don't know how
not to listen.

Traci Leigh Taylor 2010

Introduction:
Learning to Sing - Momma Traci

This book is the journey I have taken since my son, Daniel, came out when he was 15. I wanted to get to know this stranger I lived with; I wanted to understand him, his friends, and his world.

When he was in high school, I became "Momma Traci" to his gay and lesbian friends. I have met, interviewed, and received letters from people of all shades of the rainbow who felt safe and felt compelled to share their stories with me. This book is more than just *my* journey. This book is a collection of their songs—songs of strength, songs of freedom, many times songs of fear and oppression, but always songs of truth.

In the beginning, I wanted to call my book—*You can sing* because to me the ultimate gift was to have a beautiful voice. Now I feel brave enough only to sing out loud to my dogs and sometimes with Daniel. It wasn't until I started writing this book and examined my own life that I remembered that I loved to sing when I was a child, sitting next to my sister on the piano bench as she played. But I lost the courage to sing amidst our family turmoil.

When Daniel went away to college, he gave me a CD called, *Yes, You Can Sing!* by Pepi Lemer. It was a sign to embrace my voice and move forward with my literary dreams. My nest was empty and it was time. I took writing classes and joined a couple of writing groups.

As I look back, I can see plainly that writing this book became more than telling my friends' stories; it was my version of singing and coming out of fear.

In 2009, Daniel was touring gay and lesbian film festivals with *The Big Gay Musical*, an independent movie he starred in. He was in front of a group in Washington, D.C., doing a Q&A about the movie when he was asked once again, "How does your mom feel about you being in gay movie?" This time he said, "She loves it. In fact, she is in it. And she is writing a book about us." He called and told me about it.

That first night after his call I felt excited, but then I couldn't sleep. I had no idea where to start. Daniel suggested that I go through his school annuals, pictures, letters, and journals stored in our barn attic. I spent several days going through his boxes. I put everything into files.

Still, I felt there should be more. Daniel suggested that I talk to his friends. I got some names, a digital recorder, and a red briefcase, and I started interviewing.

Each interview opened another door to more people who were gay, lesbian, bisexual, or transgender, and to their friends and mothers. Their stories became part of me. I dug deeper and began to understand the connection between my life and those I had interviewed, and why I cared so deeply and knew their stories had to be heard.

I visited a LGBTQ homeless center in New York and a LGBTQ youth center in Portland, Oregon. Daniel posted requests on Twitter and Facebook asking for LGBTQ individuals to write me with their stories. This was the turning point. I received letters from LGBTQ people around the world revealing their struggles of coming out. Many people—not just kids—have stories to tell, and this project allowed them to express those things they have had to hold inside, their unspoken words.

From those afraid to come out, I asked for the letter they wish they could give their parents. Their letters were heartbreaking and compelling, each furthering my understanding of their deep conflicts and fears, and each illuminating my son's journey as well.

In their struggles, I revisited my own challenges and found my voice. These pages offer a glimpse into the lives of many brave people. Their transparency and authenticity are at once hopeful and inspiring. I am grateful to those who opened up to me and trusted me as their "Momma Traci."

My hope is that this book will answer questions and bring under-standing. For the parents and friends of LGBTQ individuals, may these stories illustrate how acceptance or non-acceptance affects these important people in their lives. Most of all, I hope this book will give a voice to all the songs I have heard. It is truly beautiful music.

Author's note: Some names and other details have been altered to ensure the anonymity of interviewees when requested.

Part One

It takes a village

The path that got me here — Momma Traci

Mother's Day 2012

I awoke to the clean smell of ocean air, the roar of the waves, and a bell ringing a ships' warning. Down the stairs I went, toward the aroma of fresh coffee and breakfast, and to Mother's Day gifts from my husband and daughter. A clear blue sky enticed us to a walk on the beach, with a brisk spring wind that sprinkled us with sand and billowed our jackets like sails. Renewed, but with cold hands and faces and pockets heavy with shells and rocks, we returned to our beach home to enjoy a lazy Sunday.

Amanda, my daughter, snuggled up in the papasan chair with a blanket. Her puppy curled up in her lap to sleep. My husband, Steve, and I shared the couch and a blanket as the fireplace warmed the room. We decided to watch a movie.

"Mom, you choose," Amanda said. "We'll watch whatever you want."

I pulled a folded piece of paper from my purse—my bucket list of gay movies suggested by friends: romantic comedies, dramas, and documentaries all classified under the LGBTQ section of Netflix. Those I'd already watched had lines through them with stars and notes.

While I knew my family would watch whatever movie I chose, I imagined Amanda rolling her eyes and Steve saying, "Not another gay one!" I decided on a straight movie. As *Mystic Pizza* played, I felt as if I were floating in limbo somewhere between the straight and gay world, and my mind traveled back to the path that got me here.

Daniel was born in Alaska when my son, Joseph, was eleven and Amanda was nine. We moved back to Oregon just before Daniel's first birthday to be closer to my aging parents.

When Daniel was just a toddler, I realized he was different than other boys his age. He was more sensitive, and he became very interested in "girlie" things. I found him in his sister's room when he was two years old, enthralled with dressing and play acting with her Barbie dolls. I was scared he might be gay.

These were the stereotypical qualifiers, and my son seemed to exhibit them all. I called my sister, Janet. She was living in Alaska with her second husband and two children—but she had been married before, at eighteen, to man she didn't know was gay. The marriage was short and ended badly—it turned out he had only married Janet because his psychiatrist advised him that marriage would cure his homosexuality.

Janet and I talked frequently about my "different" son, but soon my fears quieted when Daniel began to spend his days riding his red and blue Big Wheel up and down the hill. I told myself I had been overreacting. But Amanda continued to discover her dolls in Daniel's room, and he still appeared proudly in front of us dressed in girls' clothes.

When Daniel was four, he wanted a Cabbage Patch Doll for Christmas. Despite my hesitation and his father's dismay, I bought him a male Cabbage Patch Doll dressed in a camouflage shirt, pants, and hat. "Buddy" became Daniel's constant companion.

The relationship between a stepparent and stepchildren can put a strain on a marriage. My older children and my husband fought constantly which drove my husband and me apart. Soon after Daniel started kindergarten, my husband and I divorced and agreed to share custody of our son.

Daniel's dad soon remarried. His new wife had three boys of her own, all close to Daniel's age. Daniel and his father begged me to let him live with them. I gave in and gave my ex custody.

That was the biggest mistake I ever made. At first, Daniel was happy having young brothers at home, instead of living with two teenagers with me. Within a year, though, problems arose between Daniel, his new brothers, and his stepmother.

I was working as a representative for a company that manufactured craft products and was often traveling. Daniel spent every other weekend with me, always ending with him crying all the way back to his father's place on Sunday night. I would play a cassette tape of Bobby McFerrin's "Don't Worry Be Happy" in the car to console him, but even today Daniel says that song makes him sad as he remembers that long ride home.

If I could go back in time, I would have turned my car around the first time he cried. I would have fought sooner to get him back.

By the third year, Daniel's unhappiness had escalated. I quit my job and sought full custody of Daniel. His father didn't fight me. I bought some red cowboy boots and got a job working in advertising at a country radio station.

For the next several years, Daniel had problems making friends in school and was often picked on. I tried getting him involved in t-ball, but most games ended in tears. Daniel wanted to take dance lessons, but I worried he would get picked on even more. I enrolled Daniel in karate but just before class, suspicious headaches and stomachaches kept him home. He was happiest creating dance videos of himself with the used movie camera I bought him for his birthday.

But he was miserable in school. At parent-teacher conferences, his teacher scowled as she told me he had problems fitting in with the other boys. She suggested counseling.

Working at the radio station was a lot of hours but had perks like tickets to concerts. For Danny's birthday, I took him to see Clint Black and we went backstage for pictures. We taped a radio advertisement starring Daniel and a local DJ, and he seemed like a pro.

The divorce decree had split the bills between me and my ex-husband; but when he had financial problems and stopped paying "his bills" I was still held responsible and they came after my paychecks. I was forced into bankruptcy. Amanda moved in with a friend, and Daniel and I—with our three cats and a gerbil—moved into the basement of my younger brother, Kevin. Adding insult to injury, I totaled my car on the way to my brother's house.

The basement was dark and damp with two little windows that peeked into the side yard. We went to sleep at night surrounded by our possessions in cardboard boxes. We could hear Kevin and his wife's yelling and heavy footsteps overhead. I felt as though I had returned to the confines of my troubled childhood.

Within six months, however, I'd saved enough money to move into a shabby apartment. At work, the business manager decided to take some of my accounts to entice another salesperson—he only took accounts from the women on staff. I stood up to him and won, but I made a plan to leave. Within a year and a half I had gone to real estate school at night, gotten my license, quit my job at the radio station, sold my first house, and moved into a nicer apartment in a better school district. Daniel started fifth grade at Hazeldale Elementary, where Mrs. Carpenter entered his life.

He seemed happier—he was getting better grades and began to excel in art and science. His project won an award in the science fair. He entered the school talent show with his unicycle and dance routines and even made his own costumes. He had discovered the stage.

The next year, Daniel started showing interest in a girl in our neighborhood and my worries about his being gay disappeared. Daniel was overjoyed to have Mrs. C again as his teacher for sixth grade.

Around that same time, I met my current husband. Steve is a general contractor, and I was showing a house he had built. Steve and his realtor went to a local restaurant and bar on Wednesday nights, and he invited me to come along. After a few dinners, I began bringing Daniel. There was country line dancing, and Daniel joined in alongside the adults. He shined. He was asked by the line-dancing teacher to enter a contest at the state fair. He won first prize.

The summer before seventh grade Daniel and I moved to Hillsboro, a suburb of Portland, and I began saving money to buy a house. Daniel continued to do well in school, but he still had few friends. I convinced myself it was just a phase. Daniel became more involved with theatre and participated in all the school plays. His first was *A Christmas Carol*—Daniel was Tiny Tim. He carried a crutch, held together by a simple wing nut. During a performance, the crutch collapsed as he walked across stage—but Daniel held it together without missing a beat.

He became best friends with a neighbor boy, Adam, and they were together all the time. Then, all of a sudden, Adam stopped coming over and Daniel would not tell me why. A few weeks later Daniel came home late from school, crying. He told me that Adam and some other kids wrote "FAG" on his locker.

My instinct was to go to the principal, but Daniel insisted I leave it alone. I didn't even consider that my old fears could be true; I was still in my denial phase. Years later, Daniel explained that he and Adam had both been picked on at school and called "fags." They had confessed their feelings to each other. But a couple of weeks later Adam decided take the attention off of himself by telling everyone that Daniel was gay.

At just the right time in his life, Daniel met Kim Sandstrom. She had formed a teenage acting troupe called Hart Attack, and Daniel joined in giving productions at local schools. The Hart Theatre became his second home—he took tickets, built the stage for productions, and made it on stage himself at the dinner theatre. He felt like he finally fit in. He and Kim are still friends today.

In October 1996, my 15-year-old son finally told me he was gay. We had purchased our new home and were finishing up cleaning our old apartment. I was standing barefoot on the kitchen counter wiping off the top of the kitchen cabinets. Danny walked into the kitchen, his head down, his hands deep in his blue jean pockets. He just stood there. Finally he looked up.

"Mom, I need to talk to you."

"Not now, Danny. We need to finish," I insisted.

"Mom, this is important. I need to tell you something, now."

"What?"

"Mom, I think I'm gay."

I didn't say anything.

"Mom, *I'm gay*," he repeated. I eased myself down to the kitchen floor and steadied myself against the counter.

"Danny, you are too young to know," I reasoned.

"Mom, I *am* gay, and I just had to tell you," he said with finality.

I didn't want to believe him. My upbringing had taught me that being gay was shameful and perverse. I had a cousin that lived with us for a summer when he was 18. One night, my mother and sister got him drunk, put makeup on him, and dressed him in women's clothes. They put a scarf on his head and tied it under his chin. They laughed and called him a queer.

But I loved my son. I felt a burden of guilt that perhaps how I raised him had caused him to be gay. I worried how others would treat him and, selfishly, I worried how others might look at me. Most of all, I was afraid of what this meant for my son's life.

I soon realized it was not a choice, he could not choose to change. In actuality, I was the one with a decision to make.

I pushed his words aside and continued to clean the apartment. I packed up the vacuum and cleaning supplies and dropped off the apartment key with the manager. We started back to our new home and to our Sunday family night where Amanda and Steve were waiting with pizza. We stopped at the video store to rent a movie. Daniel was unusually happy as he jumped out of the car and extended his hand for the money for the movie rental. I stayed in the car, not wanting to see anyone. After the pizza—and starting my second glass of wine—I sat in the dark living room next to Steve and my daughter. Daniel was sprawled on the carpet with his pillow in front of the TV. He had chosen *The Birdcage* and I alone was all too aware of the symbolism. Amanda and Steve laughed on cue with Daniel as we watched the gay couple in the movie pretend to be an average, conservative family—with one of them in drag to play the wife—all for the benefit of their straight son's fiancée and her parents.

As I watched this outrageous, stereotypical gay couple I wondered which partner my son would grow up to be like.

The next day, I still felt the sting of his words. My heart felt like it would hurt forever.

When Danny came home from school he asked, "Did you tell Steve?"

"No, I was going to put an ad in the paper."

I told him I was sorry. I wasn't really angry—I was confused and hurt. I felt deceived. He said he couldn't tell me before because of the gay jokes he had heard me tell and laugh at. Oh, God, how I must have been hurting him all that time! He was eager to answer questions and share information. But I wanted to go slow. I really didn't want to know everything.

He asked me if I accepted him, and I said, "Yes, I love you." He hugged me several times, and told me he loved me.

The next day he went to school, and I felt like I was in shock. My mind was a slow-motion movie of Daniel's life.

I sat at my desk at my home office and tried to find a hotline or counselor to call. I didn't know what to do. I must have left a message somewhere, because Jan, the mother of a gay son, called. We talked for a long time. My heart spilled out, and I cried.

Later, Steve showed up at the house and wanted to know what was wrong. I was afraid to tell him, but I asked him to sit down. I told him to *please* be careful with what he said to me. If my life was a play, and Steve had a part, it couldn't have been written better. He said it was okay, and that Daniel needed to know that we cared for him the same way. In a couple of days, I was due to travel with Steve to his brother's wedding. I was afraid to leave Daniel, but the plans were already made. Amanda's roommate would stay with Daniel, and Amanda would house-sit at Steve's.

Steve and I went with his family to Cape Cod for the wedding. We rented a big house and each couple, his mother, and his sister each had their own rooms. I was on the verge of tears the first few days and wanted to be alone. I felt as though my Danny was dead, that my son was someone I didn't know. I worried that Danny's life was a lie, and that I didn't know my own son anymore. I was in mourning for the man I thought he would have grown up to be.

Steve, his brothers, and I went into Providence, Rhode Island, to go shopping. I wanted to get gifts to take back for Daniel and Amanda. Providence, from what everyone was saying, was a gay community.

The gay jokes started, and I felt hurt and angry. I told Steve I wanted to wander around by myself, shop, and people watch.

Right away I found a wind chime for Amanda. I wandered through several more shops searching for a gift for Daniel but only found myself lost in tears. If I didn't know who Danny was anymore, how could I know what he liked? I decided on two journals—one for Daniel and one for me. I hoped we could write about our feelings and let each other read them.

Wanting to get comfortable with the people my son identified with, I sat in a coffee shop and just watched and listened. I wanted to be close to these people and see what they were really like. It was a whole new world for me.

I called Daniel every day. I longed to get to know him all over again. He had to have a strong soul to have kept this inside. I finally was beginning to feel relieved. No more wondering, just accepting him and loving him just as he was. There had been a wall between us because I had been trying to make him into something that he was not. I hoped we could start again.

When I got home I gave Danny his journal. We kept our journals under our mattresses, and we read each other's words. On paper, we could share the things that were still too difficult to talk about face to face, at least for me.

I told Amanda about Daniel. She acted only mildly surprised. She said she felt he was too young to really know and it was "just a '90s thing." She asked, "Does he realize what he is choosing?" I told her it wasn't a choice, but she insisted it was.

Daniel came downstairs. He knew I had told her. They talked—and even teased each other. He went upstairs and she turned to me.

"So many people will hate him and want to hurt him. I am scared." We cried.

When I hunted through the attic in preparation for writing this book, I didn't find the journals Daniel and I had shared. I remember asking him personal questions and then sometimes waiting several days to read his responses—because I was afraid of what he might tell me. But Daniel was eager to share, to let me know who he was and how he felt. Sometimes his words scared me because of the people he knew and places he had gone—like an underage, gay nightclub in downtown Portland. Sometimes his answers made me sad because of the things he had heard me say about gays. He told me it hurt him.

But sometimes his answers gave me peace: He had known he was gay as far back as he could remember. It was no one's fault; it was just who he was.

It was 1996 and only a few gay characters were on TV or in movies, and they were framed as freakish. The fight for gay rights had begun but was not yet front and center. My journey was just beginning. All I knew was that I loved Daniel deeply. I accepted him. I just wanted to be a part of his life, and to understand.

Coming to terms with who I was — Daniel

I interviewed my son twice. These were the most difficult conversations I experienced while compiling this book. During all the interviews, I was brought high emotional peaks and low valleys. I felt the pain in these stories. I saw the wounds and the joys of their journeys. But with my own son, I felt blindsided as I listened to him express the pain of his early years. It made me wish I had done many things differently, listened more, and asked more questions. I was also in awe over the small, forgotten moments that had impacted him greatly—like a particular Christmas gift of long ago that assured him of my acceptance. I found out who had been important in his life, and how these people inspired and strengthened him. It had truly taken a village to raise my son.

Daniel's Story
Daniel Robinson, 29
New York City, New York
January 2011

When I was about three years old, I discovered my sister's Barbie dolls. I was overwhelmed with joy and curiosity. But when Amanda caught me, she said I couldn't play with them because they belonged to her. After my sister went to school in the morning, my whole day centered on getting upstairs into her room and getting to her dolls. I fixated on the beauty of them and the possibilities of their different outfits; it was exciting and it felt inherently right to me. I loved all of the shapes, colors, and textures of their clothes, dressing them and acting out their lives. I enjoyed smoothing their hair and posing them in glamorous stances.

I was also inspired by my sister herself. When she was on the dance team, I loved watching her at practice. I knew I wanted to be a dancer, too. She was always drawing, painting, making collages, and decorating her room. And I would think, "I can do that, too," so I would try. I really looked up to her, but in her eyes I was just her bratty little brother who annoyed her and got into her things.

When I was six years old, my parents got divorced and I moved in with my father, my new stepmother Shirley, and her three boys. My parents thought it would be best for me to be around other kids my age, because my brother and sister were ten years older. In this new family I was clearly the odd one out. I didn't play football, basketball, or baseball like they did. All I wanted to do was dance. Shirley and her boys constantly put me down—if I was upset and would cry, they would laugh at me. When people came over to visit, they embarrassed me and told people I liked to play with dolls and that I wanted to be a little girl.

My dad wasn't aware of what was happening when he wasn't home. It was like living with pit bulls. When my dad was at home, they were in a cage. My dad and Shirley would fight all the time and I always assumed it was about me. Their fights never seemed to resolve and my dad would tell me to pack my suitcase and we would stay at his wood shop. I liked it because I wouldn't have to be home with the boys pretending to be interested in the things they were. While my dad was working, I would be on the floor, covered in sawdust, searching through wood scraps and eager to create something. My dad made wooden shelves, cabinets, peg boards, and quilt racks for stores and craft shows. I liked making candle holders, little animal cutouts, and cars and trucks with wheels.

I would also film my own shows in the shop with a video camera that Mom gave me. I would even create elaborate sets. I remember when the movie Sister Act II came out. I got a poster of Whoopi Goldberg and the soundtrack of the movie. I put the poster on cardboard and cut out the mouth of Whoopi and stood behind it and lip-synched to all the songs on video—my own little variety show.

Most of the time, though, I didn't feel like I was able to be a kid when I lived with Dad because I had to spend so much time defending myself from Shirley and her boys. Despite this, I am still thankful I lived with my dad, Shirley, and her boys—the time spent with them was merely a strengthening vehicle for the time ahead.

When I was nine years old, I moved back in with Mom. I was lonely because she worked a lot, and both my older brother and sister had moved out of the house. I spent a lot of time by myself. I wanted to be me and investigate the creative part of myself. The first Christmas back was the best Christmas ever. She got me the ice-skating Barbie and Ken dolls. They had skating outfits and skates. Ken had a silver jacket, and Barbie had a glittery skirt and top. My mom had a date over and he asked, "Oh my God, your son has a Barbie doll?" I knew we wouldn't see him again.

During my fifth and sixth grade years we lived in an apartment, and I went to Hazeldale Elementary School. My teacher, Mrs. Carpenter, was divine. She was always open and never talked down to me. She made me feel very special. All my other teachers before would tell me to act like the other boys as though there was something wrong with me, but not Mrs. Carpenter. She was one of the most inspiring teachers I have ever had. Other teachers seemed only interested in our just learning our lessons and fitting in, but she inspired us to excel at being ourselves.

I ran into her at the airport in New York a few years ago. We got to spend some time together and she returned the following year with her husband and saw me on Broadway in the production of Hairspray. She hadn't changed—she was the same person with the same encouraging smile. She also came to the opening of a movie I starred in, The Big Gay Musical, in Portland. She even came to a birthday party I had in Portland a few years ago and brought me a copy of a story I wrote when I was a student. It read, in part, "Mrs. Carpenter will always be my friend even when I am older and she will never be forgotten . . . she will always be in my heart." It's still true.

From there we moved to Hillsboro, outside of Portland, and I started school at J.B. Thomas Junior High School. Most of my friends at the time were girls. I tried to make friends with boys, but it would always get to a certain stage and they would get uncomfortable—I think because they would figure it out. It wasn't that I was attracted to them, or that I made moves on them. I think it was just the way I thought. I was always in an artistic place. That school year, I was miserable. I felt like there was no one like me. Then I joined band and began playing the saxophone. We would go to the high school for band practice, and there I met a kid named J.R. He was out, flamboyant and comfortable in his own skin. He was the first out gay guy I ever knew. He inspired me to accept myself so that it didn't matter what other people thought of me.

In eighth grade, I got involved in theatre. It helped me get through the tough times in my life because it let me escape from judgment into art and become someone else. At this time, rumors of my being gay were brewing, and I was constantly being picked on and teased. I hadn't admitted it then, but I was starting to come to terms with who I was.

I wrote my best friend a letter to tell her that I was gay. She left it in her locker and her locker-mate found it and told everybody. People just didn't know how to respond. There was name-calling, homophobic slurs written on my locker, and ignorance from school staff members. I knew I wasn't changing, and I knew I wasn't going back in the closet, so I was open about it. A girl asked me a question: since I was gay, did that mean that I was attracted to lesbians? I thought to myself, *this is only the beginning.*

While all of that was happening at school, my mom and I were preparing to move into our first house. We were cleaning the apartment we were moving out of. I walked into the kitchen where she was standing on top of the counter, wiping down the top of the cabinets. I asked her, "What would you do if I were bi-sexual?" There was a pause, and I knew there was no turning back. I took a breath and told her I was gay. No more words were exchanged. That evening on our way to the new house, we stopped at the video store, and I jumped out of the car to pick the flick. I was feeling so good and so relieved that I finally told her. The movie I picked out was *The Birdcage*.

A couple days later, she and her boyfriend left on a trip to see his family back east. When she returned, she brought us each journals for us to write in, so we could read each other's thoughts.

Finding each other again — Mrs. Carpenter

After interviewing Daniel, I knew I needed to go back and talk to the people who were early influences in his life. Daniel's favorite teacher, Mrs. C., has made her way back into Daniel's life in the last few years, and she was pleased to reflect on her relationship with my son. In 2009, I invited her, along with thirty-five other family members and friends, to the opening of Daniel's movie, The Big Gay Musical, at the Portland Gay & Lesbian Film Festival. I drove to the theatre with Amanda, and was surprised to see people lined up around the block to get tickets, and nowhere to park! I expanded my search for a parking place, but I was not familiar with downtown Portland and all the one-way streets.

After ten or fifteen minutes I began to panic. I thought about calling Daniel, but what could he do? I was almost in tears, afraid we were going to be late for the opening of the film. Just then, I got a call on my cell—it was Mrs. Carpenter. She and her husband were standing in a parking spot right in front of the theatre, holding it for us. It seemed like a miracle they even knew we were out there searching.

Mrs. Carpenter
Daniel's fifth and sixth grade teacher
February 2011

As a teacher, I want to be there for every child; and I'd like to think I make a positive impact on them. You really don't realize the impact you have made as an elementary school teacher. The time we have with them in elementary school is so short, and after they walk out our school doors on to junior high and beyond you may never see them again.

That's why I felt so very blessed when I ran into Daniel as an adult, because he was a kid I remembered so vividly, so special to me in my heart. I hadn't seen Daniel in years, and I didn't know what had become of him but had often wondered. I was in the Portland airport in 2008, and coincidentally Daniel and I were both on our way to New York. I was in line, and I heard a grown man yell, "Mrs. Carpenter!" I turned around and saw very tall, good-looking young man coming towards me. I thought he looked very familiar, like a former student, but children who are eleven or twelve years old often look much different when they're adults.

He said, "I'm Daniel. I was in your fifth and sixth-grade classes." Instantly I remembered him. He gave me a big hug. I asked what he was doing, and he informed me that he lived in New York. We boarded the plane, and when we got off, we caught up with each other again. He told me he was in a play. He asked if I had ever heard of Hairspray. I laughed and said, "Uhhh . . . yeah!" It is so exciting as a teacher to see my kids as adults, grown-up and successful in whatever direction that they are going.

I was in New York for a formal training program to take some of my students to Washington, D.C. My schedule was very tight, but I made special arrangements to have some time to spend with Daniel. I didn't have time to go to the show, but he took my friend and me to his theatre, and took us backstage. My friend, who was involved in theatre, was absolutely beside herself. She was thrilled to be able to stand on that Broadway stage. Daniel took us to different places, including the restaurant Vynl, where we met some of his friends. It was a special time I will never forget.

The following year, I took my husband to New York for his fiftieth birthday, and we spent several days with Daniel. We saw him on Broadway in Hairspray—it was great. He was so cute. He told us to go to the stage door after the show and they would let us in. We went to the stage door, and there was a crowd of people there. Even though I didn't want to push my way through, my husband encouraged me to let them know that we were there to see Daniel. I got the attention of the man guarding the stage door, and told him that I was Mrs. Carpenter. I hardly got the words out of my mouth when the man said, "Oh, you are Daniel's teacher! Daniel said you were coming!" He let us in, and we saw Daniel coming down the stairs with someone else. She also knew I was Daniel's teacher. She said he was waiting for us, and that she thought it was so nice that we came to see him. Everyone treated us so kindly.

That first time I saw Daniel in New York, I didn't know he was gay, but I sensed it. We were walking down one of the streets, and I asked him how old he was. He replied that he was 25, and I asked him if he was in a relationship. A smirk came over his face and he asked, "You know I'm gay right?" I said, "Yeah," and we kept walking. He told me he was in a relationship with someone older—and I sort of teased him about it.

I have many gay friends and relatives. Back when Daniel was in grade school, I knew some people that I thought were gay but it wasn't something I ever talked about. Now, it is more mainstream and not completely hidden.

Daniel was very creative with the projects he did in school. He had that sense of being excited when he was presented with the opportunity to create. He would light up and fly with it. He always wanted to share the things he created and loved with me. When Daniel was in my fifth-grade class, he and some other students were having some problems with reading. I set up a program where they would have a first-grade reading buddy. I would meet with Daniel and the other fifth-graders in the program at lunch time and teach them all kinds of reading strategies, like things to do with the first-graders when they didn't know the words. Then Daniel and the others would meet with their first-grade reading buddies. In turn, they all became better readers. Daniel did very well as a mentor with younger children because he had such a kind heart.

Daniel had two friends in the classroom, girls, and at the end of the year, they presented me with a book that they had created of all my daily fashions. Every page had a picture they had drawn of me in different outfits. I still have it somewhere.

Daniel would jump at the chance to help me after school or at lunch. Each of my students has their strengths and their distinctiveness, and I hope I am the kind of teacher that celebrates those things—those things that make them who they are.

Since seeing Daniel in New York, I have seen him on a couple of his visits to Oregon, and we occasionally text each other. The last time I saw Daniel was when my husband and I came to see him at the Portland Gay & Lesbian Film Festival for the opening of The Big Gay Musical. I loved the movie and listening to him introduce it.

Meeting Daniel as an adult and realizing that he remembered me has had an impact on me. It makes me remember that when I am with students, every word—whether it is feedback I am giving them, talking to them, or redirecting them because of their behavior—everything you say has the capacity to make or break them. I always remember that I have a responsibility to support these children and to help them grow into their true selves.

A Note from Mrs. Carpenter:

Our school district recognizes the diversity and worth of all individuals and groups. It is the policy of our school district that there will be no discrimination or harassment of individuals or groups based on race, color, religion, gender, sexual orientation, gender identity, gender expression, national origin, marital status, age, veteran status, genetic information, or disability in any educational programs, activities, or employment.

A place of acceptance and discovery — Kim

Kim has continued to be in Daniel's life through the years. In 2005, Daniel flew to Portland to choreograph a dance piece for Dance West, a group he had performed with during his senior year of high school. He dedicated a piece, "My Juliet," to Diana—Kim's daughter who died in 2004, and with whom Daniel was very close. When Daniel was in junior high school he had wanted to play the role of Romeo at Hart Theatre, with Diana as Juliet; she got the part but he didn't because he looked too young.

I watched as Daniel took the CD player into our front yard and carefully worked out the choreography for "My Juliet." Then I went with him to watch him teach the dance to his students. I saw a side of Daniel I had never seen—an inspiring teacher carefully mixing instruction and praise for each dancer. Kim and I went together to the production at the Newmark Theatre in Portland. It was beautiful. As we watched the dance created for and dedicated to Diana, I held Kim's hand as we cried.

Kim Sandstrom
HART Theatre, Hillsboro, Oregon
February 2011

I was an actress in New York City years ago. Back in the 1970s, I went to school at the Academy of Dramatic Arts in New York, and followed that up with a degree in drama at Pacific University in Forest Grove, Oregon. I moved with my family to Hillsboro, Oregon, and started a small dinner theatre as a family business.

Not long afterward, I was approached to establish a standing theatre in downtown Hillsboro. My then-husband and I, my children, and a lot of community members worked together for nearly a year, and in 1994 we established Hillsboro Actors Repertory Theatre (HART) which is now in its seventeenth year. Because of my children, and my own experience as a young person in theatre, I also started an acting troupe, Hillsboro Actors Training, and a teen theatre troupe called Hart Attack. On top of that, I had my main-stage productions at HART. Many kids who were in Hart Attack have gone on to professional theatre, including Daniel.

I met Daniel about the time HART opened, when he was 13. Hart Attack was designed for teens and pre-teens who had a little acting experience and wanted to do more, but who didn't always get cast. That always bothered me—that kids wanted to do theatre, but there were very few opportunities for them. Daniel contacted me and asked to join Hart Attack. We met on Tuesdays and Thursdays after school at the Hart Theatre. Daniel was very involved. We had our own t-shirts and performed at schools and the courthouse. Daniel showed real theatre aptitude. I can't remember meeting anyone then that wanted to be on stage more than Daniel—except for my daughter, Diana.

Daniel's first show was Pollyanna, and he was wonderful. He memorized his lines quickly and was always volunteering to bring costumes and props, or to take tickets and paint sets. The one thing I remember about Daniel was that he not only wanted to be on stage, but that he wanted to understand theatre and all the aspects of it. He had a renaissance attitude—he wanted to understand and do it all. When he didn't get cast as Romeo in our production of Romeo and Juliet, he was very unhappy. He thought since he read his part the best, he should get the part. He was used to always getting the leads. He was crying. I was trying to make it a teaching moment, because this was educational theatre, and he had to see this from a different perspective—even if you have the desire and the talent, sometimes you don't fit the part. I felt bad that he had to go through that, since he was deeply hurt.

He was the kind of person I loved having come into the theatre because I knew he would have longevity—Daniel would always have the theatre as a part of his life. I also had an opportunity to be with him on stage—I was cast as his mother in Brighton Beach Memoirs, and my daughter was cast also. Daniel was perfect as Eugene, and he looked great on stage. I remember looking through the kitchen window on the set and seeing Daniel on stage, and thinking how much he owned the space and the character. I knew he would go far.

Theatre can be almost a holy ground for what it does for peoples' lives. It can root them and ground them, and be a place of acceptance and discovery. It's a place where they can learn responsibility and accountability—theatre is all of that and more. For Daniel and a lot of other teenagers, it was also a safe place. If you didn't fit in with the cliques or you knew you were thinking differently than the crowd at school, Hart was a place to explore and be who you wanted to be. I was very protective of the kids and I took the responsibility of watching over them very seriously. Hart saved a lot of kids—they had friends there and found a lot of love and acceptance. Hart still has that today.

In 2004, I lost my daughter Diana. Daniel and Diana had always been very close and in 2005 he came back to Hillsboro and choreographed a ballet with the Dance West dancers and dedicated it to her:

"This piece is dedicated to the memory of Diana Brookins (February 3, 1979 - July 25, 2004)—a great friend, beautiful mother, and a talented actress who made a lasting impression on me."

Daniel Robinson

Why couldn't I — Dawn

Once in high school, Daniel no longer seemed to be the insecure little boy who cried easily. Daniel's success—in school, the community, and the theater world—helped build up his armor. He had an air of strength as he walked the halls with his friends. When someone called him "fag," he would just block out the words or make believe they said something else.

Daniel was in his first high school play, Working, and he had a solo song. I sat in the audience as he performed at the school assembly. As the lights came up on Daniel, a male student a few rows ahead of me yelled "FAG!" The word pierced my heart—all the effort Daniel had put into this show, only to have someone try to destroy it. The teachers didn't even turn their heads to see who yelled. My pain evolved to anger. I wanted stand up and scream to protect my son. Daniel sang his solo as if he hadn't heard. Years later he admitted he had heard, and it had hurt.

It was a difficult time for Daniel, even if he didn't always show it. It was then that we found someone to talk to about our concerns about Daniel being harassed: Dawn Montgomery, the assistant principal at his high school. She was someone we could both go to. There wasn't always something she could do, but we knew she cared and was always there for us.

Daniel excelled in high school, in choir, and in theater. He was even the mascot of the cheerleading squad. One day, he logged onto a school computer—and forgot to log off. Someone then used his account to send sexually explicit e-mails to all of the football players. When Daniel found out, he was afraid of harassment or physical harm.

Dawn talked to the coach, who in turn talked to the team. Though we were assured it would be safe for Daniel to continue as the mascot, I tried to convince him to quit. But Daniel insisted on staying. He told me no one knew who was in the mascot suit and since all the cheer-

leaders were his friends, the football players wouldn't dare touch him. Daniel even went to the prom with two of prettiest girls on the squad.

In 2004, when Daniel returned to Portland on a national tour of Oklahoma, that moment in the school assembly returned to me. I contacted several newspapers to make sure it that they knew that Daniel was from Hillsboro and had been on the Portland stage many times. The Hillsboro Argus and the Portland Tribune devoted almost a full page to a former Portland actor appearing at the Keller Auditorium. I secretly hoped the boy who yelled that slur and the kids who bullied Daniel through the years saw those articles or were in the audience when Daniel stepped onto the stage with seventy of his friends and family members proudly watching.

I called Dawn and invited her to the show. She accepted and arrived at the theater with her longtime female partner. I had no idea she was gay. I couldn't help feeling closer to her, and was more appreciative of the support she provided Daniel and me.

When I asked Dawn for an interview, I was puzzled why she seemed so eager. I was not aware of the effect that a high school student—and his courage concerning his sexual orientation—had had on her life.

Dawn Montgomery, Ed. D.
High School Assistant Principal
June 2011

It was always a challenge for me to be an educator and be a lesbian. The first time I remember Daniel and his mother was when they spoke at a district-wide meeting. I don't know whose wonderful brainchild it was to have this forum for administrators, where gay and lesbian kids and their parents could talk about what it was like to be in our schools, but it was powerful. Daniel must have just started tenth grade, and I was the assistant principal at the high school.

I thought it was very brave of Daniel and Traci to tell us how hard it was. She was there fighting for him and talking about the issues that were affecting him. It had a big impact on me. I had not *officially* come out at the time. It was really powerful to hear their stories and their experience of what it was like to be in our schools. I realized we had to make some changes.

The high school had just opened that year, and it was just ninth through eleventh graders that first year—seniors stayed at their home schools. The district had pulled kids from different schools in the community, and it was a difficult time for everyone. Daniel was picked on by the juniors because he was only a sophomore, but also because he was gay. It was awful. We had all these kids coming from different schools, trying to fit together. Some kids were totally insensitive to other kids who were different, and especially to anyone who showed any signs of being gay. We had so many fights that we pulled in an additional assistant principal mid-year.

I remember Traci coming to me about a particular teacher who had said some things that were insensitive to gay and lesbian kids, and she was concerned about the effect it would have on kids who were not out. Eventually, we developed policies and put up signs that said we were accepting of everyone. Not every teacher elected to post the signs and talk about the issues, but many did. Those signs are still up today: "We DO NOT tolerate verbal or physical harassment at our high school, particularly when action is based on race, sex, national origin, religion, age, disability or sexual orientation."

Those were the days when we didn't have any gay and lesbian clubs. I recall a teacher approaching the principal and offering to start a club for gay and lesbian students. The principal was uncomfortable with the idea, and it took some convincing to get it approved. It really was necessary because the gay and lesbian students needed a way to support each other.

An important thing happened several years after Daniel graduated. The drama director proposed producing the play, *The Laramie Project*—the true story of the murder of Matthew Shepard, a 21-year-old gay college student who was tied to a fence, beaten and tortured, and then left to die. *The Laramie Project* was shown at high schools and universities around the U.S.

It was controversial, and felt personally risky to me because of the relationship with my female partner. I spoke with a couple teacher-leaders in the school to get a read on the staff support for this venture. Ultimately, I went to the superintendent and told him we had a plan—to have a community forum to discuss the issues concerning gay and lesbian kids. Then, we would show the play.

I told the superintendent that I knew it was a risk, but the kids needed it. He trusted my judgment, and it went great. We posted it in the community newspaper as a play with an informational session and presented it after school. It included a panel of community organizations—including GLSEN (Gay, Lesbian & Straight Education Network)—to discuss the issue and how to support our students.

Another high school in our area tried to do the same thing a few years later, but it was cancelled because of the unfortunate community outrage over the play. A local newspaper reported that the high school had banned *The Laramie Project* because the principal felt the sexual content and use of profanity was offensive. The article went on to say the people in the theatre community felt that it was banned because a gay character was featured in the play.

Many high schools now have what is called "The Day of Silence" that recognizes gay, lesbian, bisexual, and transgender youth who opt to be silent for the day as a way to show how they are silenced in the community and in the world.

During my teaching career, I had some very hurtful things said about me. During the '90s, when several anti-gay ballot measures were proposed, a community member told me what a parent had said to them—which was very condescending to me—and I was really upset: She had said that she didn't want her child in my classroom because she was sure I was a lesbian. It was dangerous time to be a teacher, an educator, and have it known that you are gay or a lesbian—and it still is in many schools and districts.

Knowing Daniel and seeing how brave he was, and how supportive Traci was, helped me see that the only way we are going to change
things is for people to be who they really are, whether they're talented
like Daniel or in a position of authority like me. If people are going to
judge you, or if you don't get some leadership jobs because of it, so be
it. We have to change things by being out and confronting the issues.

It was a difficult transition to be out in my position of school leadership. I was not out to parents and students, but I started bringing my
partner to games and school activities. I didn't advertise it. I introduced her as my friend, (not) as my partner as I do now. But I didn't
hide it either, and to anyone who had any kind of radar, it was obvious. One of the reasons I began to come out was because I had seen
how brave Daniel was. If kids at such a young age could come out and
be who they were, why couldn't I?

Part Two

Branches

Sexuality on a sliding scale — Jeremy

When Daniel was in high school, he had a good friend named Jeremy. He was a few years older than Daniel. He had moved from Boston and had been living with friends, working, and taking some classes, but Jeremy ran into some financial problems.

He lived with us for six months, and we became close friends. I remember his favorite outfit: a light blue polyester jacket, matching bell-bottom pants, and tan furry platform boots. When we would go shopping together his clothing and feminine mannerisms drew attention and comments, but we would giggle as though we shared an inside joke. He helped me with my own coming out as the mother of a gay son and as an advocate for the LGBTQ community.

Jeremy was into photography. He loved taking black-and-white photos, and he took some of me. First, he did my make-up as I laid my head in his lap. He styled my hair with his gentle, long fingers. I dressed up like a dance hall girl, and the photos he took that day are some of my favorites of myself.

He has had a hard time with his self-worth through the years, and as a result has been in several unhealthy relationships. But now I can see happiness and success in his life. Many mornings, he sends me a sweet text message with a picture of flowers or his pets. I am very proud of "my son," Jeremy—he really lives what he believes.

Jeremy, 35
Boston, MA
June 2010

I must have been in the first grade, or maybe before, when I found a dress and put it on. My father saw me but didn't say a word. He just walked out of the room. I was scared, and I knew I had to get that dress off. I found my grandma, and she helped me to take it off. Her relationship with her son, my father, was a close one, and she knew he was temperamental. She didn't want him to hurt me.

My parents split up when I was five, and I went to live with my mother in Boston. I was popular with the kids in school. In the second grade, I was on the playground at recess with a girl named Natalie and one of her friends. Another girl approached us and asked me, "Are you a boy or a girl?"

Natalie said, "He's not a girl or a boy. He's a girl-boy."

When I was in third grade, my mother re-married and we moved to Houston, Texas. It was traumatizing, because my femininity was a much bigger deal there. By the fourth grade, I knew I was different from the other boys. I had always been more interested in playing Barbie dolls with the girls than playing with trucks.

I remember being teased about the way I held a book when I read—my wrists were always limp. The boy sitting next to me pointed at me and laughed. I didn't realize what I was doing was a "gay thing."

I started to get picked on. To distract the other children, I would be imaginative. I would make up stories. I told them I had nine names including my grandparents' name, my mother's married name, as well as my own. I told them I knew French. When they would ask me to say something, I would make up words. As long as I was entertaining, I didn't have to worry about being picked on.

When I was eleven, I had my first sexual experience with a girl— my next-door neighbor. She was older, 13, a bit wild and a unique person. Her parents were white, but she was black—her grandfather was black. She instructed me what to do, since I had no idea. She was very romantic; she even lit candles. I think it was the first time for her, and that she was experimenting. We went all the way, but I wasn't really old enough for anything to happen. I remember feeling funny afterwards, but at the same time I felt like I was experiencing something new and different.

I did like boys, but I wasn't interested in baseball or things like that. When I played with the other guys I couldn't hang out with them in the same way that I could with a girl. The first men I was interested in were not boys my own age, but teachers. I would picture myself sitting in bed with them, wearing bathrobes.

I had a really close friend in the fifth grade. Cedric. We did all sorts of fun things together. He was my best friend and we walked home together every day after school. We wrote letters back and forth. I wrote letters to a lot of people, and I still do. But there was one particular letter—it wasn't sexual. It was about him being such a good friend to me. He had the letter in his dresser with the others, and his father found them and he became concerned. He called my mother and asked her to have a conference with him. My mother told him that she didn't think there was anything wrong but she would make sure I wouldn't write letters to his son anymore. It was very embarrassing. We stayed friends, and he thought his father being upset by the letters was dumb. Cedric moved away, but even before that I began feeling like something was wrong with me.

I hadn't felt like that when I lived in Boston, so I wanted to move back. I missed my father and my cousins. I loved my mom and my brother, but I didn't feel like I would ever be treated right living in Texas. There would always be questions about my sexuality. I used to go to bed at night and pray to God to take away my attraction to boys, or to let me wake up to find myself changed into a girl.

I started acting out so I could move back home with my dad. I went to a grocery store with some friends and stole a little stapler and some paper for my letters. Two officers caught us, and they called our parents. It supplied enough tension that my mother decided it was time for me to move back in with Dad in Boston. I felt like there things would go back to normal. People would accept me, and my problems would all go away.

I started seventh grade. My dad asked if I wanted to be in choir. I knew it would draw attention to me because I would be a first soprano. Instead, I got involved in drama and excelled in writing and art. I was getting straight As. I had a girlfriend, but rumors about me being gay started. It wasn't that I wasn't interested in girls—it was just that I was starting to think about the possibility of being with boys.

My dad had started a new family, and it wasn't working out with me being there. I moved in with my dad's parents on their farm. My grandmother told me later that she had tried to counteract my femininity. She would get eggs that had more male hormones and feed them to me. I have to give her credit for being so creative in using homeopathy. She would suggest that I not wear color-coordinated socks and shirts or talk in a feminine voice. She was instrumental in showing me how other people perceived me.

When I was 15, my mother relocated to Boston, and I moved back in with her. Soon afterwards, I had my first sexual experience with a boy. I was staying overnight with my new friend, Todd. He suggested that I sleep in his bed instead of on the floor. I woke up and he was holding me and touching my private places. I touched him as well, but that was all that happened. The next morning, I had to go to church with my mom's parents, who attended the Reorganized Church of Jesus Christ of the Latter-Day Saints. That was extremely mortifying. I knew what I had done was unacceptable. When I got home from church, I wrote in my journal about my experience with Todd in an obscure way. I left it on the kitchen table in the hopes that my mother would find it and talk to me about it, but the journal entry never got read.

I felt the only way to correct my sexuality would be to take extreme measures. I decided to attend the Church of Jesus Christ of the Latter Day Saints to prevent myself from becoming homosexual. In the Mormon Church, homosexuality was an abomination. I had a good Mormon friend, and I started going to church at her ward. I would go to seminary before school in the morning. My friend introduced me to two male Mormon missionaries. We made dinner for them, and afterwards one of them approached me. He said, "I have a fire burning deep inside of me, and I want to help you."

I ended up having an intense relationship over the phone with this 21-year-old missionary. We became very close. I had wanted someone to read my journal. I asked him if he would read it. Part of me wanted to cover up the journal entry about Todd, but part of me wanted him to read it so someone would finally understand what I was going through. Terrified, I called him and asked him if he had read my journal. He said he had, and he wanted to talk to me about one particular entry. He had found it! He wanted to know exactly what had happened, and when I told him, he said he understood. He emphasized that if we were ever to discuss anything of this nature in the future that I should be careful to never write it down.

He told me there were ways to heal this portion of my life. He told me that when he was back home with his male friends, they would go on camping trips. They would just cuddle together in a sleeping bag, sharing affection without being sexual. He suggested that we take a camping trip together.

We would meet at church and find a private room where we could embrace one another for long periods of time. This would cause me to have an erection, which I would always try to hide. I finally asked him if he got excited when he was holding me, he said, "Yes, and it is normal. When we are together and holding each other, that it is our time 'to collect'"—that is what we called it. Sometimes he would write me letters saying, "I need to collect," with a smiley-face next to it.

Once I came over to visit him at his place. We went into the back room where we proceeded to hold one another. He reached down into my pants and began to hold me. I started crying, because I knew at that very moment it was over. We had crossed the line. His face was beet red. He pushed me away. He said, "You are the adversary. You have to leave now."

I didn't understand what he meant when he called me "the adversary." I tried to be friends with him after that, but he said he couldn't. He said he would get in trouble and lose everything he had.

I was still in high school, and I really didn't know where to go from there. I had several long-term relationships with girls that were somewhat sexual. About that same time, Cedric called to tell me he was gay. I told him it was okay. I was glad he told me. He was amazed that

I was so accepting. I didn't tell him about my experiences. I was still trying not to acknowledge my feelings for men.

The Mormon Church was trying to convince me to become a member through baptism. My mother didn't want me to convert until I was eighteen. They sent two elders to my home to persuade my mother differently. When my mother refused, they threatened her with my excommunication. My mother slammed the door in their faces.

A few years passed. Two women, missionaries, asked if I was still interested in joining the church. We talked for several grueling hours, after which I told them everything. They suggested that the only solution for me was to meet with the mission president. I met with him in his office, and I begged for his assistance to remove my sexual desires towards men. I wanted to become a member of the church and to straighten my life out. I told him what had happened with my missionary friend years before. I wanted was to live my life righteously. Before he could place me in the church, he would have to excommunicate me. After one year they would reevaluate my status.

I left, bawling, with my Bible in hand. I didn't think I could go on. Something inside of me told me that it was finally time to tell my mother. I went home, and I poured my heart out to her. She was very understanding and accepting.

A few months after this, I met a guy. We had each been seeing girls but started having a sexual relationship with each other. One day, he came to me and told me we couldn't have a relationship anymore because it was wrong, even though he was the one who started it. When I was 18, I met another guy who told me he was bisexual. We started seeing each other and began talking about a long-term relationship. I had moved back in with my dad, but he didn't have a clue about what was going on.

My grandmother came to visit me, and she noticed a hickey on my neck. She asked me about it, and I lied to her. I felt so bad, because I had never lied to her before. I broke up with my boyfriend.

I was still doing well in school—in art, drama, and singing—but it was a confusing time. I was constantly teased about being gay. Many kids called me a fairy, which was very painful. Some of my friends would defend me and say I wasn't gay. I never came out to anyone at school because I didn't think it was necessary.

I wanted to go to college to focus on singing and opera. The only way I could be myself was to move away from home. I found an art college in Portland, Oregon, and moved there.

This gave way to the best experiences of my life. I learned so much about myself and about being okay with whoever I was. I was free to dance, dress like a woman, or perform as a woman. I started going out, first to The City and later Evolution, an underage gay nightclub. It was a magical time for me. I went out with men and with women. I even had a long-term relationship with a lesbian woman.

The first time I remember seeing Daniel at the club, I noticed how he really shined. Daniel and I performed together at the nightclub, and we became friends. I came to his house many times. I started having roommate problems, and I needed to move out. Daniel and Momma Traci insisted I move into their home. She was so nurturing and outgoing, and that was something I really needed. Together, we could all just be who we were.

Even though I adored Portland, I was amazed at how difficult it was to find acceptance, especially in the older gay community. The wrong haircut, the wrong clothes, or even the wrong conversation could get me some dirty looks. When I would go out, I would often dress androgynously, which disturbed some people because they couldn't label me. I never made it easy for people to define my sexuality, which made it challenging for others to relate to and accept me.

I had someone ask my advice on investigating homosexuality. How could they find someone that would be willing? To be honest, finding a same-sex partner isn't that different from finding a partner of the opposite sex. The connection lies between two souls who are willing and eager to cross that intimate boundary.

I don't really consider myself gay. I reject that label. I believe human sexuality is on a sliding scale—some are more one way than the other. The value of a relationship does not come from sex. Saying you are homosexual, heterosexual, bisexual, or even asexual is basically saying that everything you are revolves around sex.

I believe in love. Sex is only a small part of love. Who would give up the opportunity to have a relationship with a beautiful man or a beautiful woman? Building a relationship with someone includes many dynamics that are more important than sex alone.

September 2013

I am now about to turn 38. I came back to Portland because it was the happiest place I ever lived.

I moved here from Boston where I was in a five-year relationship with a man. It was the first time I had been in a same-sex relationship for such a long period of time, but it was an unhealthy relationship. We were a toxic mix together.

My living circumstances in Portland were not what I expected. In less than four weeks I was in an emergency situation where I needed to find a place for myself and my pets. I was afraid I was going to have to live on the street. I had started dating a gentleman, and he offered for me to move in with him. I accepted.

In the next five to six months my eyes were opened to what a really unhealthy relationship looked like. I worried about my own safety and felt helpless. After daily phone calls with Momma Traci, I realized I needed help. I think in a same-sex relationship, many people do not set their standards as high as with the opposite sex. Growing up in a small town, it seemed unlikely I would find someone like me. I was willing to settle because I didn't feel there were a lot of options.

It was difficult to finally realize I had to get out of that relationship. Momma Traci was able to get hold of someone that directed me to a foundation called Bradley Angle. A caseworker opened my eyes to what I was experiencing. I had moved around a lot as a kid and never felt like I fit in. I didn't realize I was being abused because abuse was so familiar. Bradley Angle also helped me financially and made it possible for me to move into my own apartment with my pets. I no longer lived as a victim but forgave and moved on with my life.

Currently, I am a board member of the county health department and a member of the advisory council where I help raise awareness for the LGBTQ community. The person I was in an abusive relationship with was not honest with me, and I didn't find out until almost too late that he had HIV. I always used protection and have tested negative for two years. Because of this, I helped bring to the attention of the health department the need to have condoms easily assessable to everyone in all of their clinics.

I am now in a healthy relationship with a woman, Jessica. We had been in a relationship with each other before and have been friends for years. We came back together and brought the things that worked. Since we both had spent much of our lives in same-sex relationships it has been challenging to be accepted in the LGBTQ community. It is like reverse discrimination.

My hope all along has been to have the members of the LGBTQ community be accepted. I really do love someone for who they are. There is no boundary because of gender. It is about what's going on inside of them, not outside. If you love one another it shouldn't make any difference.

The Sound of High Heels — Danny

My son suggested Danny would be a great person to interview. I sent him a message through Facebook to introduce myself and explain my project. He agreed to an interview about his coming out story. Driving to his apartment in Portland, I felt very nervous. This was the first time I would interview someone I'd not met before. Danny met me at the door and introduced me to his boyfriend and their two cats. Charmed by his wide smile and dimples, I felt my uneasiness fade as he took me into his story.

Danny Thorn, 32
Portland, Oregon
March 2010

I didn't know what gay was. I didn't even know what the word meant. I would hear people say "gay," "queer," or "fag," but it wasn't until I was in the fourth grade when I found out what those words meant. Somebody called me a fag, and I asked some kid what it meant—he told me it was when boys liked boys. I don't remember the feelings that I had, but they definitely weren't toward girls. I hadn't explored my feelings toward boys because I feared them more than anything else. They would tell me, "You're such a fag. You never play sports or anything." I stayed away from them because I didn't want to hear that. I knew it was negative.

I was one of three boys. My parents got divorced when I was ten, and Dad took all of us. I had one older brother and one younger. I was the one with a head on my shoulders. I always went to school an got good grades. I was the outgoing one.

In seventh grade I tried dating girls, and I even had my first kiss. Eighth grade was the last time I had a girlfriend. I really liked her, but it didn't even last a week. I had some girl friends that I hung out with and we started going out dancing in Portland, to this place called The

Quest. My curfew was midnight, but it wasn't long until I started staying out later and later. My dad was always in bed by then, so it really wasn't a big issue.

When I started high school, I had a realization that I might be gay. In the town where I grew up, a small town in Oregon, it seemed like there wasn't a single gay soul. There wasn't anyone even close to being stereotypically gay.

In my freshman year I went with one of my friends to a dance practice for the all-girl high school dance team. I really liked it because I love to dance. After the practice, I asked the coach, "Could a guy be on the dance team?"

She replied, "I don't know. We've never had a boy on the dance team before."

"Can you find out?"

She went to the administration to do some research on the rules. There was nothing in the rules that said guys couldn't join the dance team. She said, matter-of-factly, "If you would like to start coming to practice, here's the schedule. You're on the team."

I didn't realize at the time what a big step I was taking. I started going to dance practices and still going to the club in Portland. Then we discovered an underage gay nightclub in Portland, The City Nightclub, before it became Revolution. The girls and I would go one Friday night to The Quest and then the next Friday night to The City. I hadn't danced with a guy or even explored being interested in a guy. When I went to the gay nightclubs I would dance with the girls, or just by myself. Typically it was a mix of people dancing alone, with only few couples here and there.

It was a real shock for people to see a boy on the dance team. The guys mostly had a problem with it, but the girls thought it was awesome. The girls on the team, the girls I went to choir with, and the girls I had classes with loved it. It was kind of awkward when we did assemblies. When I did my first assembly with the dance team, in front of the entire high school, you could just hear this murmur above the music. When I did the splits, you could hear the whole audience say, "Ahhh!" I heard another guy yell, "Oh my God, I bet that hurts!" That's when I knew that I was different. Things would never be the same again.

I was on the dance team all through high school. I was lucky because I had an older brother in school with me, and some of my cousins acted like gangsters. The kids in school knew my family, so I didn't get picked on much. There was some name-calling, but I never got beat up. I started hanging out with kids who were the outcasts—they were called the "grunge." I had long hair and wore flannel shirts and ripped jeans. The administration thought we were a cult—one of my friends even drove a hearse to school. It was just a rebellion thing.

I started doing a little bit of acting in my junior year—along with being on the dance team and choir and going out to the clubs. The City Nightclub helped me feel more comfortable with myself. One night I met a guy there, and eventually we were dancing. I think we kissed. I came off the dance floor and one of my friends asked, "Oh my God, you danced with a guy. How was it?" On the way home they asked me, "So, you're gay?"

My only reply was, "Yeah, how could you not know? We've been going to a gay club for a couple of years."

Another friend said, "You never said anything! You never danced with any guys before, and you never talked about it."

"I don't really don't know. I guess the subject just never came up."

So they were the first people I came out to, just before my seventeenth birthday.

Shortly after that, I came out to my best friends, Diane and Addie. I used to go to church with Diane and her mom and grandparents. My dad was Catholic, but we only went to Christmas Mass and Easter Mass. Going to church with Diane made me feel like I belonged with her family. I went to the youth groups every Wednesday and even sang a couple of times in front of the congregation.

When I told Diane and Addie, they took it as a matter of fact, as if they already knew that I was gay. I think everybody in my high school, even everyone in town, knew I was gay—everyone except my dad.

I had a friend, Nicky, who started coming to our school when I was a junior. Everybody talked about him being gay. He was the stereotypical gay: skinny, lanky, and very feminine looking. He had a crush on me and he used to write me letters, some of which I still have today. In one of the letters he was playing coy, saying he had a crush on a guy and didn't know how to tell him. I wrote him back asking, "Who is it?" I knew it had to be me, since I was the only other gay guy in school. He was very awkward. Nicky got picked on and beat up by other students all the time. At the time, I was still trying to be accepted, and still trying to accept myself, so I didn't associate with him—except through these letters. I feel really bad now, and I have apologized to him for that many times. We are best of friends now and we see each other often.

The summer before my senior year, I went to my first Gay Pride event in Portland. I went with two lesbians—the first out gay people I had met in my town. We spent the whole day there, and I got to meet a lot of new people. Just seeing guys with guys and girls with girls—holding hands and feeling comfortable—was amazing. I bought some pride rings: six rings that wrap around each other. You could get them in either rainbow colors or in silver—I got mine in silver. I wore mine to Texas on our family vacation.

When I went to Texas with my father and younger brother, I told my cousin I was gay. She took me out to the bars down in Mexico and to a salon to get my hair bleached white.

When my dad saw it, he asked, "What did you do to yourself?"

It was the day before we were going back to Portland. Dad came from Texas from a manly upbringing, and I think the combination of my white-bleached hair and the "'70s retro" clothes I was wearing was too much of a shock.

He gave me an ultimatum: "You are not getting on the bus with me with that hair." I relented, and agreed to get some hair dye to cover up my white hair. I went to the store and got blue hair dye. I dyed it, washed it, and walked out of the bathroom.

Dad was livid. He asked, "What did you do to your hair?" It didn't sound like a question. My hair was now a sea green to teal blue. It looked really bad.

He took my hand and dragged me out the door, telling me, "We're going back to the store, and you are getting black hair dye!"

I had to go into the store by myself with my nasty colored hair, and finally I dyed it black. On the bus going home to Oregon, I had black dye all along my forehead and on my hands. It was embarrassing.

When I started my senior year, I decided that I didn't care—I am gay and there is nothing I can do about it. I was going to be open about it. If people asked me, I was going to be honest. If they didn't like it, that was their problem.

In English class, we made collages about ourselves. We took cutouts from newspapers and magazines and glued them onto a piece of cardboard. I started by cutting out grunge and fashion stuff from magazines. I found an article for a movie about a high school teacher played by Michelle Pfeiffer in Dangerous Minds. The page was all black with a bunch words in the background that you could barely see. They were all racial slurs and names. The words "queer" and "spic" were right next to each other, and I cut them out to put on my collage. You would have had to be up close to see them. When I put it up on the wall, and I remember thinking that a lot people are going to see this, but I didn't care.

No one ever said anything about that collage, but from that point things changed. I started dressing different—I wore a t-shirt that had a smiley face which read, "Have a Gay Day!" I threw myself out there for everyone to see. To my surprise, I got a positive reception. I became more popular and started getting invited to parties. Some of the guys had problems with it, but their girlfriends would shut them up.

That same year, I had gone out to the club to go dancing with my girlfriends, and they decided to go home early—but I didn't want to go home yet. I had been talking to this guy, Josh, who I had met the week before. I asked if he would give me a ride home. The girls left, and we ended up dancing all night until the club closed at 4 a.m. The owner of the club was helping the homeless gay kids stay off the streets, so he kept it open late. Josh gave me a ride and when we got to my place, we kissed goodbye. My dad happened to be awake. He must have heard us drive up and looked out the window, but I didn't notice. I went inside to find my dad walking down the stairs.

"So where were you?" he queried.

"I was at the club."

"Well, who brought you home?"

"My friend, Josh."

"I thought you were out with some girls."

"Well, I was, but they left early, so Josh dropped me off."

"What the hell were you doing kissing him?"

I didn't know what to do. I didn't say anything. I just brushed past him, running up the stairs, thirteen steps. I have always remembered the thirteen steps to the top of the stairs. I got undressed, got into my bed, and pulled the blankets over my head.

My dad came in soon afterward. I am not even sure what he said. It was something about kissing guys, and I don't know what else. Then I heard him say, "I'm giving you a ride to work in the morning." He left and went back to his bedroom.

I worked on Sunday mornings at a shoe store, and I had to get rides to work because I didn't have a car yet. Dad gave me a ride to work the next morning. I was very uncomfortable, sitting in the car, staring out the window, neither of us saying anything. He dropped me off. All he said was, "I'll pick you up after work."

The day went by too fast. When I closed the store, Dad was outside waiting for me in his car. I got in, and he started driving, past our turn, out of town, past the next town, and out into the boonies. He started talking. I was staring out the window, shaking and crying, because I didn't know what to expect.

Finally, he said, "You know, I don't know what this is. I don't understand it. I tried to keep you kids out of drugs. I've kept you out of gangs. I've kept you in school, and I've put food on the table. I worked and worked, and I never thought anything like this would ever happen."

He started cursing God and blaming himself at the same time. He told me a story about when he was younger, a time when he was hitchhiking home. A guy pulled over to pick him up, and he started hitting on my dad—which didn't go well. Dad said he got out of the car and beat the guy up, and left him on the side of the road. He told me that God must be punishing him for the things he had done in his life.

I was shaking. Then, he said something that surprised me.

"But, I love you. You are my son, and I am going to be there for you—no matter what you need." That was the only time I've ever seen my dad cry.

I know it was hard for him, because of the expectations he had for all of us. He made me feel comfortable. I was touched. I knew then things were going to be okay, and that I didn't have to worry anymore, because my dad had been my biggest concern. I didn't want anyone else to tell him. Later, he told me his friends had told him before that I was gay, but he didn't believe it. For a year after that ride home, he didn't bring it up. He didn't say a thing about it. Our relationship grew stronger, and we began to talk more.

The next year, I moved out of my dad's place. I was dating this guy, Noah, and we had been dating for about four months. One day, I was talking to my dad on the phone while Noah was visiting.

"What are you doing?" Dad asked.

"Just hanging out with my friend, Noah." I told him.

"Oh, your boyfriend?" I was surprised. At first, I didn't know what to say, but I realized I didn't have anything to hide anymore.

I said, "Yeah, my boyfriend."

"Oh, that's good."

I didn't say anything more. I just gave him space to take it in. He would ask me questions like, "Why do you tweeze your eyebrows?"

or "Why do you paint your nails?" I would give him an answer, he would accept it, and that was the end of the conversation.

My dad has been my inspiration. He taught me values not just by telling me but by the way he lived. My dad always worked hard and kept food on the table, clothing on our backs, and a roof over our heads. He took care of us. He has always been our rock. He has always been strong.

When I was old enough to work, I made a conscious effort to make enough money to pay for my own things and to help my dad. It wasn't that I didn't need him. I knew he was there if I needed him. I just wanted to help him out. I knew how he struggled to pay the bills and take care of us. These days, my relationship with my dad is great. He comes over and visits my boyfriend and me and sometimes takes us out to breakfast or lunch. My being gay is not an issue anymore.

After my parents divorced, it became a battle to see my mom. She did come over a few times to take me and my brothers out for the evening. Sometime we would sneak off—there was a school behind us and we would meet back there and visit for an hour. She moved on, got married, and had three more kids. I lost contact with my mom and her side of the family from the time I was 12 or 13 until I was 21. When we finally did reconnect, I went to her house for Thanksgiving. I found out a lot of stuff about my dad that I didn't know. I took it all with a grain of salt because they both had their issues. I never have blamed either one of them for what happened between them. Life just happens and people grow apart.

She already knew that I was gay. She had heard it from someone in the family. We kind of talked about it. She had always been very religious and she sent me letters with little scriptures but they were always uplifting. She was just like me—we are one and the same. We have the same soul. She is very accepting of everyone.

I cherish those moments of having her at my house and meeting my boyfriend, Donnie, and seeing them dance together and making tamales with her. She was amazing. I even took her to the club once with one of my friend's moms. She was out there dancing, just soaking it in and enjoying our time together. She was a great woman.

She had heart problems, and she passed away in 2006.

I have been fortunate not to have any major hiccups in my life. I have a lot of endeavors and always want to try something new. For the last three years, I have committed myself to two things: cooking and acting. I love to cook. It is my passion. I am really technical about it, and when my boyfriend cooks I will tell him he is doing something wrong. And I love to act—I have been doing that for five years now, including some traveling shows.

As a gay man, I have gone through many phases. I went through a phase where the louder I dressed, the better—that was my feminine phase. I never wanted to be a girl. I was just attracted to the clothing, the makeup, and the primping. I still love looking at women's shoes and dresses—especially the shoes. I love walking in heels—they make me feel sexy, and the higher the heel the better. When I put them on I carry myself differently. I like the sound they make when I walk and the heels click the floor.

The last time I dressed in drag was in the Rosebud & Thorn underage gay pageant. The contestants model evening wear, do a performance, and answer questions. Then the audience votes for their favorite. The winners become the ambassadors of the club's gay youth and organize fundraisers and put on shows/performances. The winning female illusionist (drag queen) is crowned the Rosebud, and the winning gay male is given a medal and is the Thorn. I got the title of the Thorn, but deep down I wanted to be the Rosebud.

I have a good gay friend, and every day he dresses like a woman even though he doesn't want to be a woman. He doesn't want to go through the change. He has a husband who is straight. They met when my friend was dressed as a woman. His husband is in love with him, and this is the only relationship he has ever had with a man. It's not about being a boy or girl. It's about love. In the end, it's about finding somebody you connect with, and finding joy and comfort with that person. It's about finding that right person that just fits.

April 2014 Email

Momma Traci,

Currently I run the lights at a fitness center, they have dance club lighting when people do Zumba and I am working as a server at a gay owned restaurant. I have also gotten licensed in Zumba and have been leading songs with my partner. We are a dynamic duo on the stage. It has been a great fitness journey for our relationship.

My hope is to land a cush day job so I can get back into acting and performing. My goals for this year are to take up the aerial arts, silks, trapeze, partner acrobatics and physical theatre stuff. My dream is to one day grace the Cirque stage. I will also be pulling out my alter ego persona, and I hope to perform at the local bars. The drag scene has changed so much in Portland, and I am happy to have a place to express my creativity. Best of all my partner and I have been together for 12 years now and our love has only gotten better with age.

Danny

Just wish I'd done it sooner—Ryan

It had been over twelve years since I had talked to Ryan, one of Daniel's friends. He used to come to our home when Daniel was in high school. Ryan had been different from the other boys who visited. He needed more than acceptance—he needed family.

We met at a restaurant near his work, and when I saw him I instantly recognized his shy smile. I was greeted with a warm hug from this boy who had grown into a man.

Ryan
Portland, Oregon
March 2010

I was a normal kid. I played soccer, played with trucks, and played in the mud. At the same time, I had a lot of female cousins, and we played with dolls. When they came over, we would play in the basement where my mom had a huge storage room full of canned food and other groceries. We would play "grocery store" and pretend to buy the food, paying for it with monopoly money.

Growing up, I had more friends that were girls than boys. I was just more comfortable with girls as friends. As I got older, girls at parties wanted to play "seven minutes in heaven" in the closet, but I didn't.

I'm not sure when I first knew I was gay. I guess I was 11 or 12 years old. My best friend in school was Brandon. We started going to school together in kindergarten. We wanted to do everything together. We hung out all the time, and the other kids would call us gays and fags.

In the fifth or sixth grade we had our first kiss. We weren't sure if it was wrong. He was Italian, and his family was Catholic; my father was Catholic but my mother was Presbyterian. I hadn't really ever been told by my parents that being gay was wrong, or that gay people were bad, but still I wasn't sure. We moved from Portland a few miles away to Milwaukie when I was 11, and Brandon and I continued to stay in touch until we were about 17. Then we drifted apart.

The majority of my mom's family felt very strongly against gays. They lived in a small farming town in Eastern Oregon with a population of less than 300. If you weren't white, straight, or a farmer, then you were nothing. I already had a problem because I was a city boy.

Every other weekend, we would visit my mother's family. My brother was five years older than me, and in the summer would stay there and work on their farms to make some money. When I was 13, I started driving a grain truck and a combine for my uncles, and sometimes I would help my cousin's wife by watching her two boys, who were six and nine, when she took lunch out to the crew.

The next summer, my cousin approached me and said, "You are gay, and gay people molest children. I am going to find out if you molested my kids."

I don't know how he knew I was gay, or why he thought I would do such an awful thing. I pleaded with him to believe me, that I never touched his boys. I denied that I was gay—because to him that meant that I was a child molester. There was a big fight and my parents got involved. My cousin pressed charges against me, and I was arrested and put in jail. I was placed in a tiny cell by myself due to the fact that I was under the age of 18; but by state law I was still old enough to be tried as an adult.

They interviewed my cousin, his wife, and finally the boys. The boys both said all we ever did was play outside with their trucks. They let me go, and nothing came of it, but it was an awful time in my life. I felt so alone, embarrassed, and ashamed. I felt that it would never be okay to come out as gay. Everyone would think I was a child molester, and things like this would happen all over again.

I was not a religious person, but I remember praying every night for help. I wanted it all to go away. I even thought about ending my life. I went through counseling—which was recommended by an attorney—and a doctor stated that I didn't have a tendency to be a child molester. I was honest to the counselor about being gay, and he helped me to feel better about it. But I still couldn't bring myself to tell anyone.

Everyone in my mother's community knew everyone else, and eventually they all found out about the charges. It caused a huge rift in the family. Nothing was ever the same afterwards. For years after that, I was terrified to come out to my parents because they might disown me, or not accept me—or even worse, they might believe I really did molest those children. I really didn't understand what the term "homosexuality" meant, or what being gay was. I had kissed a boy, and hung out with a boy. I liked a boy, but I hadn't thought about dating or getting married or having kids with a boy.

This incident ended my relationship with my mom's family, except my grandmother who never turned her back on me. She has always loved and accepted me. She never treated me differently, but she has never spoken about what happened or about me being gay. It also broke my mom's relationship with her family, except for her mother and her sisters.

When I was 19, I saw Brandon again. He was dating Daniel. They broke up, and Daniel and I started hanging out. No one in my family knew I was gay, but I think that they suspected. Daniel wanted me to go with him to the underage night club in Portland, but I wasn't sure. I was afraid people would see me there. I finally agreed, and I met a lot of nice people who are still my friends today. I am not sure what I was worried about, because if they were there they were probably gay, too.

I remember coming to Momma Traci's house with Daniel and talking to her. It was the weirdest thing that she was so understanding and open and involved. It was amazing to me. I needed that, because I was moving towards my gay life, and I was losing some friends. It wasn't that my straight friends turned on me, but it was hard to live in both worlds.

One night, Daniel called me while I was at home in our basement with three of my girl friends. Daniel asked me, "Do they know that you're gay?"

I said, "No."

"Why don't you tell them?"

"I don't know." I was really starting to sweat.

"Just tell them you're gay, right now, and that's that."

So I turned to my friends and announced, "I am gay." They looked at me for a second or two, not sure what I had said or if I was even talking to them, and then continued talking to each other.

Daniel asked, "What did they say?"

"They went back to talking with each other."

Daniel insisted, "Say it again."

I was getting tired of this conversation, so I relented. I turned to my friends again. "I said, I am gay."

This time, they heard me. I had to get off the phone because they wanted to ask me some questions about it, but they were all fine with it. That is how I came out to three of my closest friends.

I started telling my other friends. All of the girls were fine with it, but not all the guys. Daniel wanted me to come out because he knew that if you just say it, it really doesn't mean the end of the world. It's not as big a deal as it is in your head. Without meeting Daniel and Momma Traci, I don't know how long it would have taken me to come out. Maybe I would be 31 and still in the closet. I am glad I came out—I just wish I had done it sooner.

It wasn't until I was 22 that I came out to my brother. I came out to him and his girlfriend (now his wife) at a bar in downtown Portland. My brother's band was playing, and after their set we sat at the bar and ordered some shots. After a couple of shots, my brother's girl-friend looked at me and asked, "When are you going to finally admit that you're gay?"

Shocked, I looked at her and then at my brother. I said, "Fine, I'm gay!" I think she sensed that she had pushed me a little too hard, so she hugged me. We ordered another round. It didn't make any differ-ence to either of them, and it's been fine ever since.

I don't remember ever telling my parents that I was gay. I think they just knew. Once, I heard my mom on the phone talking to my aunt about me, and my mom was trying to tell her nicely to mind her own business. A short while later, my dad grabbed the phone from my mother and told my aunt, "This is my family, and this is none of your business. Either you accept it, or you don't, but we don't want to discuss this with you anymore." He hung up the phone.

My boyfriend and I have been together for almost nine years. He has gone to all of my family functions and he has always been welcome. Even that first Christmas, my mom had presents under the tree and a stocking on the mantle for him. She never asked if he was my boyfriend—it was just assumed. I have always had a close bond with my parents. I still live within a couple of miles from their house. My mother passed away last year, but while she was alive we would talk every day. The last couple of years before she died, she would call after having a couple of glasses of wine and ask me questions about being gay, but I'm sure she didn't remember it the next morning. She asked me once if we were planning to adopt, and I told her that I might, someday. I wish I had been able to give her grandchildren before she died.

This last year was the first time since I was 14 that I attended my mother's family's Christmas party in Eastern Oregon. My mom was dying of cancer and she wanted me to deliver her presents. A lot of the family wouldn't even look at me. I felt branded and I left after only a couple of hours. When I got home, my mom was in the hospital. She died two weeks later. I didn't feel good about going to the family Christmas, but I felt like it was one of my mom's final wishes. She had always wanted to me to go to see if it would work.

Since that time, things in my mom's family have changed. One of my cousins just moved to Portland and came out as a lesbian. The family seems to accept her. What is really strange is that they are more accepting of her gay lifestyle than of my cousin who married a man from Africa.

Living in a town of less than three hundred people, who are all white and straight, there can be problems accepting people who live differently. I have struggled for years about how my family could believe horrible things about me and then turn their back on me. It has taken me a long time, but now I believe that they just don't know any better. I do miss my family, and all the things that we used to do up on the farm, but family isn't just blood relatives. My family includes my long-time friends, their families, and many other people in the gay community.

I am thankful that my grandmother has always been here for me. She has continued to come for visits when no one else would. She says she doesn't care what the others think—she loves me, and she loves my boyfriend. She is 94 now. We have gone up to her place to stay with her, and she has been to our place to visit. She was even with my boyfriend and me when we picked out our first house. She told us, "I think you two will make this home really nice." And we did.

Part Three

Metamorphous

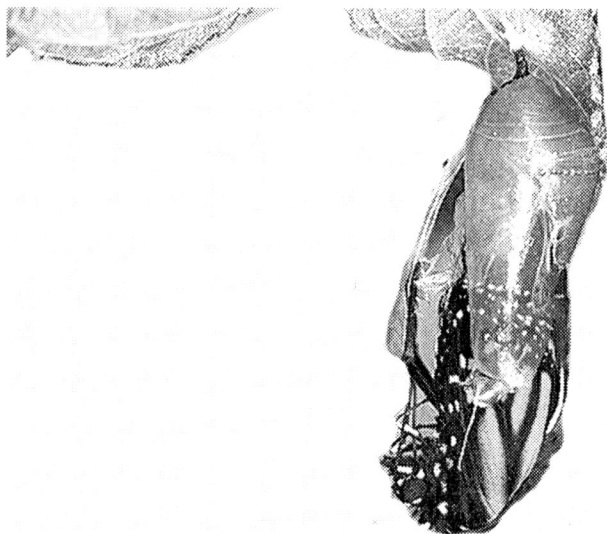

A family evolving —
Marisa, Anthony, and their mom Rita

I met Marisa, her brother Anthony, mother Rita, and their dad when Daniel was in high school. Their lives evolved through the years as Anthony and then Marisa came out. I was privileged to interview Anthony, Marisa, and Rita and to hear their stories for this book.

Marisa was one of Daniel's best friends in high school. Along with their friend, Thomas, the three were inseparable. My first memory of Marisa was when she was on stage, a cute little dark-haired girl belting out a song in a voice much bigger than she was. As an adult she is beautiful, animated, and bursting with happiness. She brings out the little girl in me, and I love her.

Anthony is Marisa's older brother. I sat next to his mother, Rita, in the auditorium of Century High School to see Daniel, Anthony, and Marisa appear in Working. Daniel and Anthony sang a duet together. It was beautiful. I knew he was gay, and I was very aware that his mother didn't.

I liked Rita instantly—Marisa definitely was a younger version of her mom. When Rita and her husband were having problems dealing with Anthony being gay, I talked to them. Rita reflected back her love of her son but her husband seemed upset and I felt like I had to choose my words carefully with him. Years later, Rita and I met at Anthony's apartment near Portland State University. We shared our feelings of love and acceptance of our children, and we became friends.

I found out Marisa was gay when my husband and I were visiting Daniel in New York. He was putting on his own show in 2009 at the Duplex, Looking Back on the Yellow Brick Road: A Celebration of Musical Theatre. Daniel, Marisa, and others performed songs from Daniel's favorite musicals. It was fantastic. Marisa's brother and parents were there, too, and afterwards we all celebrated at a restaurant nearby. I noticed several significant glances between Marisa and a girl I didn't know. Daniel whispered to me that Marisa was gay. I didn't feel shocked, even though I would have never guessed. Marisa was finding her true self. Marisa and Daniel's dear friend Thomas is not related by blood, but he is also integral to these stories. He was a sweet young boy who was always cast in the school plays as a comical character actor, and the memory of his crazy grin and antics still makes me smile. He used to come to our home, sometimes just to visit with me—until his mother called and told me to keep Daniel away from him. She thought Daniel was making Thomas gay.

Marisa, Anthony, Rita and Thomas continue to be entwined closely with Daniel and me. They are like family.

Singing her heart out
Marisa, 27
Portland, Oregon

(1ˢᵗ part of her interview) November 2010

I was a freshman when I first met Daniel. He was a year ahead of me at Century High School. Daniel was already out; everybody knew he was gay. We were in the middle of the academic year, and the school had just started a drama club. Our drama teacher, Mr. Bradley, told us our club team leaders would be Daniel and two other people. There was something about Daniel that just shined. I felt like I was just a kid compared to him and that we would never be friends. I would see him in the hallways and I'd say, "Hi," but he didn't know me. In high school, kids sort of stick to their own crowd.

Then we put on our high school's first musical, *Working*. I was cast as the waitress and Daniel got the lead role. That was my first role ever. I was into singing at that time, not acting. Because *Working* was really all individual parts, we had individual rehearsals with the director. The entire cast had not met until we started building the set.

At the first dress rehearsal, I was really nervous to sing in front of my friends and everyone. After I sang, Daniel said to me, "Marisa, that was really good." I remember being impressed that he knew my name. It was the first time he had ever talked to me. I would often stay and watch him rehearse, and I thought he was really talented. I was very shy then, but I wanted badly to be in his circle of friends.

During performances, before I went onstage, Daniel would say, "You've got this—go out there and sing your heart out." He was always supportive. Getting to know him was kind of like being in his club.

After we finished *Working*, we started talking to each other more but we really didn't spend any time together until Daniel and my brother, Anthony, got to know each other. My brother wasn't out yet, but I knew. I think I knew he was gay before he did. He wasn't into girls—he was into boys, and he had always been very feminine.

I saw Daniel at school one day and he asked me if my brother was gay. I told him that he wasn't. I didn't want to tell anyone that my brother was gay unless he gave me permission. Daniel smiled and had this look in his eye like he already knew. Soon after, he and I started hanging out, and we started getting closer. Daniel was always nurturing to me. He always believed in me and he always told me I could do anything. Whenever I voiced doubts about my singing or acting he always told me to shut up, that I could do it. I never had a crush on Daniel. I just cared about him—just like I cared about Thomas.

When it came to Daniel and Thomas, I just liked being close to them. The three of us were in choir together. I remember one night Thomas and Daniel came over to my house the night before we had some big choir event in the morning. We stayed up playing games until around 4:30 a.m. We had to be in Portland by 7:30. When we got up and showered, we felt like we were hung over even though we had not been drinking. We did make it there on time, though.

We all came back to my house afterwards around noon. The three of us took a nap together in my room, and when it got hot I took off my jeans. It was nothing sexual—they were like my brothers. So there

I was, sleeping between two boys in my underwear, and my mom came in my bedroom and saw us. Later, she would tell me that she thought that it was really sweet—then she went to close the door and stopped. Even though she knew that they were both gay, she still had the mentality—since they were boys and I was a girl—that it wasn't right.

Then, there came the debacle with Thomas. Thomas had a friend, Diana, who he talked to a lot. He told her about sitting on a couch in the auditorium with Daniel, on the stage with the curtain closed—and one thing led to another. Daniel and Thomas kissed, and eventually made out. Thomas was a Mormon and felt guilty and confused about what they had done. One Friday night, when Diana was over at my house helping me with a film project for a class, the phone rang, and it was Thomas. I began to ask him how he was doing, but he cut me off.

"Can I speak to Diana?"

"Are you alright?"

"I need to speak to Diana right now."

I gave her the phone. As she began to talk to him, her face dropped. She walked into the other room. Five minutes later, she came back saying, "We need to go to Thomas's house right now!"

I didn't understand. "Why?"

"He's going to hurt himself."

"What are you talking about?"

"Marisa, he's gay. He says he's got a knife. He's going to hurt himself."

I didn't know what to do, but then I remembered my brother was home. I ran upstairs to his room.

I ran in, exclaiming, "Anthony! Thomas just called and he's gay and he's going to hurt himself. We have to go get him." He grabbed his keys and started putting on his shoes.

He said, "I know what he's going through—because I'm gay, too."

All I could say was, "Oh, sweetie, I already knew that!"

He smiled and I gave him a big hug, then he left with Diana. I stayed home in case Thomas called back. Soon they came back with

Thomas, but he wouldn't even look at me. They told me they sneaked into his house, got him, and sneaked out. His parents went to bed early, around eight.

Anthony ran upstairs to get a first aid kit. Thomas had toilet paper wrapped around his wrists and there was blood everywhere. He'd been scratching himself until he bled. My brother held his hand while Diana was tending his wounds. He hadn't used the knife yet—he had wanted someone to stop him.

That night, Diana told me what had been going on between Thomas and Daniel. We all fell asleep together in the living room and we took Thomas home the next morning.

I've always felt protective of Thomas, and I would get upset when I would see that he was wearing long-sleeve shirts. Later I found out he had started cutting his legs, shoulders, and stomach where he could easily hide it. I couldn't understand what would drive someone to that. I just didn't understand why he would put so much energy into hurting.

Another night, Thomas called Daniel and told him that he had a knife to his stomach and was going to kill himself. Daniel called 911. The sheriff showed up at their house and woke his parents up. After that, his parents made him go to the bishop and confess all of his sins, and he told the bishop that he had fooled around with Daniel. That was when his mom called Momma Traci and told her that Daniel was making Thomas gay—and that he wasn't allowed to see Daniel anymore. We didn't see Thomas in school again for a long time. I guess I got mad at Daniel for that. I felt like Thomas's parents found out about him being gay because Daniel called 911.

In my sophomore year, I started to come out of my shell. Mr. Bradley didn't want to give me leads in any of the shows because I was too reserved. He said he wanted me to give more, but I really didn't understand what he meant. I always held back because I didn't want to mess up.

Daniel was the one that taught me "more." I had always separated acting and singing like it wasn't real life. Daniel taught me that acting is real life, just bigger. He used to tell me to just have fun with it. For the school's talent show we decided to perform a few things from *Rent*. Daniel sang *What You Own* with Anthony. Momma Traci sat next to my mother for the talent show. As they watched Anthony and Daniel sing, Momma Traci told my mom how great it was to have a gay son. Momma Traci knew Anthony was gay, but my mom didn't. I think everyone knew but my parents.

Next year, Daniel and I decided to try out for parts in *Jesus Christ Superstar,* which was to be performed in downtown Portland. It wasn't a high school production, but we tried out anyway. The next day we found out that both of us got parts. My parents were really worried that I would be going into Portland, the big city, because the rehearsals were at night. Daniel told them he would be with me and would drive me home every night. That's when Daniel had that red truck of his. I loved that truck. It had a Hawaiian hula girl on the dashboard.

That's when Daniel introduced me to Idina Menzel's music and gave me her CD. I still have it. It's completely worn out and scratched because that's all we listened to. Daniel would even have me sing some of the songs to other people. I always felt important around him, like I had a purpose.

While Daniel was in his senior year, he was going to Century some days and to a liberal arts school on the others. I was at Century and I would have choir and then lunch—an hour and forty-five minutes to-tal. I would go to choir, check in, and sneak out, and Daniel would pick me up. We would drive around for a while and then he'd drop me back off.

His art school was performing a dance to Fame and he told one of his teachers that they had to hear me sing. When I performed for them, they gave me a singing part. Daniel picked me up and took me to practice, and I got to perform with them. He was always trying to get me involved in opportunities, to get me out there.

At the end of summer, I ran into Thomas one day and he gave me a big hug. He just said, "I love you, Marisa."

I said, "I really love you, too." I wondered why he hugged me so tight. Then he disappeared—his parents sent him away. I would call to talk to him, and they said he wasn't there. He wouldn't return my calls. I think they sent him to Maryland and then to Utah. They must have thought that if he were somewhere else, he wouldn't be gay.

One time I called and his mother told me, "Thomas doesn't live here anymore, and I would appreciate you not calling here." No one knew where he was. No one knew how to contact him. He was gone for a long time.

Daniel had left for college in Arizona, and Thomas had been gone for about seven months. Out of the blue, there was a knock on my door and there was Thomas, standing in front of me. He had borrowed his mother's car. I remember crying, "Why did you leave me?"

He hugged me. "I'm sorry, I'm sorry." That's all he said. We drove around for a little while and picked up Diana. She was so happy to see him, but she could be very confrontational.

"Okay, what's going on? Where are you?" she demanded.

"I'm right here."

Diana persisted. "No. Tell me the truth, where are you?"

What he said next shocked us. "I know there is a woman out there who is meant to be my soul mate. I know now I have desires to be with men, but they are roadblocks to my journey to be with the one I'm supposed to be with."

Finally we parked in front of our house. I had to go inside. I asked if he was going to come to school the next day.

"Yeah, I'm going to come by and say hi to everybody," he said. I went upstairs to get ready for bed and pretty soon the phone rang. It was Diana, and she was crying.

"Oh my God, we weren't supposed to see him. He was supposed to be at his sister's place. When Thomas took me home, his dad was waiting on my doorstep. He practically dragged Thomas to his car and told him that he was never to see me again. Then they drove off." She was hysterical.

We didn't see Thomas for a long time. He didn't come back to Century. He didn't graduate with us. A year or so later he came back. He told me he didn't get to go on a mission because they said he had sinned; and he was devastated by that. It had always been his dream and they took that from him. After I went away to college in New York, he called me and told me he was so much better. He said that he wanted to see me, and that he missed me. He said his parents were not accepting of him. They kicked him out of their house and told him when he was dying of AIDS that they would take care of him.

He got his own apartment. He was working and saving money to go to New York. A few years later he went to Thailand, where he decided he would no longer deny that he was gay. When he came back, he brought everyone gifts, but his parents would not accept them—because the gifts represented something not Christian.

Thomas came to New York for a while, and then he went to Africa to help children—but he got scared and came back because he heard that if the Africans think you are gay, they will cut your hand off.

His sisters always loved him anyway, but his brothers would not allow Thomas near their kids. They said he was a pedophile. They would say awful things to him. His parents acted strange around him and said they were fine with it, but deep down I'm sure they thought he'd burn in Hell. It is so sad that his parents let their religion destroy their relationship with him.

These days Thomas is back in New York. He was dating someone whose parents are Jehovah's Witnesses and don't accept him, so it kind of gave them something in common. I don't know why Thomas seems to date guys that are real assholes. Maybe he doesn't think he is worth anything better, but I know he is.

"It's showtime!"
Anthony, 31
Portland, Oregon
June 2011

In junior high I realized that something was different about me. I didn't know anything about being gay, but I knew something was off. I continued to ignore it. I thought, "It's nothing, it will go away." I would even sneak Playboy magazines into the house and look at the pictures of women to try to force myself to be attracted to them. But it didn't work.

I was at a junior high school dance and was slow dancing with a girl. She leaned toward me and kissed me—and slipped me her tongue. I backed up, pushed her back, and said, "I can't do this. I have to go." I took off and just ran. It shocked me. During high school I dated a girl, but I was just going through the motions. I wasn't really into her.

I think everyone around me knew that I was gay—except me. When I finally came out to my friends in high school, they told me they knew. They were just waiting for me to figure it out, which made it easier for me when I did. I didn't get a hard time in high school because I was gay. I was never bashed or beat-up. I guess I just lucked out. Some of my classmates were verbally hostile to me, but nothing really dramatic happened.

I started to get to know a little more about gay people in my senior year. There was a boy named J.R. who was very flamboyant and very out. My mom and dad didn't want me to hang out with J.R., "that flamboyant frilly boy," because they said everyone would think I was a fag, too. That was when I was in marching band. I played the saxophone and was in youth band for the summer. I also started taking voice lessons in high school. My dad encouraged me to do that. I would come home from voice lessons so frustrated and mad that I just wasn't getting it. I would want to quit, but my dad wouldn't let me give up. He gave me the push I needed.

But that wasn't the same story when it came to color guard. J.R. was in the marching band and color guard. Color guard had a lot of gay people in it. This is where I started to be exposed to gay culture. I remember the day I decided to convert over to the "color area," which involved rifle and flag twirling. I didn't want to play saxophone anymore. I wanted to do something different. I liked how color guard looked, how they moved and performed, and I wanted to try it. I felt at ease with it. I started color guard the summer after I graduated from high school. My dad was furious. He said he didn't want people to think that his son was a fag.

My dad and I kept fighting over this silly color guard thing. I ended up doing it anyway. I only got to do it for a few years, but it was fun. Recently my mom told me that Dad felt so bad for being so upset about it. She told me that he was practically crying because of the way he had treated me.

Around that time I met Daniel. I was just out of high school—I was 18, and Daniel was 16. By that time I knew I was gay, but I hadn't told my parents. The idea of telling them scared me. I was afraid my parents wouldn't accept me, that they might kick me out and leave me alone to fend for myself. I felt really comforted being around Daniel, because I felt safe talking to him. Daniel, Marisa, Jeremy, and I used to hang out at Momma Traci's house.

Sometimes I would go to the underage club in Portland with Daniel and Marisa. I was slowly getting into the gay scene and as far as gay nightlife that was all there was—the underage club. One night a guy from high school was there—a guy who was always really hostile to me in high school.

He walked up to me and asked, "What are you doing here?"

"I'm here with Daniel."

"What, are you gay?"

Daniel jumped in. "No, he's straight."

But he figured it out anyway, telling Daniel, "No, he's not. He's a fag."

I didn't say anything. I was really shy and hadn't come out of my shell yet. I looked up to Daniel because he was so confident. I admired him as a performer, too. I thought he was really talented. I thought that if I was around him enough, maybe I could learn to be self-confident, too. I wanted to be able to do what he was doing.

Right after I was out of high school, I told my sister that I was gay. When I told her, she was actually happy. That was the night we went to Thomas's house because he hurt himself. I remember seeing the scars on Thomas's arm and thinking it was really sad that his parents didn't accept him. It's hard to grasp that any parents could not be accepting of their own children and would shun them just because they are gay. People will love who they love. It is energy you are attracted to. If it's a man, that's fine; if it's a woman, that's fine, too. That's just how it is.

My dad was the next family member who found out, but it wasn't intentional. He had been on the computer and had looked at my online history. He found pictures of guys, and then he found an explicit e-mail. He approached me about it and sat me down. He said, "I have some confusion. What is going on?" I simply told him that I am gay. We both started crying. He told me that it was okay, and that he still loved me, but asked me not to tell my mother.

I really don't remember how I came out to my mom. I think my mom already knew, but she just didn't want to believe it. They both had a hard time accepting it. Thank God John was around at the time. He was my dad's best friend. John is gay also, and he really helped my parents through the process. We call him our fairy godfather, and we say that I'm his fairy godson. John guided them to be more accepting. John used to tell me that no matter what happens, things are going to be okay.

Confidence is the most important thing I have learned. My parents were insistent that I go to college right away after high school. They kept pushing me, so I went to Portland State University for a year. I fumbled through it. I wasn't ready. But I auditioned with Daniel for the talent show at Century High School. My choir teacher from high school was there. After we were done, my former teacher looked over at me and asked, "What happened?" He was so shocked when he heard the sound that came out of me. In choir, the voice was there but I didn't how to use it. I was shy and was afraid to sing loudly. I didn't have any confidence then, but it was beginning to grow.

Marisa and Daniel moved to New York and started at AMDA. I thought, "That is what I want to do." I loved the idea of being able to learn to act, sing, and dance all together at the same place. I got a call from Marisa—she wanted me to audition to get into AMDA. She told me she knew I could get in. The second I got off the phone I went online and filled out the application and picked my monologue and song. Some of my classmates and even some of my teachers at PSU helped me with my monologue to get it prepared. I worked with my voice teacher to get my song ready. I remember going into the audition very confident. I sang, followed by my monologue, and I walked out of that audition floating on a cloud. I had an interview right after that and I was so sure of myself that I told myself, "I got it"—and I did. I got my letter of notification a week later. I spent two years there and graduated.

Immediately after I graduated from AMDA, I took a summer theatre job in Auburn, New York, and I did three shows. After that I did children's theatre. I liked the kids and it was fun, but the whole experience of doing the children's show was not pleasant. Amelia Bedelia Goes Camping was an hour-long show with several acts. There were only four people on stage, and I was on stage the whole time except for costume changes. The people I worked with were not pleasant to be around, and the manager was a control freak, a big child. Everyone was always was arguing, and they talked behind each other's backs. We were crammed into a van for six months, traveling from town to town. It was the most grueling job I have ever had, and I will never do anything like that again.

I then had a chance to sing with the New York City Pops Choir. I even got to sing in Carnegie Hall.

After that I fell into a rut. I was working in a chocolate shop in the West Village and it took up all my time just to pay the rent and bills. That was all I did: Go to work and go home, go to work and then back home. I was miserable, and I was shutting out everybody around me. I wasn't doing what I came to New York to do.

I knew I needed to go back to school. I tried one semester at Mannes Music Conservatory. I couldn't afford to go any more, but I got to meet some wonderful people. I had a great voice teacher there who helped me with my voice and added a whole new layer to it.

I moved back to Oregon and am back in school now, and it is going great. I received scholarship money, which is a real honor. I am getting a Bachelor's in Music with an emphasis in voice. After that I plan to go to Portland Community College for the two-year Sign Language Interpretation program. Being a certified sign language interpreter will enable me to combine theatre with interpreting and will help me communicate with my younger sister who is deaf. I do miss New York, but I don't miss the struggle. I know singing or something else will take me back there someday.

When my sister Marisa came out, I was surprised. When she was dating a guy, she broke up with him, and she told me that he was distracting her and keeping her from her goals. I don't think that was the case. I think she was dealing with her feelings. Marisa told my mom first, but she didn't tell my dad right away because he was having some medical problems. Marisa was performing every Wednesday night at Therapy, a gay bar in New York City, and she was dating Teresa.

Once, Mom and Dad were in New York visiting and they went to see Marisa at Therapy. They had just seen her performance and they were both having a lot of fun. The whole place was swarming with gays and lesbians, and Marisa hugged Teresa. Marisa looked up at Dad and his smile just went away. At that moment he had realized his daughter was gay, too.

I'm very open with my parents now. I have asked them to watch gay movies with me. I want to expose them to as much as I can so they feel comfortable.

There are gay men that don't come out until in their 30s. It just boggles my mind that they confine themselves that long. My dad's friend John was married, had two kids, and lost one child to a car accident before he came out. His daughter doesn't talk to him, and he isn't allowed to see his grandchildren because he is gay. John is in his sixties, but he is full of life and energy.

I wasn't ready to come out until I was 18. The moment I came out, everything was in place. It was meant to happen. These days, kids are coming out when they are younger than I was.

When I was younger, and people were mean to me because I was gay, I would just tune it out. I tried to not let those things bother me. My Catholic upbringing made me feel bad at first because I was gay— now I question religion. Parents can destroy their gay child when they instill guilt in them because of their religious beliefs. Sometimes it is so bad they will kill themselves.

The last voice teacher I had in New York was really good at teaching confidence. He would tell me that when you are up on stage and you are presenting your piece to stand up and present it. He would tell me to be fearless, to "get up there and fart it out." The classes I took at AMDA taught me to just be me. Now I can walk into in a room where I don't know anybody and be comfortable. As Debbie Reynolds said, "Chin up! Boobs out! It's showtime!"

Supposed to feel like
Marisa, 27
Portland, Oregon

(2nd part of her interview) November 2010

I consider the word "gay" as universal, applying both to gay men and lesbian women. When I was a kid, I used to have fantasies about women I liked. I wanted to be close to them, but I didn't know how, so I'd imagine they were my mother. I didn't think of it as a sexual thing. I was always comfortable saying, "She is beautiful," but I was never comfortable saying the same thing about a man.

I didn't date much in high school. I was a virgin until I was 16. I am a sexual being—I enjoy sex. I even enjoy sex with men. It's just that when it comes to companionship, I prefer women. I like the softness and the closeness, and I like the connection I feel with them. With a guy, it was always like they just want to hurry up and do it. I loved my first boyfriend, and I truly thought I was going to marry him someday, but there was something else I wanted. I didn't know what it was.

We were together for two years. After that I dated another guy for two years and I can say I loved him, too, but still I wanted more. I have never met a man that I've been completely infatuated with.

One reason I'm more attracted to women is because they are more fun to look at than men. Now that I am older, I do appreciate a good-looking man. Daniel is a beautiful boy, but there have only been a handful of times that I have been floored by a man. I never thought I could be a lesbian because every lesbian I ever knew of or saw looked like a boy, and I didn't want to look like a boy. I like makeup, having my hair long and my nails done, and so I couldn't be a lesbian, could I?

The first woman I really liked was Joyce. She was a co-worker while I was working at a hotel in New York. She was big and beautiful. When I discovered that she was a lesbian, I thought, "This doesn't make any sense, because she looks so feminine."

I worked with another woman, Holly, who was born and raised in North Carolina, and she had a thick Southern accent. She was 38, and she was beautiful. She was stunning. You would never guess she was a lesbian, but she loved women. Whenever she saw a hot girl who came into the hotel she would come up to the front counter and ask, "Which way to . . . ?" It was an excuse for her to check the girl out. Afterward she'd say something like, "Damn, I just had to see that one up close." This blew my mind because she was pretty and a lesbian. That's when I knew that I was wrong—not all lesbians were dykes who ride Harleys.

I was always flirting with Joyce, but she had been in a relationship for five years. One night she asked me if I wanted to kiss her. Of course I said, "Yes." She told me to hurry up, since she had a girlfriend and might change her mind.

I kissed her. I remember being so excited and feeling so good. I thought, "This is what I'm supposed to feel like." Something lit up inside me. Eventually, though, Joyce chose her girlfriend over me. I was heartbroken. I couldn't eat or sleep, and I lost a bunch of weight. I quit working at the hotel. Joyce asked me if it was about her. I told her, "No," but she really was the reason I left that job.

I had to start looking for another job. I was looking for a place I saw on Craigslist when I walked past Garage Restaurant & Cafe, a jazz restaurant in the West Village. I asked the hostess if they were hiring. They were looking for a hostess, and I got hired. That turned out to be great because practically everybody working there was gay—the manager, the bartender, and one of the servers. It was a really friendly place.

The Duplex Cabaret Theatre, a famous gay piano bar and cabaret, was across the street and the Stonewall Inn—where it is said gay rights liberation began with the Stonewall riots in 1969—was right down the street. Fate had led me there. I felt like I was starting a new life. Nobody knew who I was or that I had had boyfriends before.

That is where I met Teresa, the liquor distributor. She came across very harsh, but you had to get to know her. I was immediately attracted to her, which was strange because she was beautiful and yet masculine. She had been out for years. She was comfortable in her own skin and she knew who she was. When I met her, I felt the kind of feelings I had felt when I kissed Joyce.

Teresa and I started seeing each other. She would tell me that she had been unhappy for a long time and didn't like the idea of going through life without getting to know me. We were together for two years and we broke up many times. I was only 21. She was 16 years older and had been burned a lot in her life. She was very supportive of me, like Daniel always has been. She told me I had great talent and she encouraged me to be out there performing—but at the same time, she would never tell anyone that we were dating, which made me feel like she was ashamed of me.

I remember talking to Daniel about kissing Joyce and then about Teresa. I had explained to Teresa how important Daniel was to me and that I loved him. But when I introduced Daniel to Teresa, she didn't like him. I think it was because he didn't give her the approval she thought she needed. Daniel is hard to read. When people meet Daniel, they want to be part of his life. Maybe they are a little jealous. I feel like I'm lucky because Daniel is part of my life, so it really hurt me when Teresa didn't like him. How could she not like my Daniel? She was the person I was supposed to spend my life with, and he was an important part of it.

One year, before the gay pride celebration in New York, I came out to my brother. I said something like, "I have something to tell you. I like girls." He gave me a big hug and welcomed me to the club. He said that he figured that, based on the guys I dated in high school.

"What's the matter with the guys I dated?" I asked. "They were funny."

"Yeah, but most girls don't look for funny. They look for hot!"

I told my mother that I was gay when I started dating Teresa. I told her I had something I need to tell her, especially before I told my father. When they had come to visit me, I was really distant, and I apologized to her for that. I had been seeing a woman for a year and a half, and I'd felt like I couldn't tell her. I explained that Teresa wasn't the first woman I'd been with sexually, but she was the first female I had been in a relationship with.

I said, "I guess that means two out of three of your kids are gay."

She replied, "No, I think it might be three out of three, but we will let your sister figure that out later." I think she was joking.

I knew Mom would be upset, but ultimately I knew she would only love me more. That's the way she is. She's a true mother and I'm her baby. With her kids, as with everything else, she has always shown love instead of anger. I am lucky to have my mom, great friends, and my brother. When I jump into anything head first they never let me drown. I have surrounded myself with the people I want to be like, people that are truthful to themselves, like my Daniel.

Teresa told me that I could do what I wanted, but just not tell her. Once I went out with one of her friends, and she found out about it. She said she never wanted to see me again because "you don't date your girlfriend's friends." We got back together and we broke up again. This happened over and over. I had a need to have her acceptance and I didn't know why. I guess she reminded me of my father. I was constantly seeking her approval. When we were together we had fun, but it wasn't meant to be. Still, I will always love her.

I didn't really get to tell my dad that I was a lesbian. He found a letter I had written to Teresa while he was visiting in New York. About a year later, we were fighting by email over something. He mentioned something about skeletons in my closet, and he said I wasn't being truthful with him. I figured out what he meant, and I responded that if he wanted the truth, yes, I am a lesbian, my girlfriend's name is Sarah, and I love her very much. He said he wished that I had come out gracefully. The "gracefully" part really made me mad.

We don't get along, and it's not because I'm a lesbian. It's always been his temper and how he calls me names. He hurts people with his words. I truly wanted to tell him in person, but it ended up happening by email.

Sarah and I decided we needed a break from the city, and we moved back to Oregon. It was only supposed to be for the summer, but it ended up to be longer. We were staying with my parents to save money with the goal of moving back to New York, but we didn't get along with my father. We finally had a big blow-up fight and he kicked us out. We had to use our savings to rent an apartment in Portland. I was very angry and bitter. I hated being in Oregon because it reminded me of my father and the stress of family conflict.

We moved to Minneapolis to be close to Sarah's family. I love living here. I love the people I have met, and I love Sarah's family. Her father is supportive of all the kids, even if they change their plans to follow a new dream. I wish my dad could understand that.

I have researched the MacPhail Center for Music, a performing arts center here where people can take lessons in music with professional artists. I would love to play the guitar and piano better. I want to start at the beginning with piano, guitar, and voice. I love to write as well— I have books and books filled with poetry and thoughts. I want to put my words in motion. I can hear rhythms and beat in my head. I'd like to be a songwriter. These are my goals right now.

I have been with Sarah for a little over three years now. I've never been with anyone who understands me the way she does. She's the only person I've ever wanted to let in. I want her to be a part of my life forever. I trust her with all of my heart. We have started talking about a domestic partnership. It's definitely not the same as marriage, and doesn't give us all the same rights, but at least it gives us some. It makes us angry that we can't get married, but I know it will be legal someday. We are already married in our hearts.

That's the way God made them
Rita, 56 (mother of Marisa and Anthony)
Portland Oregon
June 2011

During college, between 1975 and 1977, I had several friends who were gay. My parents didn't like me hanging around with them. They said being gay was a sin. Even still, I kept spending time with them because they were my friends, and they were fun. I was going to college in Texas, and we would go across the border into Mexico to go clubbing and dancing. Throughout the years, I have worked with many gay and lesbian people, and I've always felt that they were some of the nicest people I've ever known.

When the kids were little, we had a friend, John, who was married with kids and going through a divorce. He had hidden being gay for a very long time. When my husband found out, he was angry—not because John was gay, but because they had been friends for such a long time and John never shared it with him. I couldn't understand what difference it made. As I looked back on it, I think that God sent John to us as a friend to help us with what was to come. At the time, Anthony was 12, Marisa was nine, and Christina was six. I suspected that Anthony was gay, but never Marisa.

When Anthony was little, I would see him playing with his cousin's My Little Pony dolls and press-on nails. Even though he was also into the Transformers toys that I would buy him, I still wondered if he might grow up to be a gay man. When Anthony was eight, my husband got him into baseball. Anthony didn't like baseball, but his dad—who was a little league coach—insisted: Anthony was going to play baseball. Anthony wanted to play the violin. His dad agreed, because he loved music, too—but Anthony still had to play baseball.

I really started questioning his sexuality when Anthony got into junior high, and later into high school. He was gorgeous and had lots of friends—lots of girls that were friends, but no real girlfriends.

When Anthony was a senior in high school, we held a quinceañera for Marisa, a Hispanic coming of age tradition. He brought a girl to the party, but he ignored her all evening. I asked her if everything was all right.

She said, "No. I like Anthony, but he doesn't like me the same way because of his problem."

"Problem?"

"Yes, but I can't talk about it. I guess I'll just keep trying."

Anthony was in choir and marching band all through high school. The summer after he graduated, he wanted to start color guard. I thought it was fine, but my husband became very angry. He said that it was a thing girls do. He didn't want any son of his doing that "rifle-twirling, faggoty bullshit." I remember his words clearly, and I am sure that Anthony still remembers them, too.

When Marisa was a freshman in high school, she got involved with the drama club. She would go to auditions and hang out with all the other kids in the club. I met all of Marisa's friends from drama club—they were working on a set for a play. Daniel came up to me and introduced himself. I thought, "What a nice boy, and good looking, too!" I remember telling Marisa, "Daniel is such a nice boy. I would let you date him."

"I thought I wasn't going to be able to date until I was 17?" she said.

"But Daniel is such a nice boy. Your dad doesn't have to know."

"Danny is gay."

"Are you sure?" I asked.

"Mom, he is openly gay. Everybody knows."

I was disappointed, but Marisa just shook her head and laughed.

I didn't tell my husband for a long time that Daniel and Marisa's friend, Thomas, were gay. When I finally did tell him, he was fine because he really liked the boys.

I met Daniel's mother, Traci, when Marisa, Daniel, and Anthony were performing on stage at the high school. Daniel and Anthony were doing a duet. Traci told me how wonderful it was to have a gay son. I wasn't sure that Anthony was gay, and I didn't know that Traci already knew that he was.

I found out for sure about a year or two later. He had told one of my nieces that he was having a hard time telling us. He didn't realize she would tell everyone. My sister called to tell me that she had heard a rumor that Anthony was gay and she thought I should know. She had heard it from her husband, a dentist, who heard it from his receptionist, who heard it from a friend—it really got around.

I was mad that someone would spread that rumor about Anthony. I followed the rumor back to my niece and called her. Even if it was true, she still didn't have his permission to tell everyone. I told my husband, and he was really angry at my niece. When Anthony came home, we sat him down. My husband didn't say anything. I told Anthony about the rumor and asked if it was true.

He said, "I've been meaning to tell you for a long time, and I guess this would be a good time. Yes, I'm gay."

I started crying. "I guess I always knew, but I'm sorry that it had to come out through your cousin."

He said that he was scared to tell us because we always said that it was wrong to be gay. He was scared that we were not going to accept him.

I told him we should respect gay people. It wasn't up to us to judge them; it was up to God. I explained that I wasn't crying because he was gay, but that I feared for his safety. I told him that there were many people in the world who don't accept gay people, and many who want to hurt gay people.

A few days later, Traci came to our house. I guess Marisa had called Daniel, and Daniel called Traci to visit us for moral support. She brought us some pamphlets about being gay as well as a book by Ellen DeGeneres' mom, *Love, Ellen: A Mother/Daughter Journey*. I still have those pamphlets. I made copies and have shared them with lots of other people. One of my sisters has a son that just came out last summer.

Traci talked to us, and it made me feel better; but my husband was difficult to talk to. Our gay friend, John, has been so supportive and has helped us so much. My husband did a lot of research. He read a lot of books and finally came to the realization that it was okay to be gay, that God loves all of us, and that it's not a sin. We started going to an Episcopal church that is very inclusive of the gay community. We became big advocates of the gay community. We even marched in the Gay Pride parade.

There was a boy that Marisa and Daniel hung around with who was also in the drama club, Thomas. He was gay and it was really tough for him. His parents sent him away when they found out. I just don't understand it. I always thought if I ran into his parents one day, I would tell them how wonderful their son was, and that I knew God loved their son just like he loves us all.

But I worried all the time about Anthony's safety. I wanted to talk about it with my family, but my husband wouldn't let me. He said I shouldn't be telling other people that Anthony is gay because it was not my place and it was personal, even though I knew Anthony wouldn't mind. I don't go around telling everyone, but if the opportunity arises, I do. I didn't get to tell my mother—I wish I could have told her before she died. My sister says our mom knew anyway, and that she was okay with it. I haven't told my dad, but I think he knows.

During Marisa's senior year in high school, I had an inkling that she was gay. I can't really explain it. It was a mother's intuition. I remember going shopping with her at the mall, and I would comment about the good-looking guys and point them out. She never seemed that interested. I kept telling myself, "Your daughter is not gay." By this time, I knew about Anthony. After high school, Marisa moved to New York to go to AMDA. My husband and I visited her every year and met all her friends, and then my thoughts about her being gay would come back again.

After she graduated from AMDA, she performed in singing competitions in gay bars and would always win. We went to listen and encourage her. She had lots of gay and lesbian friends. By then I was pretty sure she was gay, but I was just waiting for her to tell me. She started seeing a boy in New York, and they dated for almost two years. When I saw them together, I never saw sparks. I thought it was just a cover-up or that she was confused.

Then Teresa came into the picture. Teresa was kind of masculine and had lots of tattoos, and Marisa talked about her all the time. I knew for sure then that Marisa was gay, but I didn't confront her. I wanted her to tell me. My husband had the same feelings but conceded that we could be wrong.

Marisa ended up telling me on the phone. She said, "Mom, I've been waiting for you to come for a visit. I really wanted to tell you this in person. Mom, I'm gay."

All I could say was, "I know sweetheart, and it's fine."

Marisa quickly added "But I'm a lipstick lesbian."

"A what?"

"A lipstick lesbian, that's a lesbian that likes makeup, does her hair, and likes to look pretty."

I found myself smiling.

The next year Marisa started dating Sarah, but I hadn't told my husband that she had told me. He went to New York and took them to Atlantic City for the day. Later, he called and told me how much fun they had, and how much alike Marisa and Sarah were. He said they were like two peas in a pod. He really enjoyed seeing them laugh and seeing how happy they were.

If I could say anything to parents who suspect their kids are gay, I would tell them to just look at their son or daughter and realize how wonderful they are. It shouldn't matter if they are gay or lesbian or whatever. We should love our kids unconditionally. It doesn't change who they are. If I had the chance to snap my fingers and change them from being gay, I wouldn't. They were born this way.

I wouldn't change Christina either. She is deaf, and that is who she is. Recently, she thanked me for not giving her cochlear implants. I told her that I didn't think it was my place to change who she was. When she was in sixth grade, she came home from school signing to me that she wanted to be in the school band. I asked her why she wanted to be in the band since she was deaf. She got so angry at me. She reminded me that I had told her to never let her deafness stop her from doing what she wanted. She signed to me as she pounded her chest, "I can't hear the music, but I can feel the music. My friends are in band and I want to join, too."

We let her join the band and she played the clarinet. We got her a private tutor who also knew how to sign. She was like any other kid—she played the scales over and over in the beginning, and not very well. But just before Christmas I came home and heard someone playing Jingle Bells, and I thought it was her teacher. I walked into the family room and found Christina playing, and it was beautiful. She did great in band, and even ended up doing recitals in nursing homes.

Christina and I have talked about Anthony and Marisa being gay. It is difficult for Christina to accept because she goes to a fundamentalist Christian church. She would say, "Mom, being gay is a sin." I told her that she had been misinformed. I asked if she knew that one in ten people are born gay. She believes that being gay is a choice. I asked her if she chose to be deaf. I explained that Anthony and Marisa were born gay—and that's the way God made them. Christina has come a long way, but she keeps asking questions. I think a small part of her still believes it is a choice, but I am hoping she will come around.

Recently, we had a family gathering and Anthony brought his boyfriend. His boyfriend was talking to my dad, who is now 86. They were making conversation—about my dad growing up and about music—and my dad said, "I'm glad that Anthony has a partner in his life. You guys should get married."

I finally understood — Momma Traci

Having a teenage son is a challenge—having a gay son even more so. Who could stay overnight? A girl, or a boy, or was neither an option? I admit I invaded Daniel's privacy when I found that he had been visiting sexually-explicit sites on our computer. I talked to him about it and even tried to block the sites, but he always seemed to find a way around them. Then, I started getting into his email before he came home from school. If I saw a request for his picture from someone, I would send them a picture of an ugly overweight guy. Recently I told Daniel about what I had done. He thought it was funny, but I am sure he wouldn't have felt that way back then.

In high school, Daniel was strong-willed and independent. He would stay out past curfew, talk back to me, and sneak out. With the emotions of a teenage girl but the libido of a teenage boy, he was a nightmare combination. Life with Daniel was an emotional roller coaster. I warned him about older guys trying to take advantage of him, and I worried about him constantly. But he continued to stay on the honor roll and he was actively involved in activities like drama productions.

In 2000, Daniel left for the University of Arizona to study dance. I flew to Tucson with him to help him get moved in. His roommate seemed fine except for the boa constrictor she had in a big glass tank in the living room. That gave both Daniel and me the creeps. When Daniel opened the freezer to put away his groceries, he found a bag of dead white mice with long pink tails and little pink feet. He carefully moved his frozen food to the opposite side of the freezer away from the snake food. When we turned on the TV, only even-numbered channels would come on. His roommate had blocked all the uneven ones because they were "bad luck."

The next day we visited the dance department and met his teachers. Daniel was excited and eager to start. The last night I was there we snuggled up next to each other and cried ourselves to sleep. We had been so close, it was hard to be apart. I returned to my empty nest.

The newspapers and television reports were filled with stories of gay bashing and AIDS. I couldn't protect Daniel anymore, and I constantly worried about him. But Daniel loved his school, and I looked forward to talking to him on his phone each morning as he walked to class. After about six months his roommate's snake got loose and she couldn't find it. Daniel moved into a small place of his own, and I flew back to Arizona to help him set up.

After a couple of days of cleaning and buying what he needed to live on his own, we went to the video store to rent some movies. I was looking over the musicals, trying to find the first one I fell in love with: *Seven Brides for Seven Brothers*. Daniel approached me and exclaimed, "Mom, they have gay movies!" We spent the next two days, sitting side-by-side on the floor in Daniel's apartment, watching gay movies.

We watched *Bent*, about two men in a concentration camp—in love, but not able to touch, kiss, or even hold each other. Their lives consisted solely of passing each other as they moved rocks from one pile to another, day after day. They could steal only a few moments standing next to each other, joining their hands and their love only in their minds. Daniel and I held hands as tears ran down our faces.

Watching these men in love but not able to love freely, my eyes were opened. My life had been so consumed with worry about my son that I had never understood his need to love and be loved, freely and openly. I finally understood.

From a caterpillar to a butterfly — T.J. / Jaia

I remember my first trip to New York City in 2002. Daniel had moved from Tucson to attend the College and Conservatory of Performing Arts (AMDA). He had already been there one term and was moving out of the dorms and into an apartment he would share with Marisa.

When I got there it was raining, hard. I took a taxi to his dorm and found students huddled out front under the overhang with their soggy boxes and luggage. Inside, the hallways were jammed with students moving in and out.

Daniel took me upstairs to meet T.J., his new friend. He was lying on his bunk with music plugged into his ears, reading a copy of Out. T.J. looked up at me with a wide smile and we began talking as though we were old friends. I fell in love with him right away. When I left he gave me a big hug.

The next evening was an AMDA school production. Daniel was amazing, masculine, and graceful. T.J. was an incredible dancer, but I remember thinking that he just didn't seem to fit as male.

My return visits to New York to visit have always included spending time with T.J. When I saw T.J. on stage as Jaia it had only been two years since we first met. I was amazed by his beauty and grace as a woman. It was just a drag show—but there was so much more to come.

T.J., 27
New York, New York
June 2010

I remember when I first met Daniel at school at AMDA in New York. I was in my room sitting on my bunk bed in school housing, watching an episode of The Real World. My roommate was showing Daniel around and introducing him to people because he was new.

Daniel saw the TV and said, "I love that show!" I asked if he was a dancer—immediately we had something in common. I was going to perform in the dance workshop—sort of a talent show students audition for—and I suggested he should, too.

We did three dance workshops together. After we got to know each other, we would dance all the time and choreograph programs for other students. We really clicked. We would go dancing to the clubs, down to Chelsea and Greenwich Village. We were going-out buddies.

When I graduated in February 2003, Daniel left school early to do a European tour of Grease. I did a tour with a children's show for a couple of months. After that I was in tours of Rent on and off for about three years playing multiple parts.

Daniel and I had a lot of ups and downs in our friendship, but every time we were in town we would hang out together—going dancing especially—and we started getting closer. Unfortunately, all the guys I was interested in always turned out to be straight. I felt a different connection with Daniel. We would go to Barracuda, where I now have one of my shows. Going to see our friend, Candis Cayne, was the highlight of our night. It became a ritual for us.

When we went to see her show, I would think, "What was her life like? It seemed so amazing." She inspired me. If she could transform from a man into a beautiful woman—and be happy and successful, going for her dreams—then I could, too. She transitioned many years ago from a caterpillar to a beautiful butterfly.

A transvestite is a straight man who wears women's clothing for sexual pleasure. They don't want to live their everyday lives as women or become women. A transgender person is someone that identifies as the opposite gender of their gender assigned at birth. Your sexual orientation does not determine your gender, and vice versa.

I used to dream about being a girl when I grew up. I always thought that someday it would happen. I loved being with men, but not as a man. I loved it in a "feminine woman way" more so than in a "masculine, gay male way." In all of my relationships, I had always played the female role, and that is how I had always been treated.

Throughout high school and later at AMDA, when I had nothing to do and had no money I would go to Barnes & Noble to lounge and read all the gay and transgender books I could find.

I am a woman. I was just born a boy.

I've always liked men and I have always felt a connection to them. At the end of the day, what truly matters is if two people in a relationship love each other. There is such a wide spectrum of gender and sexuality. At one end, there are masculine gay men that don't identify with anything feminine and at the other feminine, straight men only attracted to women. There are billions of people on Earth and there is no way we can be exactly the same and like the same things.

When I was small I liked to play with dolls—and maybe even dress up in girls' clothes. However, if you continue acting feminine, others begin to look at you that way. Daniel is a very masculine gay man. As LGBTQ youth, we learn how to play the game. Daniel might be gay, but he likes to project himself as a straight, butch, masculine guy. For myself, I like to be seen as feminine. I could have lived in my head as a woman and pretended to live the rest of my life that way, but I decided to do something about it. I embrace the woman I was meant to be.

I had been performing on stage as a woman, Jaia, since 2004. That's when I started doing drag and dressing female. I went back and forth between male and female just fine for a few years, but then I came into the city and started doing my own gigs. I was in a gay relationship with one of my boyfriends, and he loved my Jaia persona, but we lived our lives as gay men. Finally, I was thinking to myself, "Do I really want to do this outside of the stage? Will this affect what I really want?" I didn't like going back and forth. I really didn't want to be T.J. anymore juggling this dichotomy.

My boyfriend and I broke up. We knew it wasn't going to work. I didn't want to be a man anymore. When I got ready to go out or for a show, I dressed as a woman. That's what became normal. I didn't go out in men's clothes anymore.

The first person I told about my thinking of changing my gender was my roommate, Bobby. We were roommates at AMDA and have lived together ever since. He has always been very supportive of me and has never judged me.

He told me that whichever way I was going, he loved me—and that I was fabulous either way. He told me that I had to explore it, since you never know until you do.

I think that is what a lot of parents fear: the exploration factor. Maybe they think that if you explore it, you will go ahead and do it, and it will change everything forever. That is not necessarily true. I had to decide for myself.

I discovered that I can really be who I am, the woman I have always dreamed of being, and still accomplish what I want as an artist. My goals in life have been to be who I really want to be and to entertain. I don't want to give up one for the other.

Jaia

I hadn't seen Jaia for almost a year when I attended the New York premiere of The Big Gay Musical, Daniel's movie. Jaia had legally changed her name and she looked different—but it was more than makeup, hair, and clothes. She really looked like a woman. She was a knockout. A couple of days later, Daniel did a video shoot with her. It must have been a funny sight: Jaia dressed to the hilt with two suitcases of costumes, Daniel with his video equipment in one hand and a garbage bag of more costumes, and me with two more garage bags of even more costumes as we crossed Manhattan in a taxi and two subways to our destination. It was a perfect day.

During one of the costume changes, Jaia told me she had been going through hormone treatment and I could see it in her face and her body. A new woman was blossoming right before my eyes, transitioning from a caterpillar to a beautiful butterfly.

Jaia, 29
New York, New York
September 2011

Daniel and I have been so lucky. We have seen and done a lot of things that most people have not. We have been able to go different places, and we have been able to be ourselves. Life is so much more than your sexuality and your gender.

Daniel and I have an interesting friendship. We may not see each other for a while, but then we are right back together. At first when he started AMDA, I had a crush on him. People were always asking me if he was single and about his sexuality. I got a little protective of him and would tell them, "No, he is straight. Leave him alone." Then he is starting telling people that he was gay.

Our relationship could have been a trivial one but I am glad we got to this point. Daniel is family to me. He is my brother—and now I am his sister.

Part Four

Yellow Brick Road

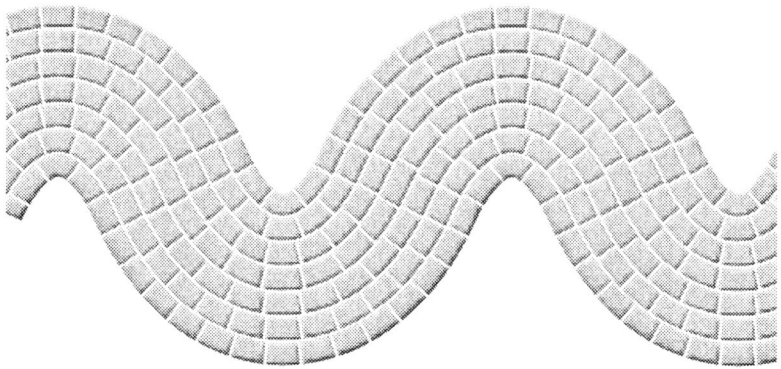

Bringing Me Closer — Chad Allen

Steve and I have a condo on the Oregon Coast in the small city of Depoe Bay, the whale-watching capital of the world. Bud was an old sea captain who lived across the street from us. He was outspoken, far to the right politically, and a fearless member of the city council. When he saw us in our yard, he would bolt across the street to regale us with the political dramas of Depoe Bay. His stories were always lengthy, and often a repeat. But Bud was kind-hearted and always there to offer help and advice with charm and a winning smile.

One year, Daniel was coming to Depoe Bay and he was bringing his boyfriend, Chad. I wanted them to meet Bud, but I was unsure how Bud would react. One evening, after listening to a couple of Bud's stories, I told him that Daniel was gay and that he was coming to visit with his boyfriend., and that I hoped I could bring them over to meet him.

Bud's blue eyes sparkled. "Do you think they will mind that I am straight?"

While Daniel and Chad were visiting, the four of us were walking on the beach with our dogs. We could see for miles, and it felt like we had the beach to ourselves. Daniel and Chad were walking ahead of us, hand in hand. A couple appeared in the distance, walking towards us. Daniel and Chad dropped their hands to their sides and continued walking. The simple act of holding hands with the person you care for was a freedom I had taken for granted until that day.

Chad Allen, 37
Los Angeles, California
February 2011

My name is Chad Allen Lazzari, but I go by Chad Allen. When I started acting, casting agents thought my name was too Italian. They told me to use my middle name because it sounded more like a "white American boy."

I started acting when I was five, mostly doing commercials for McDonald's and Mattel toys. I did almost every "He-Man and the Masters of the Universe" advertisement for years. My first television series came when I was eight—I acted on St. Elsewhere for four years. Then, my acting career took off. I worked on several series: *Webster*, *Webster's Best Friend*, *Our House*, *My Two Dads*, and *Dr. Quinn, Medicine Woman*.

I knew I was different from the time I was a child, even before I could relate to the concepts of sex and sexuality. When I was five or six years old, in one of my acting first jobs, I was enamored with the male lead. I wanted to be so close to him, and I dreamed that he would take me away with him. It wasn't sexual, but it was an attraction. There was a book that someone wrote a few years ago called—*When I Knew* by Robert Trachtenberg—mostly celebrities talking about when they first knew they were gay. The writer came to me with some photos from the show I did when I was five—until then I hadn't known the actor I'd had a crush on was Alec Baldwin, before he was famous.

When I was growing up, I would get teased. I would do a shooting for a show and then go back to school. That was quite unusual for a child actor then, but my parents thought I should stay connected to my real school. By the time I started high school I was a teen star. I was on all the teen magazine covers—it was my picture that girls had on their bedroom walls. So in high school, half the kids would follow me around because they wanted to be close to me, and the other half—mostly older kids—would pick on me. They would beat me up in the hallways and call me names like "faggot actor." I don't think the word "fag" was directed at me for being gay but it was derogatory, the worst insult you could call someone. I don't think they thought I was gay, but I was an actor and that was enough.

I was trying to fit in. I did date a few girls, but only half-heartedly. I only had sex with them a couple of times. I remember knowing I was attracted to my male friends, and when I would hear the way the guys would talk constantly about sex and girls, I just didn't get it. I didn't see what they were so excited about. It wasn't until the first time that I kissed a guy I was really attracted to that something burst inside of me. I finally understood why guys spent all their time talking about chicks, seeking their attention and wanting to get laid. I understood it perfectly.

In my young mind, this guy and I were going to be together forever, and I didn't care who knew. I was very naïve, and he was terrified. It wasn't until I was 17 that I had my first sexual experience with another guy, the cousin of a girl I was dating. He was older and in the Navy, stationed nearby. The ex-girlfriend found out later, and I don't think she was very happy about it.

I have four brothers and a twin sister. I came out to my sister when I was 17. I had moved out of the house and into a hotel while I was working on *Dr. Quinn, Medicine Woman*. I came out in my personal life and started to explore that side of me because I was on my own. I was meeting gay friends for the first time. I had a really close friend, Heather Tom, an actress and a daytime star for many years on *The Young and the Restless*. All of her male friends were gay, so they took me under their wings. I fell into this tight-knit group that was like family. We took care of each other. We did our share of partying and running around Hollywood, but we were a family.

After *Dr. Quinn* ended, I came out publicly. I was 20. A guy I dated briefly took pictures of us kissing in a friend's swimming pool and sold the pictures to a tabloid magazine for a bunch of money. They put an article about me being gay in the magazine, with the picture of us kissing on the cover. I wasn't out to my family, but I knew that I had to tell them before the magazine was published. I went to my parents' house, sat them down, and told them I was gay. I told them everything I had ever wanted to tell them. I explained that everyone was going to know because of the magazine, so I recommended that they tell the rest of the family so they wouldn't be embarrassed when they got a million phone calls.

It was one of those amazing experiences, as is for most people when they come out of the closet. It was a pivotal time in life, to finally express who I really was. I am very close to my mom, but when I came out to her, she cried. It seemed like she thought she should cry, though. She said, "Well, I always thought you were too cute to not have a girlfriend." My dad started crying, too, which was weird since he is very stoic. I had never seen him express emotion.

A friend recommended a wonderful book *The Family Heart: A Memoir of When Our Son Came Out,* by Rob Forman Dew. It is written by a mother and about how her child's coming out changed everything.

I read it for myself and then I gave it to my mother. I think it really helped her. Still, she had to hide it from my dad. He is very Catholic and had very definite ideas about what was right and wrong. He didn't want this "acceptance thing" going on.

Coming out to my parents brought us closer together. I don't think it's possible for a parent and a child to be truly close if the child hides something as important as this. It may be horrible coming out—for a lot of people it is—but most of the time the good that comes out of it is fantastic.

I was brought up in a male-dominated world. The first time I had a straight friend, a guy who knew I was gay upfront and didn't care, that was huge for me. He just wanted to hang out and have fun, just like my brothers and guy friends in high school. It was such a validation to be open and to be a guy's guy, because that is who I am. It meant the world to me. Up until that point, I thought there was no way those two worlds could ever exist together, and that scared me. But he was the coolest guy. Skeet Ulrich has now become a famous actor, but we had a blast together even though he was totally straight and I was gay. Sexuality didn't change anything.

March 2014 email

Momma Traci,

I am currently studying psychology at UCLA, and I am working on LGBTQ issues. I helped to launch an online confidential counseling space for LGBTQ students on campus. I am also looking at Ph.D programs.

Xo
Chad

Friend of Kenny — Kevin

A few years ago, my husband and I visited Daniel in New York while he was on Broadway in a production of Hairspray. This was my husband's first visit to New York. He was amazed at how friendly the city was. One night Daniel and his friend, Kevin, invited us to a picnic on the rooftop of Daniel's apartment building to experience Manhattan's city lights. Daniel and Kevin laid out a blanket for us to sit on, and they brought champagne, chocolate, and strawberries to share by candlelight. The view was spectacular. The lights of the Empire State Building seemed unreal.

We talked and told stories—it was a magical night. My husband asked Kevin why rainbows were used by gays as a symbol. Kevin told him he believed the rainbow symbolized hope that there was a place for them.

As of March 2014, Kevin is living in New York as a successful Broadway actor.

Kevin, 48
New York, New York
September 2010

I came out late in life. I officially came out when I first started having experiences with other men when I was 29. Up until that point, there was nothing, no running around at all. I knew from a very young age what my situation was going to be. When I was probably four or five years old, I knew I was different, or at least that I saw the world in a different manner. There was an innate gentleness or kindness inside me which many would probably write off as effeminate. I was called "fag" and "sissy" because I was sweet, spoke softer, and was gentler and less inclined to show aggression. My interests were more feminine than what would be considered masculine.

At that age, you are basically sexless. You have not reached puberty. But friends and family decide, based on mannerisms, that this effeminate person is who you are. You grow up knowing that you're different. When you're called out all the time, you want to know what it means, why it's bad, and why who you are is considered negative.

I knew that to have any tendencies that were seen as girlish was considered inappropriate, whether it was dancing or gymnastics or playing with a neighbor's dolls. I didn't do those things—I knew I would get picked on.

But I had two of the best friends in the world—one of the most wonderful things about my childhood. A boy who lived down the street had a total model train set, every Tonka truck ever made, and this big dirt mound in his backyard that we could play with the trucks on. The little girl across the street had all the best dollhouses and the best doll collection. The three of us were friends. We split our time between the three houses. Even though I did enjoy playing with the trains, I had just as much fun playing with the beautiful dollhouses— probably why I have a love of architecture today.

I learned at a young age to be very self-aware. I learned how to protect myself—in some cases physically—when people got mad or lashed out. I knew if I was being too effeminate I was risking being called a fag. I knew I could only be so much of myself.

During second grade I finally put a name to what made me different. We were in the boys' room and some kids were horsing around. One of them said, "Hey, you're a homo," and another kid told him he didn't even know what that meant. He explained that it's when a guy has feelings toward a guy in the way he should towards a girl. I remember standing at the sink, washing my hands. I looked at myself in the mirror and thought, "I'm a homo—that must be who I am."

I thought that this would go away, that puberty would kick in and my hormones would balance me out. At that point, I didn't understand that there was what Native Americans call the third sex: homosexuality. It's like being in the middle—you are both yin and yang.

Some people consider suicide, going to the depths, or lashing out. But I didn't. The most important things to me were family and the belief that the way you are perceived is very important. We have a very big, close, Irish Catholic family, and it is very important for us to achieve. As long as we did our best and represented our family well, whether we were number one or number twelve, it was good. It worked both ways—for our achievements and our negative actions. We knew if we started trouble it would reflect negatively on our family—on all of us. It wasn't a shame thing, necessarily. It was just that we should be proud of our family and where we came from. So I became an overachiever.

During high school I was involved in government groups, service groups, and plays, which ultimately led to my current career. I was also active in sports. But I kept a part of myself private. I'm sure people sensed I was a little different and that I was likely to be gay. Some people did not like me because of that, and they treated me in a negative way. But other people thought I was fun, colorful, and active.

I did date girls during that time. Maybe I needed to give it a chance. There was a great sense of obligation as well. That was what guys were doing, so that's what I had to do. I had very good best friends, people I projected my feelings of friendship, love, and admiration on. In reality they were deep crushes, but they were completely non-sexual. These friends were all straight. I was a very loyal, devoted, and generous friend. That's the way it went with my best friends in high school, college, and even afterward.

My father passed away in 1984 when I was 19 years old. He was an intimidating man. He made it clear that my "weakness" was not to be tolerated. I grew up in fear of how I was to be perceived and seen—by him especially. I know he loved me dearly, but when you have fear combined with love you start questioning what that love really is. Was it obligation or sincerity that I felt toward him? In hindsight I have great empathy for him. I wonder if he had lived until I was 35 if things would have been different. I don't think so. If your family decides to disown you it might be sad, but life would go on.

After college, I was a bartender in a busy, popular bar. I had a certain amount of power. It was kind of a stage and lots of good-looking women patrons found me attractive. They would throw themselves at me. I knew my straight buddies were going to wonder what was wrong with me when a hot girl came on to me. I could only keep the "I am waiting for the right girl" act up so long, so I would go on dates—and I have to admit I was not the best date. I would be purposely self-centered and rude so the woman would no longer find me attractive. That way, I was let off the hook and she wouldn't be chasing me anymore, and the guys didn't wonder why I wasn't seeing her anymore. It was a way to keep them off my trail.

It was very difficult. I can't imagine a heterosexual forcing themselves to be with someone of the same sex—they would be absolutely repulsed. Why would they do something like that to themselves? Why would you so blatantly lie about something that is so intimate and personal as the giving of yourself, even if it was just for coffee and conversation? I'm not proud of those days. I'm not ashamed of them either; but I wonder why I put myself or those women through that. It's just the way things were during the late 1980s.

I was in my early 20s, living in a house with a bunch of other guys just out of college. Some were in grad school or law school, and we were all starting our careers. I remember having a lot of sleepless nights in that house because I knew the time was going to come when my sexuality was going to be an issue. This fun, false world of post-college frat-boy life was not my world, not something that I was comfortable with. I had no role models and no understanding of homosexuality except for the negative media attention. I really didn't know where I was going to fit in. I wondered what I was going to do when I turned 27. Who would I be friends with? Was I going to be lonely? Where was I going to be?

I went to college for business. Some people made homophobic comments to me—they thought it was a way to bring me down, my Achilles' heel. I decided I did not want to be in business after all. I didn't want to live my life in suburban New Jersey—I didn't want to find myself trapped in that life. I knew I had the ability to do some theatre. I was able to get some commercial and print work right out of college, and I thought that maybe that was my ticket out.

I started taking acting classes in New York a couple times a week, and I'd walk around and get a feel for the city. The classes were in Greenwich Village, still in its heyday as the gay mecca before it turned into Chelsea and eventually into Hell's Kitchen. It felt free. I remember that feeling when I got off the subway—it was electric. In the acting classes I met gay people who weren't flamboyant. They were just who they were. But even when I moved to New York, where it was very acceptable to be gay, I was not ready to come out.

I started getting work in theatre. In that world there were out gay men performing on stage with me, as well as in the directing and artistic teams. However, there were still no gay role models I felt like I could relate to. It was a world of HIV and AIDS, which wasn't well understood. It was during the Reagan and Bush era. There were no drug cocktails to stave off infection—it was a death sentence.

There was very little understanding on how HIV was transmitted, nothing to explain what was high risk and what was low risk. It seemed like everything was a risk. My shame and the fear of contracting HIV—let alone the stress involved in coming out—kept me asexual. I stopped dating women, and I did not start having any relationships with men for five years.

But I was living in New York and waiting tables in restaurants with other gays, and I was working in theatre with gay men. I began to learn that it wasn't what we did that was important, but who we were as individuals.

During that period, I didn't meet any gay men that made me think, "That's the life I want to live." I kept wanting to find a guy like me who just wanted to have a quiet relationship, living our lives, not marching in parades or going to gay resorts or on gay cruises. I wanted something like a straight relationship—the only difference being two men instead of a man and a woman. Those good friendships I had, I kept hoping one of those would turn into a relationship.

I was getting close to my 30s and knew I had to deal with my sexuality. As I began to explore, I realized there was diversity in the gay world. I didn't want to start out by getting drunk at a bar and hooking up. I wanted to go slow. Most people start dating when they're teenagers. I needed to take those first steps.

When I was 29, I was on tour with a show and I finally met someone. We started hanging out, watching movies, and getting to know each other. The intimacy started slowly. Not long afterward, I found out that he was already involved in a serious long-term relationship. I decided to end it because I didn't want to break up his relationship, and out of anger he outed me. As upsetting as the first couple of weeks were, after a couple of months I was fine.

I started having relationships, but for the first couple of years I had very specific rules that I followed. Either I met someone and went through courtship and dating, or I wasn't seeing anyone at all. I was trying to live by a very traditional model for relationships. As I grew and accepted my sexuality, I had to learn to own my attractiveness and appeal. Before, I didn't want to be attractive to men because I hadn't been ready. I didn't want to be attractive to women, either. When I was finally out, I could walk into a room and feel comfortable to be sexy. At last I felt free about being myself.

In my 30s, some questions were being raised by my siblings. I'm sure they knew I was gay. I'm sure my mother knew as well, but she was just hoping it wasn't true. I found myself at family events feeling uncomfortable sitting around the living room with other adults. I would hang out with the kids because they didn't ask too many questions. I found myself staying away from my brothers and sisters because there were things I was not ready to discuss, but I knew I was going to have to deal with them. I had to talk to my family.

It was my 35th birthday, a birthday that I share with my sister. My family was going to take my sister and me to a Broadway show and then out to dinner. I decided that when the check hit the table, I was going to start my speech. There would be no turning back.

The show they were taking us to was Dame Edna's, a drag persona. The beauty of that is that I didn't want to use the word "gay" or "homosexual," because so often people immediately picture the sex act. It's no different than what straight people do, but in this case for some reason it is perverse. In Dame Edna's show, she refers to her fictional son Kenny who is obviously gay. She's says, "I didn't realize there were so many 'friends of Kenny,'": the hairdresser was a friend of Kenny, the personal trainer was a friend of Kenny, and so on. That became my euphemism.

So when the bill hit the table, I said to my siblings and mother, "Thank you so much. I am sorry I have been so distant from you all lately, but I need to let you know that I am a friend of Kenny's."

My siblings all got it, but my mom didn't. She asked me who Kenny was and told me that I could have brought somebody along. I gently squeezed her hand and asked her if she knew what we were talking about. She finally figured it out. I wanted them to understand that I have lived my life with the same dignity, self-respect, and faith that our mother instilled in all of us, and that I don't act any different than them. My faith has not been a deterrent—actually, it has been a sanctuary for me. I've prayed about my sexuality, and I know that there's someone out there for me. I know it was difficult for my mother, but she loves me.

After dinner, my siblings took me out for a drink. My younger sister, who hadn't been at the dinner, called my mom and asked her how it went. She told her it was fun and very interesting.

My sister said, "The reason that I didn't come was the invitation was just for the siblings and their spouses. You didn't invite my roommate, Tammy. I need to let you know that Tammy and I are in a relationship, and that I am gay."

My mother said, "Oh, Jesus!"

My sister said, "I knew you would be upset."

"No, no—it's just that Kevin said the same thing last night."

Within a 24-hour period, my mother found out that her two youngest children were gay. She saw the writing on the wall with me, but with my sister she didn't. She felt the role of women was not to enjoy sex, but just to have children. My mother felt that for my sister that her sexuality was more of a choice, so the beauty of us both coming out at the same time was that I was able to be an advocate for my sister. I explained that it was not a choice and it wasn't easy.

I felt like it was divine intervention. If my sister had been at that table, would she still have come out? Or would have she taken another six months? If she had come out first, how would I have felt? But the timing was perfect, and we both came out on our own.

My mother was more accepting of me than my sister. She felt that my sister may have been coerced. My mother blamed Tammy. She was also very upset that my sister told her over the phone.

Never tell anyone anything that important over the phone. You don't know where they are in the day or how they feel, and they can't see the seriousness and courage in your eyes.

Once I got my first Broadway show, I felt like I could come out in the world. I didn't have to play a game anymore. It used to be that you couldn't be out in the entertainment industry, but now you can. There was an article in Newsweek ("Straight Jacket" by Ramin Setoodeh, April 26, 2010), and the writer asked, "Can gay men convincingly play straight men?" That was a shallow thing to ask.

Someone blogged that the real issue the writer had was the feminine issue: Why is it so wrong for men to have femininity in their lives? Why is being feminine still perceived as a weakness in men, and why is a strong woman considered a bitch? Why are we so polarized when it comes to sweetness and toughness?

I was in a relationship with a man named Gary around the time of my high school reunion. I told my mother that I was bringing him to the reunion. She asked if I thought it would hurt my career. I thought it was important to go back to my high school and say, "Yes, I am a fag."

It was important to go back and be myself. I looked great, I had a great partner and a very successful career. I walked into that party feeling like I owned everything I am. I was received very well. The last thing they cared about was who I was dating.

The Big Gay Musical — Fred

Near the end of Daniel's two-and-a-half-year run on Broadway in Hairspray, the filming of The Big Gay Musical began, and Daniel had a starring role. I flew to New York to watch the filming. On the set, I was met with a big hug from Fred Caruso, the writer and director. He asked if I would play a walk-on role as a waitress. Soon I was serving drinks to the characters Paul (played by Daniel) and Eddie. My heart pounded as I spoke my single line, but it was the thrill of my life. During a bedroom scene between Paul and 'The Hustler," I was invited to watch the take on the monitor. The crew thought it was pretty funny to watch me lean in close, almost hugging the huge monitor. I never took my eyes off the screen.

Fred flew me to NYC for the movie's opening in 2009. My son on the big screen! The next night, I went by myself to see the movie again. This time I fully took in its message. As I was leaving the theatre, I saw Fred and he invited me to watch the movie with him again. Four young men sat down in front of me, and I could hear them discussing what they had heard about the movie. I leaned forward and told them I knew they would love it. I told them my son starred in the movie, and they wanted me to point him out to them. Their accents were beautiful—they were friends from different countries on vacation together in New York. During the scene in which Eddie's parents finally accept his being gay, the young men turned to look at me with tears in their eyes.

After the movie we stood in the lobby and talked. One of the young men told me he was 30 years old and afraid to tell his mom that he was gay. I often think about that night and that one young man. I hope someday I will hear from him, and that he will tell me that he has told his mother and that she loves him, just the way he is.

Fred and I went to his favorite piano bar. We talked about scripts he was writing, upcoming movies, and short stories I was working on. After several glasses of wine, we stood arm in arm with everyone else,

*doing kicks and singing show tunes. By the time I left I had become
the adopted mother of at least a dozen gay men.*

Fred M. Caruso, 36
New York, New York
September 2010

I was 19 years old when I first realized I was gay.

When I was maybe three years old, I was at my sister's elementary
school talent contest, and at the end everyone got up to leave. I
grabbed the microphone started singing, and everybody sat down and
listened. They loved it. I thought that was wonderful to have the attention, and from that point on I wanted to perform.

I have been performing since I was three, and working profession-
ally in theatre since I was six. I was in musical theatre, commercials,
and modeling—almost everything across the entertainment world.
When I was growing up, I was always called a faggot because I was in
musical theatre, but I always fought it. Being in musical theatre does
not automatically mean that you're gay. I think my parents prayed that
I was straight. When I went out with girls that made my parents happy. I fought the concept that I was gay until I realized that I actually
was.

When I was 19, I was living in a frat house and I was dating wom-
en. I was even having sex with women. The girl I was seeing told me
she was in love with me. I started crying, because I realized I had absolutely no feelings for her at all. That was a big thing for me, and it
started to change my thinking. The Internet was just beginning, and I
was always in political chat rooms. While browsing, I found many
"m-for-m" chat rooms. I began exploring, and that is how I began
coming out.

I wish I could have had the ability to explore my sexuality earlier. I
wish there wasn't a stigma about being gay when I was young. Who
knows what might have happened then?

The morning after I was with a guy for the first time, my mother passed away. I hate to say it, but that made coming out a very easy thing for me. There was so much I was dealing with emotionally. I knew that I was gay, even though I'd always fought with myself about it. Since these things both happened at the same time, I could only actually deal with one of them: Fine, I'm gay, but let me deal with everything else first.

I was able to look back on my life and realize that I had crushes on different guys over the years. It opened up my previous nineteen years to what it really was. I came out to everybody in my family, except for my dad. I told him a couple years later. He accepted it, but we never talked about it again.

I've always been the glue that holds my family together. When I came out to my family—and I know this sounds awful—I was hoping they would disown me. I didn't want to have to deal with them anymore. I didn't have the strength. Unfortunately, they didn't, and they kept driving me crazy for years and years afterward.

After my mother passed away, I was very depressed. When I'm depressed, I like to go to the theatre. It's always been my church—it's where I go to celebrate life and to feel better. At the time, Kiss of the Spider Woman was playing. It starred Chita Rivera. The show was described as being about "disentitlement," about a gay man whose mother was dying. I sat in the back of theatre, bawling through the entire show—but I think that's what good theatre should do for you. It should touch you and awaken things in you. It should make you think, and it should make you feel.

As I was growing up, my mentor was Charles Cragin, who was in the movie *True Lies*. We met when I was working at a theatre in an acting workshop. He was a smart, sophisticated, talented, and kind soul—in terms of who I am today, a lot of that is because of Charles. We would just talk. We had a wonderful rapport. He was sick the last few years of his life, and he died just three months after my mother did. Even though he's gone, I have a wonderful group of friends I collaborate with and who inspire me creatively. Hopefully I inspire them also.

I'm inspired mostly by music. The collaborations of John Kander and Fred Ebb provide me with a tremendous amount of inspiration—songs from the musicals *Chicago, Cabaret, and New York, New York*, as well as a lot of songs performed by Liza Minnelli.

I am very proud of my work on *The Big Gay Musical* because the big message was acceptance. The inspiration for The Big Gay Musical is twofold. I'd written a musical—Adam and Steve: Just the Way God Made Them—several years before, and I decided to write a movie because of all the people I met who have become so screwed up because of religion. I was put off by the many depressing movies about gays and religion. They all told sad stories, like a kid committing suicide for his mom to love him. I wanted to write something funny, something campy, and something crazy that could talk about religion and about being gay.

I don't know how my life would have been different if I were straight. Being gay certainly affected my art, what I do, and the message that I try to put out.

My last movie, *What Happens Next* (formerly titled, *You Can't Have It All*), is an older man's coming out story. Wendie Malick and John Lindstrom were amazing. There is a part of the gay community that is ignored—that of the older man. Most of them got married and had kids, mainly because they had to. Some men come out at 40, 50, or 60 years old, while some of them are still married.

I love to combine humor and camp with really serious issues. *The Big Gay Musical* was about loving who you are—loving yourself and accepting yourself. *The Bigger Gayer Musical*—the sequel that I am working on—is about love and relationships, all different kinds of relationships and all different kinds of love. All the trials and tribulations and the obstacles that we put up in our relationships.

Early in life, we build a list of what is perfect and who is going to be perfect for us. As we date people, we match them up against that list—this what I want, and this is what they are, and they're not this, and they are this, therefore I don't want to date them. But it might have been a perfect relationship. The characters in the sequel are not just gay people—the issues I am talking about are not just gay issues. That is the direction gay movies need to move toward. Once a gay person loves themselves, and accepts themselves, their relationships are like anyone else's.

One of the characters starts dating a dancer, who everyone assumes is gay but isn't. It's funny that people assume that anyone who is in tune with their body, has great posture, and moves gracefully has to be gay. It's discrimination, but people put them in a category. Even the gay community does this. There are a lot of straight dancers. I wanted to bring that element of conversation into the movie.

Today, many gay men are attracted to a lifestyle that involves drugs like crystal meth, clubs, and anonymous sex. I think the major causes of this are serious self-esteem issues. Many of us are brought up with inaccurate beliefs about gay people or we have been preached to about the evil of homosexuality. I try very hard to change that mentality through my movies.

Daniel and I have received some beautiful e-mails from kids who were able to come out. Because of the movie, they found the strength to re-examine and accept themselves. Many gay Christians have sent e-mails thanking me because they were able to see how religion and sexuality can go together, and they have acknowledged that God does really love them, too.

There are many different messages we can send to kids. Helping them accept and love themselves is far more important than getting society to accept them. Once you truly love yourself, it doesn't matter anymore. Until you reach that point, you are reaching out to anyone and everyone you can to find acceptance, and that's never healthy— needing that love from others. For a while you will find it where you can, but until it comes from inside you will never find what you are looking for.

I am supporting a charity called The Trevor Project (*www.thetrevorproject.org*)—the only nation-wide gay and lesbian suicide crisis hotline. The idea came out of a short film about a young boy who, when he understood that he was gay, began pretending that he was dead. The film, Trevor, was shown on HBO, and people (contacted) HBO looking for a place to call for support. That's when it was discovered that there was no place for young gay and lesbian kids to call, to have someone to talk to.

I haven't had many serious relationships in my life because I have always been very independent. I truly have been working all my life, and I love my work. My last relationship was ten years ago, but we are still best friends and I love him dearly. I need someone who accepts me, and all my craziness, but also accepts my work. When I'm working on a film, it can be fifteen hours a day, seven days a week, for weeks at a time. It is certainly difficult for any long-term relationship to put up with something like that. Maybe someday I'll find someone special, but until that time I am very happy dating my work; it's a beautiful relationship.

Ultimately, I want to keep making my dreams happen. I am a very lucky man. Every dream I have had I have been able to bring to completion. Every idea I thought was good enough has turned into something. If I keep doing that, I will be very happy.

Back to Church — Rev Matthew

During my hippie days in the late '60s, I remember being at the coast with friends on a beautiful Sunday morning. We decided to go to church. We drove around the small town and found a little white church with a perfect steeple calling to us. But we were stopped by a sign which read "No Hippies Allowed." We left, disappointed and a little angry.

I have not seen any "No LGBTQ Allowed" signs, but I know of many LGBTQ people who are not accepted by fellow churchgoers. I have found that religious beliefs are the main reason LGBTQ people are not accepted by mainstream society. These people must believe there is a "No LGBTQ Allowed" sign outside the pearly gates of Heaven.

Working as a real estate agent near several Intel Corporation campuses, I have met people from all religions and walks of life. An Indian gentleman told me the reason Intel works so well was because it is a mixture of different people—men and women from a wide range of ages and backgrounds who share and pool their ideas and create. It made me wonder why we allow religion to divide us, when we could come together for a better way.

When I began getting letters from Christian kids who wanted reassurance that God still loved them even though they were LGBTQ, I knew I had to step out of my comfort zone and find them some answers.

I found Reverend Matthew, the pastor of an LGBTQ-friendly church in Portland, Oregon. Reverend Matthew is young and handsome, a soft-spoken minister wearing a priest's collar. He told me about the history of the church. Then he told me that he was gay.

Reverend Matthew, 48
Portland, Oregon
November 2010

Our church was born out of the gay and lesbian experience nearly 40 years ago, and serving LGBTQ people continues to be our primary mission. About 80-percent of our membership would identify themselves as gay, lesbian, bisexual, or transgender, or as friends, family, and supporters: the queer community.

In many respects, we are not that different than many other churches. We have a worship service that would be familiar to most people, as well as Bible study and outreach to the homeless and hungry. The thing that distinguishes us the most from other Christian churches is our understanding of human sexuality—sexual orientations are part of human diversity. We were created as we are. That leads us to do things differently, because we see the world through those kinds of eyes. We understand how queer people are discriminated against even today, often in a very hurtful way. We bring the resources of Christian tradition and the church together with the experience of being LGBTQ.

I am an openly gay man and a Christian pastor, so I understand this from my personal experience. I have been out as a gay man for more than twenty-five years. I have been involved in the ministry since 1983. I have been an ordained minister since 2003.

I had a very early awareness of being gay. I was raised in the Christian church, so I did have personal struggle and tension. I knew I was gay before I had words for it. Some of my earliest memories are of being interested in men in a way that I began to understand was different than other boys. I did not understand it as sexual attraction, but I was getting the message that this was something I could not share with anyone.

In first grade, my best friend and I were playing on the playground, and he invited me to his birthday party. I was so excited that I hugged him and kissed him on the cheek, and he drew back. I knew by the look on his face that I was not allowed to do that. By the time I was five or six years old I understood that I wanted to love, embrace, and be intimate with other men in a way that was not considered to be acceptable.

I finally learned the word for it when I was 10. I had read the word "homosexual," and I asked someone what it meant. In my mind I told myself, "So that's what it's called."

I was raised with a religious background—not fundamentalist, but in a family where religion, faith, and involvement in church were very important. Even though I was attracted to men, I had not acted on it since there was never the opportunity to. When I started coming out in college at 18, I finally had to confront that. The first person I told was another freshman guy that I had a crush on. I thought he was gay, but he wasn't out at the time. I was very attracted to him, and it took me an hour to finally get the words out.

After that experience, I started coming out in almost every area of my life. I started attending a gay-affirming church. I had not come out to my family, but I was some physical distance from them. It was not until 1987, when I was 25, that I came out to my family. It was a time in my life when I would not deny it if anyone asked, but I just didn't know how I was going to come out to my mother.

My parents were visiting over the Christmas holiday, and my mother and I were having lunch in a mall. My mother began to express her concerns that I had so many gay friends. Then she asked if there was anything she should know. I asked her if she was asking me if I was gay, and she said, "Yes."

I told her that I was. My mother responded just like I expected. It was difficult for her because of her religious background. Since they were leaving the next day, we continued to correspond by letter. She wrote me with her religious and personal concerns, and I have kept the letters. For several months she was the only one in my family who knew.

I have two sisters. One came to visit me, and I told her. She didn't think it was a big deal. Soon, I told my other sister. She seemed surprised, but said that it was okay with her. The next time my sisters and my parents were together, my sisters cornered my mother and told her they didn't think it was fair that they knew I was gay, but my dad didn't. If she didn't tell him, they were going to. My mom told him.

A couple of weeks later I got a letter from my dad. I loved my dad—he was a great guy, but it was very unusual for him to write me a letter. He was the only member of my family who I had heard use a homophobic slur. I thought it would be really hard for him to accept. In the letter, he told me that he loved me, and that I would always be his son. He completely surprised me.

A few years later, I had a partner I was living with. My parents knew him since they had stayed with us when they came to visit. My parents were about to have a big wedding anniversary and my sisters were planning a surprise party in their hometown. My sisters and I had a conversation about whether my partner should come along. My sisters agreed that he should.

We had the surprise anniversary in the fellowship hall of the church I was raised in and where I was baptized. That night, we all stayed at my parents' home. I remember sleeping in my bed, in the house I was born and raised in—with my partner, Tim. I remembered how I'd struggled as a child, and how I could have never imagined that this would ever be possible. Yet it was, because of the love and the grace of my family.

I always knew my parents would accept me. I knew they would not reject me or disown me. I even thought that they might be able someday to accept a partner in my life. I never thought they would accept the church I was involved in. What was amazing to me was on their very next visit, after the anniversary party, they came to my church with me. That experience taught me that I should never underestimate the capacity for people to love one another.

It would be naïve for me to say that all parents will accept their children when they come out. There are many parents who will not accept their LGBTQ children because of their condemning religious background, but you can never know for sure what will happen. Many

LGBTQ children, and even adults, automatically assume their parents will be unable to accept them, but they really don't give them the chance. There is always a risk they might condemn you, just like you think. But then again they might not.

I kept the correspondence I had with my mother because I realized I grew up in that correspondence. I grew up in my relationship with her, and in her perception of me. There were things she asked me to try, like to go to an ex-gay ministry. It was helpful to correspond by letter, because I had some distance and I could think my reply through and not give her an automatic response. Our relationship shifted and changed. I told her I wasn't ashamed, I didn't feel a need to change, and I didn't feel broken or sinful. I told her I would not go to an ex-gay ministry even though it was something she wanted.

My mother has changed though the years, but I don't think she will ever go to a PFLAG meeting or march in a gay pride parade. She always comes to church with me when she visits, and so did my dad while he was alive. Several years ago, my mother was telling me about a book she had read, *Uncommon Calling*, the story of the first openly gay man to go through the Presbyterian ordination process— Chris Glaser. He was denied ordination because he was openly gay, which was meaningful for me since my family is Presbyterian. She explained why she thought my church was so important. It was one of those wonderful moments. I think we rob people of the opportunity to grow and change if we are not our authentic selves with them. We cannot make anyone love us or make them change their minds, but if we withhold ourselves from them, they never get the opportunity to know us.

I think parents' responses to finding out their child is homosexual are often fear-based. A parent that loves their child does not want them to be "eternally lost" in the Biblical sense. There is some Christian theology that has very clear boundaries, and you're not going to able to convince believers that homosexuality is not a uniquely sinful or condemnable condition.

Unfortunately, sexuality has been equated with sinfulness. It has become that any sexuality, which seems in any way different than monogamous, married, and heterosexual, is sinful. This has come from centuries of Christian theology that is not well supported in the Biblical context but is very much an inheritance from the dualism that the body and the spirit are at war. It is something that comes mostly from Greek philosophical tradition. It was absorbed by the early Christian church and it flourished. The things that are least bodily and sexual are considered as virtuous; the things that are most bodily and sexual are considered sinful.

This is the uncomfortable intersection that gay people of faith find themselves in. The primary difference we experience in our lives— whether or not we ever express it—is based in our desire for love, connection, and touch of someone of the same gender. We cannot avoid the fact that it is an erotic and sexual difference, and that always put us on the wrong side of the tracks between body and spirit.

This can be a very convoluted issue to pull apart, because it touches on so much underlying theological baggage that doesn't get unpacked, but just keeps getting perpetuated. Part of what is needed is to pull apart the equation: Sexuality does not equal sin. Gay, lesbian, and bisexuality are not intrinsically sinful behavior, just as heterosexual behavior can be healing, loving, and holy as well as broken and sinful.

There are three New Testament scriptures and a couple of Old Testament scriptures that are commonly quoted to show that homosexuality is sinful. Most of them can be readily dismissed as not applying to same-sex relationships at all. A couple of scriptures touch on and speak to same-sex behavior, and they are traditional clobber passages.

In the New Testament there are possible references to same-sex behavior by Paul in Corinthians and Timothy, but they cannot convincingly be shown to apply to same-sex relationships. There are two words Paul uses in both passages. One word is the Greek *malakoi*, which means "soft." In the context in which it is used, it certainly means immoral but it does not imply sexual immorality, and it does not specifically imply same-sex behavior. The other word he uses is *arsenokoitai*, which is unknown before Paul's use of it. The word is ambiguous as to whether it is referring to opposite-sex behavior or same-sex behavior.

There is nowhere in the Bible that condemns lesbian behavior, or female same-sex behavior. If you talk of female same-sex behavior, lesbians have a free pass. Part of that is the cultural context of the Bible. The patriarchal understanding of human sexuality in ancient times is, in many ways, different than in our modern world. The notion that women would be sexual with one another was either unimaginable or considered of no consequence. The focus is on male sexual behavior and how it is used in conjunction with women.

Two passages do speak specifically to male same-sex behavior—in contrast to more than 350 passages that speak to heterosexual behavior and what should or should not be done. One is an Old Testament passage in Leviticus 18:22 which reads very clearly, "That a man should not lie with a man as he lies with a woman." It is repeated and expanded upon that it is abomination and their blood will be upon them, which is a very clear condemnation. The New Testament passage in Romans 1:27, by the apostle Paul, speaks to a larger argument, "How men abandoned the natural use of woman and burned with lust toward one another."

We can look at these passages and ask, "What is the actual activity, in context, referring to?" I don't believe that in either of those cases it is a universal condemnation of all male same-sex behavior. In the Levitical code, the language is set clearly in the context of the worship of other gods or in rituals of other religions in the Near East that included male same-sex behavior. There is also reason to believe it would have been conceived in the ancient Jewish mind as a confusion of clean versus unclean, like many of the dietary laws.

In Romans I, Paul—being a faithful Jew—would have had a similar understanding of idolatry and clean versus unclean. His argument was not about human sexuality. His argument to the early Roman Christians was for them to recognize that they were condemning other people, and he lists all these heinous things that the *dirty Gentiles* were doing around them. He says, "Such were some of you, therefore you cannot condemn." He was working up the crowd to show them how awful it was, and then turns it back on them by telling them they had no grounds to condemn anyone.

To lift these words out of context to condemn LGBTQ people is a complete misconstrual of the context and meaning. This also reveals the prejudice that, even if someone considers themselves a Bible-believing fundamentalist, they pick and choose which pieces of the Bible they will apply. To say that these passages are a condemnation of all same-sex behavior would mean that every gay person is morally bankrupt, whereas dismissing the condemnation of many opposite-sex behaviors as not applying to our modern context reveals a double standard in our understanding and application of the Bible.

I advise anyone who is LGBTQ to find a way to come out and to be out in all areas of their lives. In one's family it is important to come out from a position of personal strength. If they are feeling uncertain spiritually, or about what the Bible does or doesn't say about this, I encourage them to take time to educate themselves. When they have that conversation with their parents, and if it goes badly, they still can have a sense of, "This is something that we are just going to just disagree about." I wouldn't want someone to go in with a sense that there will be great anxiety and fear. You need to make sure of your own understanding, so you don't crumble in the face of your parents' disagreement. Make sure you do the homework before you have that conversation. You should have heard, understood, and answered those arguments for yourself before you have them with your parents.

Don't make the mistake of confusing what people say, do, or believe with what God believes about you. Just because a church has treated you badly, don't assume God would have said or done those things. When a person, who calls himself a Christian, treats you hatefully, don't make the mistake of believing that's what Christianity is. If our parents reject us, do not make the mistake in believing that is what God is doing.

It is a very hard thing to do, and it demands the ability to have a certain detachment and an adult faith. It takes a great deal of strength, because we learn how to love from the people who raised us. Many people learned how *not* to love by the broken ways they were raised, and we make the mistake of projecting so much of that onto God.

I take issue with people making assumptions about what Christianity means based solely upon their experiences with a very narrow, small group of Christians. There is not just one Christian view on just about anything, and there surely isn't one Christian view on homosexuality.

Homosexuality and the Western Christian Tradition by Derrick Sherwin Bailey (1955) was the first book written on Christian tradition and homosexuality from a progressive view. There is diversity and a strong progressive Christian voice around this topic. Just because one church rejects you, it does not mean that all churches do.

So many queer people feel robbed of a background in religion or faith. Our struggle for justice and rights doesn't get to use religion as a source of grounding. Every other successful movement for liberation was able to draw upon a spiritual basis. Think about the American civil rights movement or even the feminist movement that were able to draw upon religious tradition. The gay and lesbian movement has in so many ways been cut off from that resource. That tradition is what enables us to say that there is a larger force at work here cooperating with me. It is the spirit of God at work for justice. Even in the face of devastating defeat, I can get up the next morning and say, 'I may not live to see this happen, but I am part of what God is doing in the world today."

I hope to see gay marriage legal nationwide in my lifetime. I think I will, but it is still a long journey. I always take heart from Martin Luther King, Jr.: "The arc of history is long, but it bends towards justice."

I just want to say to parents: If your son or daughter comes out to you, remember that they are still the same person they were a minute before they told you. They are still your son or daughter. Are you going to be different with them because of this information? My hope is that the parents would love them the same. Remember not to respond in haste, especially if you are angry or afraid. You will have your own emotional responses—you will worry, or you may have religious and theological questions. You have been given a piece of information that means you need *more* information. You need to educate yourself. There are *lots* of resources available. Be willing to learn.

Most importantly, love them and don't treat them differently. The biggest fear that a LGBTQ child has is that their parents won't love them anymore, or that it will wreck your relationship.

It is scary for a child to come out to their parents, and it is scary for most parents when their child comes out to them. It feels scary because there is fear. Fear conceals love. You are afraid that you have lost something you love. Don't deny your fears. Work through them, because they are pointing you to someone you love: your child.

Part Five

Reaching Out

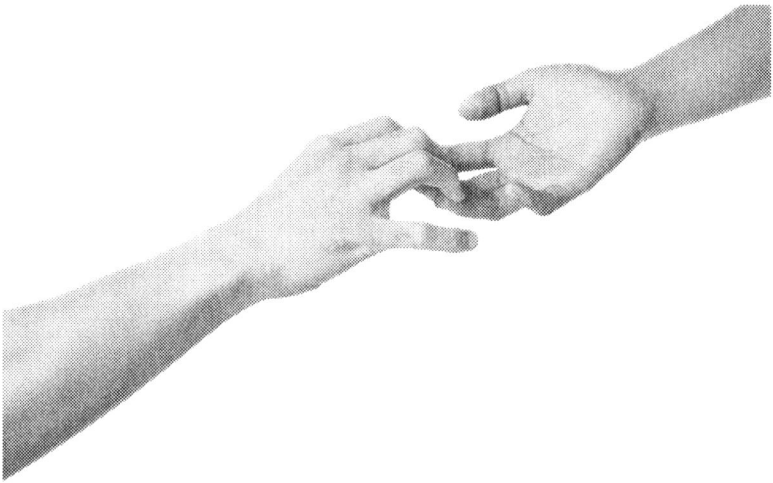

LGBTQ homeless youth center NY

Carl Siciliano
The Ali Forney Center
September 2010

Carl Siciliano founded the Ali Forney Center in 2002, at a time when there was no safe shelter for homeless LGBTQ youth in New York City. These kids were sleeping on the Christopher Steel Piers, in subways, and in abandoned buildings. The one youth shelter in the city was run by a Roman Catholic organization, but LGBTQ kids were afraid to go to a place where they were often attacked by other kids and even judged by the staff. Instead, these young people turned to prostitution for survival, and a huge number of them became infected with HIV. Their daily existence was frought with degradation and peril.

The LGBTQ community and its allies must recognize how badly our youth need support when they cannot find it at home. As more teens find the courage to come out, we must confront the reality that homophobia too frequently poisons the homes where they should be safe and loved. The Ali Forney Center (www.aliforneycenter.org) creates structures for these youths to provide the safety, support, and guidance of a healthy home.

I called and made an appointment with Carl to visit the center in Brooklyn. When I walked up the stairs out of the subway, I felt like Dorothy in The Wizard of Oz—having left brightly-colored New York City to land in a black-and-white world. The streets were almost empty of people, with business after business boarded up and forgotten. An old man on the front step of a market leaned on his broom, with the tip of a cigarette tucked in his lips, and watched me as I passed by. The center was located in an old building with tinted windows and curtains pulled for privacy. There was no sign, except one that read, "Buzz to Enter."

In a large a room filled with old couches and chairs, an array of boisterous young street kids fell silent as we entered and the counselor introduced me. I hoped the LGBTQ youth would accept me and share their stories. I told them a little bit about me and my project. Then I retreated to the windowless back office where I waited for anyone who wanted to share their story. I sat in an old wooden chair, surrounded by posters about safe sex, LGBTQ terminology, and the rules of confidentiality.

Eventually, a smiling face peeked through the doorway.

I will take your acceptance
Raciel, 18
Ali Forney Center, New York
September 2010

I think I always knew I was gay, but I had tons of girlfriends growing up. One day when I was 11, I skipped school with a girl and we went to my house. We were making out on my brother's bed and she starting taking off my shirt. I told her that she had to stop because it just wasn't working. I didn't want to even think about it.

I came out as gay officially when I was 12. I was living in New Jersey at the time. I came out first to my friend, Stephen, and then to another friend. Once they accepted me, I came out to the rest of the world.

I was living with my dad. At first, I told him that I was bi, which was a lie, but I was trying to leave him a little hope. My dad went crazy. He wanted to know what had happened to me. He said it was impossible. My dad is Cuban and was brought up in a totally different world than me. No son of his was going to be gay. He said he couldn't handle it, and he told me to call my mother. She asked me how I could know that I was gay, since I hadn't experienced anything yet. I wasn't going to tell her that I had, so I lied to her. I hated to, but I did.

I went to live with my mom in New Mexico. She had a boyfriend who was taking advantage of her, and I spoke up. I was angry that she chose her boyfriend over my sister and me. I moved out.

I bought a ticket to go back to live with my dad, but a few hours before I left my dad called to tell me he didn't want a fag in his house. That hit me like a bomb. It really hurt. I love my dad dearly, but it's like we are enemies. I tell them how I feel, and I don't hold back just because they are family. If they don't hold back, why should I? My family doesn't like that about me, and it has brought a lot of conflict between us.

I get along fine with my family now. My mom is one of those people who will accept something if other people will. She's just afraid of what people will say. She has always loved me, and she accepts me now more because she knows that it's okay for me to be gay. When I first came out, it was kind of taboo. Now she lives in Florida, and her friends and her side of the family love me because I am proud to be who I am. My mom didn't think I should tell everyone, but I am flamboyant. That is just who I am.

My dad and I have a great relationship now, but we just don't talk about me being gay. I already know how he feels about it. I don't want to inflict pain on myself. Two of my brothers didn't accept it for a while, but they do now, and my sister has always accepted me. I don't want to live with my family anymore. I feel like once you leave the nest, there is no going back.

I really feel blessed. I'm a firm believer in God and I think that everything happens for a reason. I moved to New York about three months ago. I live in the Ali Forney housing and I love it, the area is amazing. It's in a lively, young, artistic, creative neighborhood, and I live for that because I am creative, too. It has opened so many doors for me already. I am in a GED program as well. Next fall, I plan to go to college to be a fashion designer.

I have learned to accept who I am, where I am going, and I know how to get there. The staff at Ali Forney is either LGBTQ or LGBTQ-friendly, and our roommates are, too. I don't call it a shelter, because it is my home. It is an amazing opportunity that I have been given. I am in an unpaid internship at a fashion public relations firm, plus I work at a clothing store. I am starting a t-shirt company, which my case manager is helping me with. Without Ali Forney, this would not be possible.

I wish I could tell parents of LGBTQ kids to just accept who they are. It is so painful not to be accepted. Nobody should have to compromise their happiness by pretending to be something they are not. It is so stressful to be in the closet, or not be accepted. It destroys you. But first, you need to accept yourself. I have demanded respect from my family. I told my family what I heard in my favorite movie, *To Wong Foo, Thank You for Everything! Julie Newmar:* "I don't need your approval, but I will take your acceptance."

September 2012 email

Momma Traci,

I am now 20, and I have moved out of Ali Forney center from the TLP program (Transitional Living Program) where I had a job, saved money, and went to school full time. The Ali Forney helped me to get started in school and get a job. For a year I worked as an executive assistant and intern for a production company for a reality television show.

I have moved into the Green Chimneys Program where I will continue to work and finish going to school for fashion design. I am thankful for Ali Forney because it helped me to build my life.

I still feel distant from my family, but that probably won't change. I've learned that family doesn't necessarily mean blood-related. I am not religious, but I am spiritual, and God is my best friend.

Love you, Momma Traci!

Raciel

March 2014 email

Hi Momma Traci!

I've taken a break from fashion design at Fashion Institute of Technology to work and save money. I still live in NYC, where I am currently employed in the media production industry.

When I first started, I didn't think I would end up anywhere else other than in the fashion industry, but to be honest, I actually really love it! Every day is different. I'm constantly engaged and never get bored. I work for a great company and a great team where my voice is not only valued, but also encouraged. I'm humbled to have come so far in my young adult life and am excited for the opportunities that are ahead.

xo
Raciel

Learning to love himself
Michael, 19
Alabama and New York
September 2010

My mom once told me that she knew that I was gay since I was a little kid because I was always very feminine. I came out to her when I was 13. She accepted it and welcomed me with open arms, and told me that she understood what I was going through. She kept it a secret because my stepfather is very homophobic.

I also came out to my sister. When I was 18, my sister came home from school one day and apologized because she had told someone at school that I was gay. I knew then that my life was ruined. My stepfather beat me. He told me he didn't want any gays in his house and near his son, my stepbrother. Then my mom told me I had to get out.

I moved to New York from Alabama, a very homophobic state, and I haven't been in contact with any of my family since. It hurt me that my mother didn't protect me. I've been suicidal since I was 10. To make matters worse, I was born with cerebral palsy, so one side of my body is shorter than the other and is not fully functional. I have been picked on a lot.

Part of me wanted to go back home to Alabama, but the other part didn't want to take the homophobia from my stepfather or anyone else. The people at the Ali Forney Center accepted me and have become like family to me. Many LGBTQ kids who are not accepted end up killing themselves or start doing drugs. I was doing drugs for a while, but I realized I was just hurting myself more.

I have learned to accept myself. So many kids come out and don't accept themselves. They feel like they are a disgrace. When you finally meet the right people—the people who will accept you for what you are—you learn to accept yourself and starting doing something good with your life.

I am taking GED classes. I am interested in music and photography, and I want to go to college. I am involved in a group called FIERCE (www.fiercenyc.org), an LGBTQ youth-of-color organization that builds leadership qualities. It brings me happiness to know that I'm doing something for my community.

I wish my mom could see how much I have grown. I'm not a little kid anymore. I know we all make mistakes, but we have to own up to them sooner or later. I want to reach out to my mom, and my therapist thinks that is a good idea. I would tell her how much I miss her. I'm not a disgrace to our family. I am her son. When I left, she said I wasn't her son anymore because I was running away. But I wasn't running away. I was escaping.

February 2013 email

Momma Traci,

I moved back home to Alabama but I still have no family contact. I am living with my partner and his mother. I am not in school or working because of the disability caused by my cerebral palsy. Life has its ups and downs, but my partner and I stay strong together. He is an amazing person whom I love with all my heart.

Love,

Michael

February 2014 email

Hey, Momma,

My partner and I have our own apartment now. I have been having some health problems, and I just got out of the hospital. I have had some depression problems but being involved in the *Love Yourself Project* has helped.

http://www.jaylesworthloveyours.wix.com/loveyourself

Love,

Michael

The Sexual & Gender Minority Youth Resource Center in Portland, Oregon — Momma Traci

The Sexual and Gender Minority Resource Center (SMYRC) is located in NE Portland. In order to interview some of the youth for this book, I needed the approval of the steering committee and I was invited to attend a meeting.

The steering committee meeting turned out to be a group of LGBTQ youth sitting in a circle on couches and chairs in a recreational room, discussing upcoming events—including a drag show—while others around them snacked, played video games, and worked on computers. Several of the people talking were dressed partially in drag.

I found an empty folding chair outside the circle and sat down. I was amazed how orderly the meeting went and how polite everyone was. I had never been to a meeting that went so smoothly.

Someone wearing a "Staff" pin introduced me. I told them about my project, the interviews I had done in New York at the Ali Forney Center, and the letters I had received from LGBTQ people around the world—those out and those afraid to come out. I wanted their permission to do interviews at SMYRC and to offer the opportunity for people to tell their stories—with the assurance of anonymity.

They offered me the use of one of the counseling offices. I came to the center a couple of times to conduct interviews, and brought pizza for everyone to share. They were sexual minority youth 23 and younger. They were a mix of street kids, youth in temporary housing, young people in bad home situations, and some in good homes who just wanted a safe place to meet friends like themselves. What they had in common was a desire to be around people who accepted them. Being with them brought the mom out in me.

The need at SMYRC is great, and volunteers are welcome. You just need to be armed with an open mind and plenty of love to share—and maybe some pizza, cupcakes, or cookies. These kids deserve to be loved and accepted just like they are. For more information, visit their website: http://smyrc.org.

A chosen name
David, 15
Portland, Oregon
October 2010

I was born a girl, but I am beginning to transition into a male.

I think I've always known that I was different. I started questioning how I felt in elementary school and even more in middle school, probably because I liked other girls. At first, I thought maybe I was bisexual. In elementary school most of my friends were boys, but in middle school most of my friends were girls, and we didn't stay friends for very long.

In seventh grade, I realized that I didn't like being a girl—I wanted to be a boy. I envied boys and wanted to be like them. When I tried on my boys' clothes, it felt right. I started researching what I felt. I read about people that were transgender, and I realized that was me.

What gender you are on the inside is not the same thing as your sexual preference. A transgender person is someone who feels like they were born in the wrong body, that they should have been born as the opposite sex. Some people do something physically or medically about it

I think my mother already knew. Once, she asked me if I thought I was a boy. This was probably because of the way I dressed. I didn't say anything to her then. About a year ago, I wrote a letter to my mother telling her about how I felt—that I felt like I was a boy, not a girl, and I wanted to be called a "he" instead of a "she." I had chosen a boy's name: David. At first it was really hard to talk about it with her—it was hard for her, and embarrassing for me. She started investigating the subject. Soon, we both got more comfortable talking about it. She started asking me questions. These days she calls me David.

A few weeks afterward, I wrote my dad a letter explaining how I felt and left it on his desk. I told him the same thing I told my mother. I knew it would take some time for him to understand, and I gave him some resources that would help. He has not been as accepting as my mother.

I started taking hormone blockers, even though I have already started puberty. This will stop me from having my period, which is good. When I have a period it reminds me that I was born a girl. It does have side effects of acne and weight gain, but it is not that bad.

When I am fifteen, if I have letters from two different therapists and I have both of my parents' permission, I can start taking testosterone. It will change my voice and make it lower. It will also change my facial features and my body slightly. That would be great because that way I could appear to others as who I feel I am.

I have heard that people who were born male and want to transition to be a female sometimes have problems with changing their voices with hormones unless they start really early. I have also heard that the surgery for male-to-female transitions is usually very successful but not so for female-to-male. There is a saying which goes, "FTM pass on the street, but MTF pass under the sheets"—surgically you can change a man's body to look like a female and no one can tell, but you can't change the female body successfully to look like a male. The genital surgery is much harder than surgery above-the-belt. My mother has agreed to allow me to legally change my name to David, but my father is still thinking about it.

April 2011

On April 10th I turned 15. I've been on hormone blockers now since late 2010. The blockers make it so you don't go any farther in puberty. I have already started to develop, but it has stopped me from having periods. It does have side effects of acne and weight gain, but it is not that bad.

Now that I'm 15, if I can get both letters from doctors and parental consent I can start testosterone and I won't need the blockers anymore. I will still have the acne problem because it's like going through puberty again, but this time as a male.

I still need to talk to my dad about giving me permission. I'm not sure what he will do. He has been using my new name and the correct pronoun, at least to me. I'm not sure if he does with other people, but it's a start. He moved out a couple of months ago—my parents just don't get along. My brother has gotten a little better. He put my name on my birthday card—that was the first time he wrote it. Other than that, he just doesn't say my name or use the right pronoun. My grandparents are using my new name, and if they use the wrong pronoun, they correct themselves. My mom is always very supportive—she always uses my new name and the right pronouns.

I changed schools. My new teacher was not supportive and I was harassed and bullied in and out of school. Kids that barely know me came up to me after school yelling at me and cussing me out.

The doctor thought I should go into a day treatment plan—therapy and school at the same time—because I didn't feel safe from other people and I was hurting myself. I was cutting myself on my legs, where my parents wouldn't see it, but they found out. I guess I was taking out what I felt on myself—instead of handling it or taking it out on other people. When I am cutting myself I am thinking, "I can't handle this. I have to let it out." I just want to think about something else. There were times in the beginning where it was like I was punishing myself because I hated the body I was in. I haven't done it now for a couple of months.

My insurance stopped paying for day treatment because my doctor thought I was better. I changed to an alternative high school where the classes are smaller. At this school I just started with my new name, David, and I didn't have to explain anything to anyone.

He could trust me
Suzie, David's Mother
Portland, OR
April 2011

A dedicated mother, Susie drove David to SMYRC a couple times a week so he could meet with his friends while she waited for him outside in her car, reading. She has embraced her child's transition with grace and courage.

I live in Portland with my two children: David is now 15, and I have an older son who is 18.

I don't think I really ever recognized something was different with David. David was born a girl. When David was 13, she wrote me a letter, and it really surprised me. It explained that she was a guy in a girl's body, and felt that he could trust me and wanted to see if he could. I asked what I could do that would make him feel better about himself. I felt like I had to protect him. I had never dealt with anything like this before.

Looking for support, we found SMYRC. We also found Trans-Active, a non-profit community-based organization in Portland that serves transgender kids, provides education in schools, and stands up for the rights of trans kids.

My husband and I are getting a divorce. Our marriage wasn't doing very well anyway, and he just could not accept David. It was the final straw.

I didn't tell anyone in the family or my friends for about seven months. I had to be one person around everyone else and someone else when I was with David.

The hardest thing to get people to understand is that gender identity and sexual attraction are two different things. One of the things that really shocked me was how our family didn't accept it, like my brothers and their family. When I first told my mother, she told me it was my fault because I went to places like SMYRC where it was encouraged.

My other son is getting better. He wasn't using any pronouns when he referred to David, which was better than using the wrong ones, but today he used the right one when talking to me about David. I think he will come around.

David's dad is getting better, too. We gave him a pamphlet to read, and now he does use his new name, David.

David just started a new school, and it seems better. In this school, David is not remembered as a she, which is the biggest thing.

I am me, no one else
Leo, 23
Portland, Oregon
January 2013

I was born female and am gender fluid, which means my gender changes from day to day. Some days I feel male, sometimes I feel female, and sometimes androgynous which is somewhere in between. It is all about how I like to present myself. I identify as pan-sexual, which means you are attracted to people regardless of gender, but I am more attracted to women.

When I was three years old I was diagnosed with ADHD (Attention Deficit Hyperactivity Disorder). In kindergarten, I was placed in special education classes and continued in special education through my senior year even though I never had a learning disability. I was taught the same things over and over because they always taught to the lowest level.

Somewhere around the age of seven or eight, I realized that I was different than other girls my age—I was attracted to girls not boys. I accidentally discovered my uncle's pornography which may have had a hand in my sexual preference from an early age. When I was 11, I had a consensual sexual experience with a girl my age and we both found it enjoyable.

In sixth grade, we moved to Oregon. I had a wonderful teacher who was involved with my mother to help with my IEP (Individualized Education Program)—the program plan for kids in special education. I was able to take some mainstream classes. I still had behavioral issues of lashing out in anger, possibly from being educationally stifled and humiliated by other students for being in special education all those years. I found it difficult to ever get close to anyone.

In seventh grade, I moved to a middle school which was very stressful. I spent some time at the Christy School (It is now called ChristieCare), a residential center for kids with emotional problems. I was placed in classes under my level but I still learned some coping skills. My mom visited me constantly and she was supportive to the other girls there, too. My mom has inspired me to someday help kids who are reaching out. I met kids there who aged out and ended up on the street and on drugs. There should be something for those kids.

During this time my mother became involved with a man who liked my brother but didn't like me. He refused to let me live in his house. I was sent to live with my grandma. My grandma was very pessimistic. It was hard to live in her house—it was a negative atmosphere and I experienced depression.

My grandma kicked me out, and I was homeless. SMYRC was there for me and gave me the resources to get into a safe shelter. For the first time in my life I had more than just school and home—I had friends. I discovered the LGBTQ community. I climbed out of my shell. I had a place where I could express myself and my creativity on open mic night. I could dance. I could sing, talk, and express my excitement with others.

Most of my teenage years I had felt isolated because the majority of my friends were on the Internet with little face-to-face connection. At SMYRC, I finally found a place where I could have friends face-to-face. I was able to finally look inside and discover my sexuality in a safe place, knowing I would be accepted.

My mom told her boyfriend that her family wasn't a happy meal where you could pick and choose what you want—"You have to have both of my kids or you don't get any of us." She moved out.

When I was fifteen, I had a girlfriend named Casey. We never even kissed. We were just very close, more like a spiritual relationship. I was talking to Casey and another friend, Jessie, on a three-way call, and my mom picked up the telephone. We had been talking about coming out. I said "Mom, there is something I have to tell you." Then I went silent. Jessie said "Well, they are lesbians." My mom said, "And is there more to this?" My mom wasn't bothered. She wasn't even surprised.

In my senior year of high school, I was mainstreamed full time for the first time and I found myself shutting down—it was too much for me. I dropped out and got my GED. I am now going part time at Portland Community College. I really like college because the teachers are willing to work with you and make sure you are able to succeed. Recently I have become involved as a peer education with the Cascade AIDS Project. They provide twenty weeks of training about sex education, including HIV prevention, and then you can talk to youth and spread that knowledge. People in this program have gone into detention centers and homeless centers with information and resources to share.

I've been involved in Write Around Portland, an organization that provides the opportunity for people to write and publish. I have been in four anthologies which I am very proud of.

I have been in a relationship with my boyfriend, who is straight, for about four years. We live together in a friend's house where we share the costs. My boyfriend is very loving and supportive. My mom has been amazing. Recently she told me, "Boy, girl, whatever, I will be there to love and support you."

I am very lucky.

This is what Leo read on stage the night I met her at the SMYRC anniversary celebration.

(Untitled)

Is gender something that can be measured on a line? Summed into a single word for an approved group of acceptable states of being? Male, female, Trans, fluid... Should we seek out a gender and find it does not fit on this spectrum, are they not to be taken seriously? Should they stay silent, bury deep down, just choose one or the other for the sake of the happiness and comfort of those around them?

Is it possible to be my mother's "baby girl' and still be a heart pounding Bishonen I wish to be? Can I look in the mirror someday and see a girl while others see neither? Can I switch pronouns sometimes as frequently as weekly or should I keep these little personal changes to myself until I figure myself out?

I think we should throw this whole gender thing out the window, let people be who they want to be, when they want to be it. Damn the comfort of everyone else before yourself. I've lived my whole life this way; watching my words, keeping an ear out and gagging the room lest I accidentally upset one of my friends at the cost of my own comfort.

I am me, no one else. Some days I want to dress as a young girl, all frills and lace, petticoats beneath my skirt. And that's ok.

Some days I want to be a heart throb, binder upon my chest, turning my chest into pecks, suit and tie, vest, cunning smirk, absolutely handsome...and that's ok.

Some days I want to be a women, short skirts, high heels, outrageous makeup an appearance I know that will make people look twice and I love it. That's ok.

I am me, no one else and no one and nothing is going to make me ashamed of who I am and that is more than ok, it is great!

Going beyond differences
Belinda, 20
Portland, Oregon
February 2014

Belinda is a soft-spoken girl with a big heart. Our conversation at the university student union was cut short because of her job interview. We continued our discussion in my truck as I drove her there. I had some extra time, so I waited for her and was able to share in her excitement about her new job.

My birth gender was male. When I was a year old my parents got into an argument. My father told my mother that they didn't need any more children (I was number nine) and she had to kill me. My parents were Samoan, and she felt she had to obey my father because of her culture or she would be punished—which was usually abuse. She crushed my head against a door.

I was taken away and adopted by an LDS family. I grew up in Utah. I had to wear a helmet for six years to reshape my head.

By the time I was eight, I knew I was different. I would leave the house in boy clothes and then change into girl clothes which I kept in my backpack. In elementary school, I was put in special education classes because they thought my problems were something to do with my education level. I was kept in those classes for three years.

I saw myself as a girl. I would dream of being born a girl and growing up as a girl. I would take the bed sheets and curtains and make myself dresses. I experienced a lot of bullying and physical abuse from other students. When I was 11, I decided I must be gay since I was attracted to boys. When I told my mom she started laughing. I asked her why she was laughing and she said she knew, she always knew, because there was always something special about me and it would never change anything for her. When my dad found out, he grounded me: he took away my phone and my laptop.

When I was 13, I was kicked out of the church. When I was 15, my dad made me move out of the house—he became a bishop of a Mormon church, and I was an embarrassment. I was turned over to state custody and had to live in youth shelters. My adopted mom and I are very close, but not as close as I wish because of my adopted father.

As I was growing up, I was always bullied badly. My friends would tell me to stand up for myself because I am a big person—I'm over six-feet tall but I am very emotional and sensitive, and I cry easily. When I was 17, four African-American males tried raping me. I finally decided to stand up for myself: I punched two of them.

I was arrested and charged with battery as an adult. The judge said my size was intimidating and I would be a danger to society. I spent two years in jail. I was raped eleven times. I was shanked with a homemade knife in my leg and had twenty-eight stitches.

For so many years, I contemplated confronting my birth parents who tried to kill me. About a year and a half ago, I moved to Oregon to meet my birth parents and siblings. My mother was alive but my dad had passed away two years before. For the first couple of weeks, all was fine. Then I went to a church conference with them in Seattle. Afterwards, my brothers started calling me a faggot and told me I didn't belong there. Then my mom told me I wasn't the child she wanted. It broke my heart, but I had finally lost the fear of wondering who these people were and confronting them.

I am now transgender. I started taking hormones about a year ago. When I first started taking them I had huge mood swings—I was told it was like the mood swings of having a period, being pregnant, and going through menopause all at the same time. My breasts are getting larger, my skin is smoother, and my facial hair has decreased. I have also noticed some muscular changes.

Someday I would like to have a complete sex change and become a compete woman. How I see myself in my dreams—as a woman—is how I try to present myself. Some trans friends like to present themselves as very sexual, but I present myself as appropriate and professional because I don't want to put out a sexual signal.

I am very picky in my relationships. I only date straight men. That is common with a lot of transgender people. I have been in a relationship with a straight man for a year. He is wonderful.

Recently on university social media there was a "Confession" page. An individual posted a picture of me and said, "If you would rape this Trannie like the pic and if you like the pic comment on how you would do it." 274 people commented. I reported it as abuse. They took the posts down but said they couldn't trace them.

For a while, I didn't feel safe on campus. Later I posted on the site that I was happy to be who I am and would continue to walk on campus with my head up. You can say what you want, but until you are ready to be comfortable with your manhood or womanhood, please don't interfere with mine.

For me, life is like a symphony that is always filled with never-ending beauty, but only if you make it. I choose to make everything in my life—every memory, every bad event, every trauma—just part of my music. Life would be too perfect if we didn't have mistakes to learn from. I try to give to others because I just want to see people make it and become successful in life.

I am involved in HYC (Homeless Youth Continuum) to meet the needs of homeless kids in Oregon. My job is to be supportive. I work with many organizations. I teach workshops especially for LGBTQ people and share skills such as SMART Goals and coping skills. I am also involved in Safer PDX which is a program of safety tips for Portland. I take pride in myself and being LGBTQ and try to help others feel the same.

I had an adopted sister with Down syndrome who died very recently. I went back to Utah for the funeral. Before I flew back to Oregon, my dad asked me to go out to lunch with him and talk. I wished he had done that before. My dad talked about how hard it was for all of us losing my sister, and then he apologized for not being there for me. He said he didn't want to lose me and he needed to start changing because I'm still here and he was wasting a lot of time. He had been pushing me away because my differences interfere with his beliefs.

Since I got back, when my mom calls me my dad has asked to say hi to me. He had never done that before.

Part Six

Friendships

Mother and Daughter — Rochelle and Jennifer

Not everyone will accept you
Rochelle, 24
Oregon
April 2011

When I was in grade school there was a girl that I really liked. I guess it was like a crush. I remember watching her on the playground when she would play capture the flag at recess with all the boys. She always wore a sweater with three big crayons on it.

When I was in middle school I wanted to make friends with girls I thought were pretty. I thought that was the way it worked—you wanted to be friends with people that you thought were attractive. I didn't understand why I didn't like any of the boys but thought the girls were attractive. I didn't seem to have much interest in boys in middle school. I had two boyfriends but I only dated each of them for a few weeks. Dating boys didn't feel right to me.

In 2003 I started high school, and I began to question whether or not I was gay. I was 14 years old and had just broken up with a guy I had been with for six months—my longest relationship with a guy. There was a girl I went to high school with. She was a couple years older but there was something about her that drew me to her. It was the feeling I was looking for with guys but just couldn't find. I would talk about her all the time to my friends. I had never even talked to the girl, just passed her in the hallways. I remember telling my friends I thought she was gorgeous.

One of my friends asked me if I was interested in this girl. She asked me if I was gay.

"No way!" I told her. "Girls aren't supposed to like girls, and being gay is wrong."

After that day I started to wonder if maybe I did like girls. My friend's question stuck in my head for weeks. My mind battled back and forth between the wrong and the right. I was raised that being gay was wrong, and that women are supposed to marry men and have kids. I told myself that I was straight because that's what my family and society told me was right.

Shortly after, I met a girl named Katie who was also questioning her sexuality. We became pretty good friends then we started dating. We didn't tell anyone, as we were both afraid of people's reactions. I think both my mom and dad were suspicious that I might be having a relationship with Katie. My parents divorced when I was five and they worked together co-parenting my sister and me. I wanted so bad to tell my mom I was having a relationship with a girl but I was terrified that she would tell my dad. I was afraid of what my dad's reaction would be—he lived a very traditional life, and I was scared that he would disown me.

I needed to talk to someone because I was happy and it felt right, but society told me that what I was doing was wrong. It was confusing. In a time when I needed my parents the most, they weren't there because I was scared of rejection. So I told my sister, and I told her not to tell anyone.

I kind of came out to kids at school my sophomore year, but I considered myself bisexual. I told my friends I was questioning my sexuality, trying to figure out whether I was bi or a lesbian. It was around this time that a new student came to the school. She was gay. I started to hang out with her in class, then soon we started to spend time together outside of school. I started hanging out with her and her friends, all who identified as lesbians. I felt for the first time in my life that I could be who I really was.

I started to tell some close friends that I was gay. Before I knew it, my news had spread throughout the school—coming out wasn't something that happened often in my school. Some of the girls were uncomfortable around me, because they were afraid I would end up liking them. I started to lose friends—most of the straight girls didn't want anything to do with me. I soon realized that most of my friends were guys, and it was only because they thought it was hot that I liked girls. I felt like I became nothing more than a sex symbol.

I did have one friend who stuck by my side all through high school, and we are still friends to this day.

My mom found out when I was a junior—my sister told her. I was mad at my sister at first, but then I was relieved. I felt good to know that one of my parents finally knew what I had been keeping from them for so long. My mom struggled with it at first, but then she was fine. I remember her telling me that she just wanted me to be happy. She didn't care if it was a man or a woman in my life, as long as I was happy.

Having my mom find out was probably one of the best things that happened to me in high school. In a time when all teens struggle, I had to add on the fact that I was a lesbian and most of my peers and people around me didn't accept it, which made high school even harder. Having a parent to love and support me through this hard time was all I needed to keep my head up when kids were constantly trying to bring me down.

Soon I found there were more lesbians at my school. We all started to hang out together and it felt good to have other kids that were going through the same things that I was going through.

A security guard at school would harass us. One day we were all in the cafeteria at lunch. He came up to us and said he knew what was going on because he could tell by the way we looked at each other, and then he walked away. I was a good student—I always went to class and got good grades, but one time he came up to me in the hallway and stopped me. He called me by name. He pulled out his palm pilot, looked at it, and then told me to get back to class. A couple of weeks later he stopped me again. He asked me why I wasn't in photography class. I asked how he knew what class I was in, and he informed me that he knew everything and told me to get back to class.

I started eating lunch in my classroom with a teacher—one of the basketball coaches—because I was scared. The security guard asked me why I ate in the classroom with a coach when I hated sports. I had no idea how he knew such personal information. It was beginning to get creepy. I almost took it to the principal because I felt he was harassing my friends and me because we were gay.

One time in class I got in a fight with a teacher, and I had always gotten along with this teacher. The students were all getting pretty loud, and I was talking about a girl I knew who was considered a dyke—a more masculine girl. Right as I had said the word "dyke," the classroom got quiet.

The teacher said, "Rochelle, we don't say that in here."

Later, he called me to the back of the classroom. "I just want you to know the language you were using is really not appropriate, and we shouldn't be saying it in this classroom."

I said, "That is not a bad term. I was not using it in a bad way. I am a lesbian, and a dyke is a lesbian that considers herself more masculine than feminine."

In public, a lot of people stare at me if I am with my girlfriend. One time I was in the mall with my girlfriend, and a lady with her kids came up to us.

"Please don't hold hands with your girlfriend in front of my kids."

I looked at her and said. "You don't understand the society your kids are growing up in. Quit sheltering your children. I am going to hold hands with her whenever I want to. Let your kids be exposed to it now so when they go to school there isn't a large culture shock."

It made me remember this quote by Ernest J. Gaines: "Why is it that, as a culture, we are more comfortable seeing two men holding guns than holding hands?"

In 2008, when I was a sophomore in college, my dad finally found out the big secret I kept from him for so many years. Just as I had feared, it didn't go well. My dad runs a business with my aunt and uncle. My aunt found out I was a lesbian through one of her friends, and my aunt told my uncle who insisted that I tell my dad. My uncle took me to counseling, where he and I argued back and forth about telling my dad. My uncle felt that since they were brothers, worked together, and were best friends that my dad needed to know. He felt that hiding it from my dad was not fair. I insisted I wasn't ready—it was my personal business and I needed to tell my dad when I felt it was right. The counselor didn't take sides—she said we had to work it out. During the third counseling session I got tired of arguing with my uncle and walked out. The next day my uncle came to my house and told me he had decided to let me tell my dad when I was ready, but he really didn't want to hide it from him much longer.

We didn't talk about it again for a year, until I was about to move in with a girlfriend I was seeing. My uncle and aunt called me up to their house to talk to them. They didn't agree with me moving in with someone I was dating, even if it was a boy, and that I had to tell my dad. I wanted to wait until after I moved in.

The next day my dad started questioning my aunt and my uncle. He knew I was up at their house for a meeting and wanted to know what it was about. My dad told them that if they didn't tell him what was going on, he was going to leave the business.

So my aunt said, "Your daughter is a lesbian."

My dad said, "No, she's not. That is not true."

"Yes, she is. That's what this is what this is all about, and we have known for a year."

My dad called me the next day. "Is there something you need to tell me?"

"No, I don't know what you are talking about."

"Is it true that you are gay?"

"Dad, do you want to hear that your daughter is a lesbian? Is it going to kill you to have all of your big business friends know that your daughter likes girls?"

"Then we are going to go to counseling."

I told him I had had enough counseling and that I wasn't going again. My parents put me through years of counseling when they were getting divorced. I told him, "This is who I am. I have known it since I was 14 years old. Ever since I was little girl, all the weird things I used to do, it all finally makes sense. I'm a lesbian, so get over it."

After this, we didn't talk about it much. I ended up moving in with my girlfriend. A year or so later, Dad started to talk about it again, but not in a positive way. Every couple of months he would tell me that I needed to reevaluate my life choices. I would tell him that it is not a choice; it is who I am. I think he is getting more accepting of it now. For my dad, it's an image thing. He doesn't want people to know I am a lesbian because it's not the socially acceptable, traditional way to live. He wants everyone to think he has this perfect little family.

In 2009, I told my dad that I was going to leave my sister's graduation party early for gay pride. He argued with me and insisted that I not go to gay pride. I felt that I needed to be around people that accepted me for who I was—it is only once a year, and I was going to do it. He said he didn't want to open up the Sunday *Oregonian* to see his daughter's face at the gay pride festival. All his fears were for himself. He was being selfish and not understanding how important it was to me to go to the festival and feel accepted.

In college, I had taken a lot of classes on sexuality and women's studies. I had a student in class who was African-American and her family was pretty religious. Her little brother never played with trucks or dinosaurs or anything like that. All he played with was Barbies. She started crying in class when she told us her dad had said she needed to help her little brother learn to play with other toys, because he was afraid that he was going to be gay.

I think it's really sad that society has to be like that. Society puts such a huge emphasis on pink being for girls and blue for boys. Fire trucks are for boys and Barbies are for girls. It doesn't have to be that way. Just because a boy plays with Barbies doesn't mean he is going to turn out gay. It's not about that—it's about who you are. The toys your child plays with aren't going to determine their sexuality.

When I accepted the fact that I was a lesbian it began to scare me because of the idea of power. In our society, being a white male is the ultimate power figure. Being a white female you have a lot of power over many other groups but not as much as the white male. You start to lose power based on many factors—gender, race, sexuality, disabilities, income, etc. I grew up knowing where I stood in society. As a lesbian, I knew my status in society would be changed to a lower position. Most people assume I am straight by the way I dress—apparently I don't "look gay." But what does gay look like? They tell me I look straight, but what does straight look like? Sometimes I think I shouldn't tell people because I can bring my power back. This is a battle that is inside my head all the time.

I think now it is more acceptable to be a lesbian than gay. Straight girls do not like to see two men all over each other, but straight guys think it is really hot to see two girls all over each other. In high school I had a lot of friends that were straight guys. Maybe they thought it was hot, but I think they also felt like I was like one of them because I found girls to be attractive. I also find it interesting that straight women love gay men but straight men don't like gay men.

I still struggle with it now—being comfortable with myself, my dad, and sometimes other people. Dad has told me he feels like he and my mom must have done something wrong to have me turn out like this. They must have missed something with me. What he doesn't understand is that this is me. He needs to accept me for who I am and not try to find reasons why I am the way I am.

Sometimes when people ask me if I have a boyfriend, I just say no instead of telling them I am a lesbian, because I'm afraid of rejection. I am afraid they will feel differently about me and won't accept me. I don't want someone to like me or not like me because of my sexuality. Because I am going into business after college, it may always be a concern. I don't know if I will ever grow out of being afraid that I won't be accepted because I am lesbian. Especially in the work place, I worry people won't respect me. I'm afraid it will be hard for me to be a successful business woman because I'll have less power due to my sexuality.

One day one of my dad's friends told me how pretty I was. He thought his son and I would get along. My dad didn't make any effort to let him know that I wasn't interested in men. He just kept his mouth shut while I told his friend that I was too busy to date. My mother fully supports me and does not have a problem telling people that I am gay. I do think it would make a difference if my dad did accept me. I felt like my dad just wants to keep that part of me in a closet, and I have to fake a role to make him happy. It's a horrible feeling.

I have never told my dad how it makes me feel that he doesn't accept me, because I don't want to make him uncomfortable. I don't think he tells his friends. When I have a girlfriend come over he refers to her as my friend, not my girlfriend. Your parents are some of the most important people in your life, and if they don't accept you or support your decisions it brings you down. I went through a lot of stages of depression and loneliness in high school because when I needed my parents the most I was scared they wouldn't understand.

If I could tell him how he makes me feel, I would tell him that he is my father and I need his acceptance and support. I want him to be proud of me for all I accomplish in life. And I want him to be proud of me for standing up for who I am regardless of what other people think.

It's been many long years of keeping the secret from my dad, then many years of battling with him about it once he found out. Even though the battle has been hard, it seems to get better every day. I think a lot of the problem with acceptance is lack of knowledge. My father just doesn't know any different than the way he was raised. I have learned that not everyone out there will accept me for who I am, but isn't that the way it is with everyone? All I know is that I am me, and in accepting myself I have found peace. It's better to live your life being yourself than being someone you're not, even if this means that not everyone will accept you.

That moment was heaven
Jennifer, 56
Oregon
April 2011

When I first moved to Oregon, I was in the restaurant business. I was surrounded by gay waiters and they were my buddies. I guess I have always been comfortable with gay people. When I was in college I had some lesbian friends and never had an issue with it. When my own daughter came out, it affected me personally—that is when it became difficult.

I may have thought that being gay was a choice, but after seeing what my daughter has gone through I know now that is isn't. Who would choose to go through what she has? I will fight against people that who try to say it is a choice. I will also fight against the notion that you can't be gay and be a Christian.

When Rochelle was growing up, it never crossed my mind that she was gay. I don't think it is as obvious with females, especially when you have a daughter like mine who is a more feminine lesbian. The summer before Rochelle's sophomore year in high school we took Rochelle and her friend, Katie, to the rodeo. They were sitting in the backseat with a blanket over them, and I had this feeling they were holding hands. That's when I started questioning that my daughter might be gay. It was just little things, but when she was with Katie it didn't seem like the typical girlfriend relationship. There was something different.

Before Rochelle came out, she would call me to come get her from school. I thought she was just being a teenage girl, that she was emotional, but it was the way she was being treated by students and teachers. She would call me crying and make up reasons why I should come get her. One time she said she was upset about a note someone found that she wrote to a guy. The truth was that Katie's mom was upset about a note she found that Rochelle had written to Katie.

Katie's mom called and demanded a meeting between her, the girls, me, and Rochelle's dad. Katie's mother thought Rochelle was gay from what was in the note, but she didn't even suggest that her daughter could be. During the meeting, Rochelle's dad said he didn't think Rochelle was gay but if she was he would accept her, which was not true.

Then Rochelle had a girlfriend, Tristen, who seemed a little masculine. I thought maybe she was just a friend, but there seemed something different between them. One day I was sitting at the kitchen table with my other daughter. I asked her if Tristen was more than a friend to Rochelle. It was the look on her face that let me know. I told her I knew it must be true. She said yes but to please not tell Rochelle that she had told me. I called Rochelle, who was with Tristen at the time. She wouldn't talk to me, but Tristen did. I told her that I knew, and that I was okay with it. Tristen and I started texting back and forth. Tristen told me that Rochelle didn't want to talk to me about it. I told her I was here when she was ready.

When Rochelle first came out, it was hard for me but that time was short lived. My problems were mostly my own issues. I had planned that she would grow up, get married, and have children someday. It was my own selfish emotions about grandchildren and about what people were going to think. I was fine when I got over the initial shock. Those things didn't seem to be important anymore. I worried about my daughter being picked on, ridiculed, and harassed. Her life was going to be difficult.

It was about a week before Rochelle and I talked about it. I remember she wouldn't look at me. One of the first things she said was, "I am going to go to hell, aren't I?"

I told her she wasn't, and that in my mind it wasn't a sin. She told me she was seeing a counselor. I asked if she wanted me to go with her. Rochelle told the counselor that she felt good about the way I was accepting her being gay. She had been afraid I would disown her. I told her I would never do that—I loved her because she was my daughter. The counselor asked me about Rochelle's dad, but I really couldn't say how he felt.

I was worried about her dad, knowing how narrow-minded he was. I didn't want her to think there was anything wrong with her being gay. My ex-husband is not really religious but he is anti-gay—the little mean remarks he would make when he saw two men together or two women together holding hands. Rochelle told me she was walking in the park with her dad, and two girls were holding hands. He remarked that he didn't think they should do that in front of others because it was disgusting. He is very negative about those things. She has told him he makes her feel like she has to hide it, that he is not approving of her being gay.

I have told both of my parents. "There is something I want to tell you guys about Rochelle," I said. "She is gay."

They said, "Oh, good. We thought it was going to be something really bad."

I was concerned because they are from a different generation, but they were totally fine. I have one brother who lives in Hawaii, and he was totally fine. I have another brother who is a born-again Christian, and he is not accepting at all. I am sure Rochelle's dad's mother does not know. I am sure they are keeping it from her.

At work, I talk to people all day. People ask me how my daughters are and if they are dating anyone. For a long time I kept my mouth shut. Now I say something about Rochelle's partner. It is amazing how many people have a gay son or daughter or relative somewhere. It opens up a whole new conversation. People that I would least expect say, "My son is gay." I feel like a therapist. There are more gays and lesbians than we know. I think not accepting is about your own selfish issues. People are too worried about what it will look like to others.

I was so happy when Rochelle started college. She was around all different cultures and sexualities. She was finally in an environment where she realized she was okay. Her first term, she was taking a sexualities class. She was supposed to give a speech about something that described her. She wanted to know what I thought she could talk about.

I said, "You are a lesbian, why don't you talk about that?"

All through high school she wasn't accepted. Teachers and students would often make snide remarks about her. It was very negative. I told her it was a new time and she would get new reactions.

She came home and said she talked about what it was like to be a lesbian, and everyone was accepting of it. She just beamed when she told me. "Wow, I am accepted. I'm okay, and people don't look at me like I am a freak."

That moment for me was heaven.

Dear Abby — Durwood

In 2009, Daniel was at the LGBTQ Film Festival in Seattle to introduce his movie, The Big Gay Musical. Daniel's sister, Amanda, and I joined him there. Durwood was the festival's volunteer host, and he shuttled guests to and from the hotel, airport, and venue.

When I returned to Seattle a couple of years later to conduct some of the interviews for this book, Durwood graciously let me stay in his home—and he told me his story.

Durwood
Seattle, Washington
April 2011

I kind of knew I was different since I was in second grade. I had a crush on a boy named Ray. I didn't know what sex meant. I just knew I felt differently toward Ray than other boys did toward boys. I knew I had to be careful and hide my feelings. I had trouble talking to Ray, and I wanted him to be my best friend. A couple years later, we did become best friends but he never knew how I felt.

The only thing I did that was feminine was sometimes I would put on my sister's skirt and make my mother and sister laugh, but it was more of a joke for getting attention. Every year I would have a crush on another boy, and I developed the ability to be friends with the boy I had a crush on. All of my best friends through school were boys I had crushes on.

When I was a little kid, I only knew about one gay person—people called him the town queer. He used to hang out at the barbershop. My dad would take me in to get my hair cut; and when this man would leave everyone would laugh and make fun of him behind his back. At the time, I didn't know what gay was. I remember asking my dad when we were leaving the barbershop why everyone made fun of him. My dad told me that he was a guy that loves other guys and that if you ever have anyone like that who approaches you that you should run and yell for help. I asked him what he meant by "loves other guys."

"Well, he likes to kiss other guys, and if a guy tries to kiss you, run."

I said, "Well, you love me and kiss me."

"That's different."

I wasn't really picked on in school more than anybody else who was a scrawny kid. I always had lots of friends. I just didn't share my secret feelings with other people. I used to cry myself to sleep because I had a crush on a guy and there was nothing I could do about it. I used to have this fantasy that I would go to college with my best friend, then we would graduate and we would live together. I imagined how wonderful it would be to spend my life with him even though we would only be just friends.

By high school, I knew I was gay and what it meant, but I dated girls. It was a social thing and a way to fit in. I would go on a lot of double dates with the guys I had crushes on—it was my way of spending time with them. You just didn't date guys in the '70s in Georgia. A couple of stereotypical gay guys went to my high school and hung out together with a couple of girls. They had their own clique and were treated like outcasts. I knew better than to be friends with them, because then people would know that I was gay.

My parents raised me to be independent thinker. I was always comfortable in my own skin. I didn't have any religious problems with being gay because I had healthy doubts about religion. I understood the historical content of the Bible but I never took it literally. My church never stressed homosexuality—it was never talked about. I really never beat myself up about being gay. I just felt unfulfilled.

After high school, I went to Georgia Tech but I didn't seriously consider coming out until my senior year. There was a gay student club which met once a month at the student center. I remember thinking that I really should go to the meetings because I didn't know anyone else who was gay. I had a yearning to meet gay people, but I wasn't ready to come out yet.

So I would go to the student center at the time there was a meeting, but I couldn't get up the courage to actually go into the meeting. I was afraid one of my friends would see me go in. That was really stupid because my friends wouldn't have known there was a gay meeting going on.

I had planned that I would come out strong when I moved to Seattle. It would be a clean slate because I didn't know anyone there. When I got to Seattle, I started making friends but they were all straight so I postponed coming out for another couple years. I was afraid I would lose them as friends. I bought a house with some friends I worked with. It wasn't until I moved into my own place that I finally came out. I was 23. I told my best friends first—the ones I thought would be most likely to accept me. After that, I dated a little but I didn't have a serious relationship until 1990.

Every person who comes out to their parents has to figure out the right time or the perfect hook. I was born and raised in Columbus, Georgia, in a Southern Baptist family. I had a loving family, and I had no doubt that my parents would not disown me over being gay. But I also knew they would have a very difficult time accepting it and the whole concept would be foreign to them, so I postponed it as long as I could.

I used to go home to visit my parents about once a year. In 1980, I had just finished packing my bags to go back home and this fateful accident happened. My mom was an avid reader of Dear Abby. I had never read it before but I picked up the newspaper that day to read on the flight. The question to Abby was: "My son is gay and I need some advice, to get help for him or cure him of being gay."

Dear Abby's answer was, "You are the one that needs some help. You need to talk to someone to help you deal with the fact that your son is gay. There is nothing wrong with your son. You just need to learn how to accept it."

I thought this was the perfect way to come out to my mom. I clipped out the Dear Abby article and put it in my bags. My mom and I always stay up late the first night I am home to catch up. I told her that there was something I wanted to show her, and I handed her the Dear Abby article.

She read it and asked, "Why are you showing me this article?"

I said, "Because I'm gay".

She started crying. She was totally shocked and oblivious. It was a tearful night. She told me she loved me and that nothing would change that. The one thing I didn't like was when she said, "You are going to have to be the one to tell your dad. You have to tell him tomorrow."

I was comfortable telling my mom but not my dad. Unlike my mom, my dad did suspect that I was gay from when I was little but he said he would have rather gone on not knowing for sure. That was his initial reaction, but not knowing would basically have excluded him from my life. He also told me he loved me and that this wouldn't change our relationship.

It isn't just us that have to come out—our families have to come out, too. It wasn't until the next trip that I told my sister. She was surprised but seemed to be okay. I remember telling my mom how well my sister took it. My mother said, "No, she didn't take it well— about a month after you told her she just fell apart. She started crying and couldn't talk. She didn't know how she was going to tell her husband that you were gay."

It turned out my sister feared that she was going to have to choose between me and her husband. She didn't know how her husband was going to react, so she finally told him with an ultimatum. She told him that I was gay and her brother, and she loved me and if he didn't accept it 100-percent their marriage was done.

She didn't give him a choice, but he was fine with it.

I am so proud of her. My sister is very active in her very conservative Baptist church. She felt she couldn't tell her friends because she didn't trust them. This made her feel very isolated. About six months later she was out having coffee with a friend who shared that her brother had just told her that he was gay. The friend didn't know how to handle it. My sister told her that her brother was gay, too—now she had a friend that she could talk to.

I have had one major relationship in my life. I met him in 1990 and we were together for 17 years. We were very different. He was quiet, conservative in his dress and the way he acted and introspective, not social like me. He never liked it because I had lots of friends and his only friends were our friends. I always considered our differences as positive but he considered it as negative. What pissed me off was he left me when it was safe for him. He had already had been dating on the side and found someone he was interested in. I felt like I wasted 17 years of my life.

Thankfully, I had a great support system which got me through. I haven't had a serious relationship since, possibility because I am cynical about love and trusting people. It is more difficult to met single gay people when you are older. Most of my friends are younger—it is easier to be friends with someone younger but more difficult to date. Most of the people of my own age seem old to me. When I do met people my age that I am interested in, they are usually in relationships.

I have always tended to rely on fate. If something happens, it happens. I'm not lonely. I am independent, and I am happy in my life.

Just One Tweet — Momma Traci

In September of 2010 my son posted to Twitter and Facebook asking people to email me with their stories:

"My mom is writing a book "momma, I am gay" & would like to hear from LGBTQ's afraid to come out."

With just one tweet my world became larger. I received stories from all over the world, from those out and many afraid to come out. Daniel also forwarded me some of his fan mail from The Big Gay Musical. This is how I replied to those messages:

In your own words tell me when and how you came out? What happened that helped you take this important step? Did someone inspire you or hold you back to be yourself? How did your parents or important people in your life respond? Tell me about any important stumbling blocks or mileposts in your life that have affected you as a person, your career and your goals.

If you have not come out to your parents then write a letter to your parents (the letter that you wish you could write). Tell them when you knew, how you feel and how you wish they would respond. I know this will be a difficult letter to write but it may make your feel better to be able to express it even though your parents may never read it. Maybe someday you will be able to express to them your unspoken words.

If I use your story in my book you can use your first name or an alias that your choose plus your age and what city, state country that you live in. This is your chance to tell Your Story. After you send me your story please keep in touch. Always,

Momma Traci

Am I Better Off Dead? — Paul

Paul saw my son's post on Facebook. He wrote me:

"Is your book going to be about stories of kids afraid of coming out in today's world, in hopes it will help them feel not alone? To help them open up? Come out? Do you think sharing stories of people who were terrified to come out, and who finally took that step and found they had nothing to be afraid of, might help others?"

I asked if I could interview him by phone, and he called me on his cell, sitting in his truck in front of his mom's home.

Paul, 50
Tampa, Florida
February 2011

I was brought up in a small town in Michigan. When I was in first grade and was on the playground during recess, I was giving my friend Danny little kisses on his cheek when my teacher saw me and told me, "Little boys aren't supposed to kiss other little boys. They are supposed to kiss little girls."

I responded, "Nope, I want to kiss little boys." I knew then I was different.

When I was seven or eight, I was attracted to my cousin but I didn't really know what that meant. I heard older guys talking about girls, but I just didn't get it. I was afraid to ask anyone why I felt like I did, afraid that someone would find out. I saw the way some kids were picked on and called fags. I realized at a young age to keep my mouth shut. I started pulling away from people and staying to myself.

My family is Southern. I have three sisters and an older brother. I remember my brother asking my mother why she wouldn't straighten me out. They would argue about it a lot. She would tell him to leave me alone. I am not sure what my brother had picked up on except that

I was totally opposite of him. I didn't play outside or play sports. I was always in the house hanging around my mom and watching her cook. I was pretty introverted.

When I was about 10, kids started telling gay jokes and the bullying and name-calling became worse. The more I heard this, the more I stayed to myself. In junior high, I had a kid show up at my house wanting to be friends but I was afraid he would say something that would bring questions to my family's minds. I told him not to come back.

When the other boys started talking about girls, I knew I just wasn't interested. I was only attracted to boys. I heard on TV that what I was going through was a phase but I knew it wasn't. I felt isolated and hopeless. I was an average student and always wanted to be in band or drama club, but those kids were made fun of so I didn't join. I didn't want to do anything that would let anyone zero in on me or give them a reason to think I might be gay.

The people in the town where I grew up were very homophobic and still are. As I grew up, I built a wall around myself and pushed everyone away. People were afraid of me. I never got in a fight, but by high school I had a reputation that no one should mess with me. I still have a problem with being unapproachable. People say I look like I am scary, but growing up that was what I wanted—for people to stay away.

I kept it very hidden. I didn't date. Toward the end of my senior year I did have a couple of friends, Juan and David. We went to movies a few times. One time we were in line to see a movie and two guys walked by. My eyes followed them and Juan made a comment about what I was looking at, and started treating me different.

Juan stopped talking to me but David and I started getting closer. I had no clue that he was gay. After high school we worked together and watched the Super Bowl together. We made a bet on the game that the loser had to do something stupid. David lost. I won't say what it was but it was sort of gay and he did it. It was risky. I was hoping he was gay but I wasn't sure.

After he left that evening, I didn't think I would ever see him again but the next day he showed up again. One snowy evening he was stuck at the community college with a dead battery and wanted me to pick him up. I complained that it was snowing and he was 45 minutes away. He had no one else to call. I finally agreed but said I expected something in return. I was sort of teasing him. I picked him up and that night we fooled around.

Six months later, David and I moved in together in the town I grew up in. We both stayed in the closet and lived together for 10 years. I started to let my guard down a little but I still didn't tell anyone that I was gay. When I would go out with David to the country bar, I would introduce him as my half-brother. One night I convinced David to go with me to a gay bar in a town nearby. We drove there but chickened out, afraid that we would be seen.

David was getting more and more paranoid and started drinking more. Things went downhill. David's dad was a Marine. He hated me and acted suspicious towards me. I worked in the Post Office, and David worked in a machine shop. He was injured at work and was forced to go into rehab because of his drinking.

David and I bought a house and things seemed to be better for a while, but two years later I came home to a message on our answering machine telling me that he was sorry about everything. He had emptied our bank account, outed me to everyone, and left town. He went to my family and my work, telling everyone that I brought some guys home and he found out I was gay and didn't want anything to do with me.

He disappeared. His clothes were gone. He took my shotgun out of the case and replaced it with a stick and put the case back in the closet. He took every card or letter that was between us. I went to his dad, and he slammed the door in my face. I went back to the house, and my mom was there crying. She said it was okay and she loved me. She said she kind of knew. David had called and told her everything. He had also called my sisters. My dad drove up with a bottle of whiskey in his hand. He was yelling at me at the top of his lungs and calling me names, saying no son of his is going to be gay. I didn't know what to do. A friend from work came over, and she said that David went to my work place and told everyone that I was gay.

I denied it to my mom, my sisters, and people from work. There was no way I could admit it, not that day.

I moved to Florida. I couldn't sell the house right away because David's name was on it, but I was able to eventually with the help of an attorney. Before I left I told my mom and my sisters that I was gay. My mom says she accepts me, but she doesn't treat me the same.

I got transferred to a Post Office in Tampa. Best of all, I found a gay country western bar. I love country western dancing. I had two relationships while I lived there, but I have been alone since 2003.

I recently retired from the Post Office, sold my house in Florida, and was going to move to Chicago or New York but my dad was sick so I have been taking care of him. I know it is stupid because he treats me badly, but I guess it must be the guilt or the feeling of obligation.

My brother and I get along all right but we don't really talk. We have never been close. He ignores the fact that I am gay. He tried to fix me up with a girl. I think he's still in the mindset that he was in when we were growing up, when he would tell my mom she just needed to "straighten me out."

I called my old friend Buck and told him that I was gay. We were friends a long time but I hadn't told him. He didn't really like it but he seemed to accept me. He would make snide remarks. I made smart remarks back. We seemed to get along fine.

I asked Buck if he wanted to go out for a beer, but he was afraid to be seen with me. I told him I didn't wear a shirt that announced that I was gay. He told me about his nephew who was 24 and had just killed himself. Buck asked me to look up his nephew on Facebook and read what he had written before he died. It was mostly about how sorry he was, but he didn't say why.

Finally Buck agreed to go out for a drink, and we talked about his nephew. Rumors had started in the family that his nephew was gay, and that is what made him depressed. I asked Buck if he talked to him, and he said no. I told Buck that he could have told his nephew to talk to me. He said that in his family, his nephew was better off dead.

I couldn't believe that he felt that way. I asked if he thought I was better off dead. He sat there for a while, saying nothing. Then he said, "It is one thing to have a friend that is gay, but I couldn't have it in my own damn family."

That's when I decided I wanted to get involved in prevention for gay suicide. I used to stay to myself and not stand up for things, but I do now.

My sister, Ruby, asked me one time why I felt like I did. I told her it's just the way I am. She asked if there was anything about women that attracted me. She just doesn't understand at all. I thought my younger sister supported me, until I went to her house a few weeks ago for Easter. Her husband's nephew was there and I was having a conversation with him. He told me he got along with everybody except "those fruity people"—he hated them and could just kill them. I looked him in the eye and told him I was one of those fruity people. He looked shocked. My sister told me he would not be allowed back in their home. I thanked her for the support. But last Sunday I was at her house and he was there. To me that was a slap in the face.

I stand up for myself more now. I won't go back to their house.

I was just in my first gay pride parade, on top of a fire engine. I am still back at home for my dad, but I am not staying. It is too much. As soon as I get my dad situated I will move to a gay-friendly place. I will become more involved and make a difference.

Finding Peace — Leo and Mario

Leo responded via Twitter. When I found out he lived in Portland, I wanted to meet Leo and interview him in person. He is a massage therapist, and we met as his workplace.

Leo greeted me with a guarded smile and a soft voice and showed me to a small meeting room. He slumped forward as he spoke and struggled with his words, but then he relaxed into his story.

The next morning when I started my recorder to transcribe his words, they weren't there. I was embarrassed to ask if we could meet again. He gave a little laugh and said he would be glad to. We settled into the conference room at Portland's Q Center, but the recorder continued to give me problems—until his partner Mario showed up. He sat with us, and we finally had a successful recording. Thanks to my recorder, I was able to get to know two wonderful people and hear their entire story.

Will they ever leave me alone?
Leo, 46
Portland, Oregon
January 2011

As I was growing up in Montana, I thought I was like everybody else—until I reached grade school. I had made some guy friends, and I brought them over to play one afternoon. When they found out I wanted to play with dolls with my sisters, they never came back again, and they told all of my classmates at school.

My dad was concerned that I wasn't masculine enough, so he tried to "make a man out of me." He forced me to fight with another kid who had stolen my bicycle, and I got creamed. He got me into Little League, but I was awful. I hated it. He took me hunting one year and made me shoot a deer, which broke my heart—I never went hunting again.

My dad was raised by the Army and I'm not mad at him—he did the best he knew. He felt it was his responsibility to make a man out of me. My mom, on the other hand, was always concerned about what was socially acceptable and how we were viewed. That was the most important thing to her.

I really started noticing that I was different during puberty. I would always dress nice, and the other kids would make fun of me, calling me "Ken" or "Hollywood." They also made fun of me because I was deeply religious. I was brought up in the Mormon Church, and I would drown myself in religion so I wouldn't have to face my temptations—my attraction to other guys.

At the age of 12, the bishop of our church gave me a pamphlet about the evils of homosexuality and masturbation. The pamphlet told me that masturbation was a grave sin, and can cause you to be gay because you are having a sexual experience with yourself. It also said that if you masturbate, you will get used to having sex with the same sex—what they called "SSA" or same-sex attraction. The church taught that there are evil spirits all around us, and that they whisper things to us and to try to make us think a certain way.

When I was young, I truly believed that the attraction I had to men wasn't coming from me—it was coming from the Devil. When I would have these so-called evil thoughts, I would pray them away or hum hymns to myself to keep Satan away. Strangely, I became very musical because of that.

When I was old enough to date—around 16—I chose girls from other states as pen pals. It was safe because I wouldn't ever have to meet them. I did have one date with a girl during high school. We went to the prom together, and afterwards when I was dropping her off, she tried to convince me to come inside because her parents weren't there. I made excuses to leave, but she kept asking me. Eventually she gave up, giving me a good night kiss. After I left, I drove down the road, pulled over and screamed. I was so disgusted.

When I graduated from high school, the church sent me on a mission to Japan for a year and a half. I loved the county, and I really enjoyed the people. I found the Japanese fascinating. I liked the closeness of the people and I wanted to return. I didn't do well there though, probably because I wasn't pushy enough. I didn't get anyone to convert to Mormonism, which is the purpose of these missions. When I came back and told the congregation that I didn't baptize anyone, they told me that they were sure I had planted seeds of faith in the Japanese.

I didn't even think about being gay when I was in Japan. I was able to block it out because I was so busy trying to convert others. These missions are very regimented. The program controls everything you do from 6 a.m. until bedtime. You have a companion, another missionary, who is with you all the time. You do everything with them. You even sleep in the same room.

When you return from a mission, others will tell you that you will feel lonely because you are used to being with someone else all the time, and I definitely was. After I returned from my mission, I started college at a Mormon school and was living in the dorms. That was when I masturbated for the first time. I felt so guilty that I called my bishop and told him I needed to talk to him. I told him what I had done, but he wanted me to wait until Sunday to talk to him. I was beside myself—I thought I was damned for sure. I decided the only thing to do was to take a knife out to a field near campus to end my life. I sat down in the field and cried until I felt numb, when I changed my mind and returned to my dorm room.

I graduated from college with an associate's degree a couple of years later. My dad informed me that it was time for me to get married. In order to go to the highest level in Heaven in the Mormon Church, you have to be married. I did have someone in mind. A girl I worked with was a good friend, and we started dating. I had told her that I didn't want sexual feelings to get in the way of our decision to get married, and we made a pact that we wouldn't kiss until we were engaged. She went along with the idea, but really I was denying what I felt inside, and I made myself believe that it was the right thing to do.

We got married in the temple and moved to Portland. The idea of being with a female was foreign to me. It was difficult for me to have sex with her. It was even hard to think about what was going on, so I would have to take my mind out of what was really happening. I would imagine that God was helping me, with His hand on my back, giving me the ability to make her happy. My wife and I were always good friends, and we have three beautiful daughters together.

I felt unhappy and troubled in my marriage. I decided to join the Army because I wanted to die—I wanted to die for my country. In the Mormon faith, if you die in war it is an honorable death, which would mean that I could go to Heaven. When I joined the service, I was interviewed. I was asked questions—if I was gay, or if I was attracted to men. I told them no, because I believed that I wasn't, it was the Devil working inside me. I wasn't afraid to die—in fact, I wanted to, but I wasn't ever put in harm's way. I ended up being honorably discharged from the service in a little more than three years. I got a job back in Oregon and joined the Air Force Reserve.

About five years after leaving the service, I met a guy online that I knew to be gay. He and I started going to the gym together, and then on one occasion we went to a park and fooled around. At that moment, everything came crashing down on me. I finally realized I was attracted to guys, and I always had been. My world collapsed. I considered suicide again, but I knew that I couldn't kill myself—suicide puts you in Hell.

I was in the worst-case scenario because I was gay. I prayed that God would make me nonexistent. Really, I didn't think that God would turn down such a diligent prayer to snuff me out of existence like I was never there, but He didn't. I had to confront reality, and I decided to drive home. When I arrived, I collapsed on my floor, sobbing. I confessed to my wife that I had cheated on her. She wanted to know who she was. I told her it was with a guy—and she said it that wasn't so bad.

I went to the bishop that night, and they called an emergency meeting. They put me on probation, which meant I was not allowed to pray in front of other people—I could only pray in my mind. I also couldn't take Communion. They arranged to have me to see several different Mormon psychologists, whose services the church paid for.

The Mormons believe that being homosexual is a mental illness that can be cured. I was cautioned to only to see Mormon psychologists, so I went first to a Mormon psychologist who boasted a 90-percent "success" rate. He would give me massages. He told me that my father hadn't given me enough attention. He asked me to make a videotape describing to him what I thought about when I masturbated, and he was supposed to edit it and add things that would disgust me. He never got around to that. Later, he showed me my first gay porn. While it was playing, he described why he thought it was ridiculous and stupid. I stopped going to him. Later, I met some people who had the same kinds of experiences with him.

Having no success with the psychologist, I was forced to go to a program called Evergreen International in downtown Portland on the church grounds. The program is for men that have "SSA" (same-sex attraction). We were not allowed to say that we were "gay," because we were told that "gay" is a political word. We would get together once a week, like a twelve-step program for recovering homosexuals. There would be a facilitator as well as a straight missionary couple from the church there to chaperone. Sitting in a big circle of chairs, the members of the group would each tell their story of the week, like a confessional, often ending with tears. At the end of the meeting, we would give each other hugs. There was a guy who had been in the group for a long time, and he kept the wedding invitations of all the ones that "made it." I am happy to say that today he is back with his male partner.

Once a year, we would take a trip to Salt Lake City for the national get-together. There were gays from all over the Western states—a sea of gay Mormons. They taught us different ways to hold each other, in a non-sexual way. It was considered as nurturing, and I have to say it did feel good to be held. One person would hold another one and say nice things to that person, taking turns. It was supposed to be healing.

They said we were "damaged little boys" inside, and that we needed to heal so we would no longer have SSA. They explained that we didn't have good, nurturing male role models.

Sometimes, while holding one other, you got "a little happy"—but they told us not to worry, because it would go away sooner or later. I thought it was great because I realized I wasn't the only one that felt like I did, even though I thought the teachings were far off.

Many of the guys I met there—and who flunked out of the program like me—are still my friends. Successful participants stay in the group until they get married and can live a straight life. My worry is for the ones that do get married, and who—like I did—eventually realize that they are gay and break someone's heart.

While I was in the Evergreen program, we were told to tell people close to us about it. I told my parents. My dad said that he loved me, but at the same time he didn't say that he accepted me for who I was. My mom was really quiet. She asked me if anyone else knew, and asked me not to tell anyone. She didn't like the idea that anyone in her hometown would know. In the Mormon faith, followers believe that how children turn out is the responsibility of the parents. If they don't put their kids on the straight-and-narrow, the parents will be accountable in Heaven. My mom worried that the sins of her children would be on her head.

After some time at Evergreen, my wife was getting upset because I was spending so much time with these boys in the program. She was tired of it. She asked if I was ever attracted to her. She knew I would never lie to her, and I told her that I never was. She informed me that I needed to leave the house.

I was a student at the time, and I was only getting my money from the Air Force Reserve, but I paid my child support. I ended up living in my car for several months. I started volunteering for as many overseas temporary duties as I could. I put my things in storage and kept doing job after job. When my wife and I finally got divorced, the church called me into a trial in the church court. I was told this was a court of love and mercy, and that they had decided that I was no longer a member of the church. I couldn't wear the holy garments any-more, even though I wasn't anyway. They told me this was out of love and compassion, and that they hoped I would come back to the church again. I felt horrible. After two years, I finally stopped going to Ever-green. I decided that I was who I was, and that I wasn't going to change.

My coming-out process was gradual. The first step happened ten years ago when I admitted to my wife that I wasn't attracted to her. The next step happened when I was in the Reserves, in my first com-mand. My superior called me into her office. She told me that she knew that I was something, but wasn't going to say it, and she wanted me to know that it was okay with her. She told me that the master ser-geant was okay with it as well. When I heard this, I ran out to my car and cried. I was so grateful, and I was amazed.

Later, I moved to a different unit, and I had a feeling they knew I was gay and that they didn't accept me. I was a high-ranking, non-commissioned officer doing dishes for a year and a half, regardless of what I volunteered for. I was the highest-ranking, best dishwasher in the Air Force, so I got out. I was basically forced out.

I did have some short relationships with guys, some of which were abusive. I think I sabotaged myself—I felt that this was what I de-served, and it was my punishment. My feelings of guilt would come and go like waves. I continued dating when I was on temporary duty assignments, which guaranteed short relationships because they would be over when I went back home.

There was a Mormon scripture that would come to mind, some-thing to the effect of "wickedness never was happiness." I would think to myself, "If I am being wicked, then why am I so happy?" That is how I am feeling even today, but I am really not completely out yet. Not everyone knows.

I met my current partner online about seven years ago. Mario is from Argentina, but he lived in Salem, Oregon. When I would get back from an assignment, we met a few times for coffee. We took it slow. After some time, we decided to date exclusively.

I was always taught that appearances are important, so we became roommates—but with a third guy who was straight. It was like three straight guys living together, so we weren't out. Even our roommate didn't know. He moved out, and Mario's mom moved in with us, but she didn't know either.

Then came a day when he and I had a fight. We broke up temporarily. It is so hard to break up with an Argentinean man because they are so romantic. He began crying and went to his mom to tell her that Leo was breaking up with him. That's when she realized we were both gay, and it was difficult for a while. She doesn't live with us anymore, but now she totally accepts us.

One consequence of being outed was that, at the time, we were going to a church that didn't accept gays. Mario was in the choir. The congregation found out that he was gay, and he was told he couldn't be in the choir anymore. We now are going to a church that accepts gays.

When I was in the service, it was "Don't Ask, Don't Tell." Personally, I don't think it was a good idea. It made things worse. It caused witch hunts—gays would tell on other gays so they themselves could stay in the service. There were gay decoys trying to catch gay soldiers. In some places, there was a military subculture—a secret gay society on the inside. To get into such a group, you have to be brought in. These soldiers were afraid of losing their jobs, so trust was very important. It was dangerous to the military to have a secret society. I know this first-hand—I had some bad experiences with a gay superior who wanted things of me. When I refused, he threatened me. He became hostile, but I couldn't tell anyone or I would be kicked out.

I now live in Portland with Mario and my 19- and 21-year-old daughters who are both in college. My youngest daughter is 16 and lives with my ex-wife, but she would like to move in with us someday. These days, I see her every other weekend. My daughters were brought up in the Mormon Church until a few years ago, when they all saw the bigotry against gays and others, as well as the conditional love. They pulled away from it. My daughters love my partner, and they are comfortable with our relationship.

Coming out has been a gradual process for me. Now I am pretty comfortable with the fact that I am gay, but inside my guilt still causes problems. Once in a while, my feelings of self-loathing come back, and I wonder if or when they will ever leave me alone.

Fear of being deported
Mario, 30
Portland, Oregon
January 2011

I am from Argentina. My mother and I came to the U.S. on a tourist visa in 2001, and we moved to Portland, Oregon. She decided to move to the U.S. for economic issues, but mostly for safety. I did not want to come, but I knew it was going to be for the best.

When I was growing up, about the time you start having those feelings, mine were different than other boys. My parents got divorced when I was only two months old and my dad was never present in my life. Since I was very young, he would always say, "You're not going to be one of those faggots, are you?" I guess he said that because I didn't play soccer and I was feminine. I was more interested in art and theatre. In Argentina, soccer is very important. Even though I liked to play, I was horrible at it.

The other kids did not tease me about being gay—they teased me about not being macho and not playing sports. In my neighborhood when I was growing up there were not many guys so I was able to do what I liked. I would do artsy stuff with the girls. I noticed when I was 11 or 12 in school that I was attracted to guys. When I was 13, I became very good friends with a guy. My feelings became very strong but he never found out. I was devastated when he moved away. My mother thought I was devastated because of the friendship, but it was more than that.

In my teenage years I knew I was attracted to guys, but I knew I was going to marry a woman because it was something I had to do. I could never tell my mom how I felt. I was willing to live that lie because I knew I could never come out. I never had a girlfriend. I did have some intimate relationships with guys when I was 18 but they were short relationships, not boyfriends.

In my 20s I was living in the U.S. and I met a girl that spoke Spanish. I made sure I was seen with her even though she was just a friend. I could feel that she wanted something else, and I thought maybe I could make this work out.

Then I met Leo. He was my first boyfriend. We started dating, fell in love, and moved in together. We didn't live alone together, though—we lived with a straight guy and no one knew that we were gay, not even the other guy. Later he moved out and my mother moved in. Leo and I had a fight and I was upset. My mother wanted to know why I was upset. I told her that Leo had broken up with me and then the secret was out. I was 25. She told me she loved me no matter what, but she did not approve of me being gay. She has a very strong relationship with me. She never remarried or had boyfriends. Her love for me was much more than any religion, but she was still very troubled about it.

Leo and I made up. He was in the reserves, and he was deployed for a whole year. For the first six months he was stationed in California, and I went to visit him eight times. I was in the hotel talking to my dad on the phone. I had been talking more and more about Leo, and he finally asked me if I was gay. I said yes. He said he loved me, that he would always love me.

A few days later I found out that he sent a nasty e-mail to my mom saying that she made me gay. He said that if she would have made me play sports it wouldn't have happened. I know he suffered a lot internally after that because he told me he would not tell anyone. During the last phone call I had with him, before he passed away in 2007, it felt like he finally was accepting that I was gay and he even asked about Leo. I didn't know then that he was dying of pancreatic cancer.

Now my mother is doing great. She loves me and she loves Leo and sees us most every day. The church we go to accepts me and Leo. She sees that and that helps her a lot. She had to choose between her religious beliefs and me. She put it in God's hands and she chose me.

When my mom and I moved here neither of us researched it, and we didn't know that we couldn't get our Social Security cards right away or that we wouldn't have the opportunity to apply for permanent residency and then citizenship just by working here. I have worked in the U.S. for years "under the table." The whole immigration system is broken and confusing. Undocumented immigrants can't get a Social Security number but the IRS will give us a legal Tax ID numbers so we can pay taxes on a job we really should not be doing, but the IRS wants our money anyway. To get a job, employers want a Social Security number so we use one that is not valid and when our employer finds out we often have to change jobs. We do pay taxes but nothing is paid into our Social Security account that we could someday benefit from. And we still can get caught and deported.

Leo and I are always afraid I will get deported. I want to become a citizen but the only way I can is if I marry a girl.

Since I left Argentina, I have heard being gay is more open—on July 22, 2010, they passed a law that allows gays to marry. They don't call it gay marriage. The bill calls it equal marriage—equal for all with all the same rights as other married people. I have come out to my friends in Argentina on Facebook because now that my mother knows and it accepts me, it is okay.

December 2013 – email

Leo and Mario were married in Decorah, Iowa, in 2011.

In 2013, the Supreme Count repealed a key part of the Defense of Marriage Act (DOMA). Leo and Mario's marriage was federally recognized which gave Mario the benefit of immigration. Mario became eligible for a Green Card and can apply to become a citizen in three years. Mario now has an Oregon driver's license (allowed only to people who can prove legal status) and a Social Security card.

Mario hasn't been back to Argentina for twelve years, though he and Leo are making plans to visit Buenos Aires where he grew up and a village nearby where some of his relatives live. Leo said, "I can't wait to see the little dirt road village of La Paz (the Peace). I think I will find peace there."

Part Seven

Dear Momma Traci

Freedom to be me — Lee

Lee, 19
Chicago, Illinois
November 2010 - email

Momma Traci,

I am a college student in Chicago.

My story is not so much focused on the actual coming-out process and the reactions of others, but more about changes in me and my ability to be true to myself. It's more about the freedom to be me and to pursue my life's dreams and goals.

Until I met your Daniel, I had only come out to my three closest friends, and did not plan to tell anyone else for at least another year. I had always felt the need to hide my sexuality, mainly for fear of what others would think, especially in my small midwestern hometown. My repression and hiding of my sexuality led to the repression and hiding of my true hopes and dreams—dreams of what I would grow up to become. Pursuing those hopes and dreams would have revealed my sexuality. I had even reached the point of convincing myself that I would be happy enough going to school to become an engineer or surgeon because I would be able to live comfortably and never have to worry about money. Even worse, I had abandoned any hopes of continuing my experiences and education in theatre, music, dancing, and writing—almost anything in the realm of creative arts. I tried my best to think positively and see the future as full of happy times, but I couldn't stop the voices in the back of my head telling me that I was making a huge mistake. I wasn't able to be myself. I was living a lie.

I have struggled with finding any sort of self-confidence. Surrounded by classmates, dear friends, and siblings that I viewed as far more naturally gifted and able to realize their own potential, I simply took a back seat and watched as they chased their own hopes and dreams. I was afraid of disappointing not only others, such as my parents, but also disappointing myself.

I never went a day without walking down the halls of my high school wondering what every single person I passed thought of me. I thought that my physical appearance, attitude, personality, talents, and likability were all under the scrutiny of my teachers, friends, friends' friends, and those I wished to be my friends. I was always too afraid to make an impression of any sort other than shyness, because I figured that would be the safest route. In my own mind, I had no potential to become great at anything that I truly wanted to be great at. I was chasing dreams in my mind, but the rest of my body didn't seem to want to join in.

I met your son in November of last year at a Chicago film festival, where his movie, *The Big Gay Musical*, was featured. There was something different about him. Beyond the posters and trailers I saw for his movie, I knew nothing about Daniel, but he had shown so much interest and kindness in helping me to realize who I was and to live my life according to my dreams and passions. I couldn't help but want to know more about him. He had that sense of creative accomplishment yet also a passion to continue making use of his talents to create beautiful things. Those I had always known before to have great potential or talent also knew it themselves, and they loved to show it off.

However, he was someone who obviously had an incredible ability to be truly professional without letting it completely define his life. I saw albums, videos, and read articles about just some of his many accomplishments: *Grease, Oklahoma!, Happy Days, Hairspray*. These were works with some of the best dance companies, dancers, choreographers, singers, musicians, directors, writers, and performers. I was in awe at the massive amount of talent in such a kind and humble person. But once I took a harder look, I could see the determination, passion, and love he had for the arts.

Strangely, it was nothing about his talents, work experience, or the people he knew that inspired me to listen to what he was trying to tell me. It was his ability to be true to himself and his own determination to help out a stranger that made me realize that I had to stop and think hard about my own life. I tell myself that if someone of Daniel's caliber tells me there is something special about me, perhaps I should believe it. Something changed within me. I finally felt the need to express myself fully without boundaries.

Daniel and I had only known each other a few days and already he was telling me things about myself I hadn't thought about for years. I don't know if he says this to everyone trying to find themselves, but telling me that I'm genuinely special and there is more to me than even I think really was an eye-opener. Quite honestly, if he did tell that to everyone, it wouldn't matter anyway because I felt as though he truly meant it when he said it to me.

When you come from a small town where failure is frowned upon almost as much as cursing the high school football team that just won the state championship, it is difficult to listen to those telling you to follow your dreams. For many in a small town in Illinois, following your dreams only makes sense if those dreams include going to an Ivy League school to become a highly paid engineer, taking over the family business, or becoming an NFL superstar. I fully support anyone whose dreams it is to become any one of those things, but they simply aren't my own.

That fateful weekend back in November changed how I view myself. Your son helped me realize that I needed to find happiness through being true to myself. In order for that to happen, I needed to first be true to everyone else.

As Christmas break approached, I came to the conclusion that the sooner I came out, the sooner I could start feeling better about everything. I had always had an incredible group of friends and supporters, but after coming out, my perception of the love they have for me was grossly out of proportion. I truly feel blessed every day to have so many friends, family, and even co-workers showing their support. My experience coming out was met with overwhelming and surprising happiness, encouragement, relief, and love. Friends I believed to be somewhat homophobic met me with even greater happiness and support than I could ever imagine. The feeling of no longer having to hide anything has opened so many doors for me. I've met so many new people and been introduced to a world of compassion and love.

My family was, of course, the scariest group of people to tell. I knew that my two sisters and stepsister, all forward-thinking individuals, would be supportive and loving. I knew that my father, to many people's surprise, would also be supportive. I think he had known for the past couple of years. I distinctly remember him telling me on many occasions that I could tell him anything and no matter what, he would never stop loving and supporting me.

I honestly did not exactly know how my mother would take the news. I did have a feeling that after a certain amount of time she would be okay with it all. Aside from the initial event of telling her, I was incredibly surprised and overwhelmingly happy to see her progress of acceptance. Now that I've opened my mind, she has really shown me how much she loves me. Our relationship has grown beyond that of even the most bonded of mother and son.

I have yet to encounter those who hate me for being gay, at least personally. But I have definitely met those who either are in complete denial or simply refuse to be associated with me. These are perhaps the people I wish to interact with the most because those who act in fear, disgust, or even hatred of someone who is different in fact are unhappy with themselves. To not like someone—for their sexuality, race, or religious beliefs—is truly sad to me.

Whenever I am upset or feeling alone, I simply remind myself that I am actually the furthest from being alone. I cry almost every day with the joy of knowing how many people in my life love me for who I am, and who would do anything to help me succeed in any situation.

Daniel came into my life at a crucial point, one where others easily influenced me. I couldn't be happier that it was him that was influencing me, instead of someone who didn't have my best interests at heart. I've never met anyone like your son, and I celebrate your ability to love him and to raise such an amazing young man. I pray every day that I will make someone feel just as special as he has made me feel about myself.

Lee

Close your eyes and open your heart — Bridget

Bridget, 25
New Jersey
November 2010 - email

I am bisexual, but I lean toward being most attracted to females.

When I was about 14, I started feeling a weird connection with some of the females in my life. I knew I had a deeper feeling for them but I didn't fully understand it. When I was 16, I told my mother that my best friend had a girlfriend. My mother freaked out and told me that when she slept over I couldn't close my bedroom door.

About a year later I told my best friend that I had feelings for her. We became intimate that night and that's where it all started to whirlwind. She became my first girlfriend. We lasted for a year until she cheated on me with a man. During our relationship, I was in denial. The only people who knew we were in a relationship were the both of us. I didn't tell anyone until nine months into the relationship, and then I told our mutual best guy friend.

After we broke up, I started coming out to the people closest to me but it was years later that I told my parents.

After my first girlfriend, I identified myself as bisexual since I was still interested in males. I've loved and enjoyed my sexual encounters with men and still find them attractive. I just find females more attractive. It's easier to connect with a female when you're a female because you think alike. It's so complicated but so simple at the same time. I don't think that someone who isn't bisexual or homosexual can ever fully understand it, but they can accept it. When people ask me why or how, I usually tell them to close their eyes and open their heart. When you talk to someone intimately and you are unaware of sex, you can fall in love with that person whether they are male or female, it doesn't matter—it is what's inside that counts.

While I was in college, I met another female who piqued my interest. I had been single for three years and she took me by surprise. I was absolutely in love with her as much as she was with me. Two months into our relationship, I told my parents. She did the same. For years, I had nightmares of my mother finding out because I didn't think she'd understand, that she'd hate me and blame herself. Sometimes I would "hypothetically" ask her what she would do if one of her kids was gay. She said she would think she did something wrong. This pushed me to conceal my secret.

I told my father first. We went for a walk down the street with the family Yorkie. I asked him if he loved me, and he said of course. I then asked him if he loved me no matter what, and he responded without a doubt in his mind. I then told him about my current girlfriend and about my first girlfriend. He told me that as long as I was happy it didn't matter. I cried and we hugged. It was probably only a five-minute conversation.

Then I walked upstairs to tell my mother. I walked into her bedroom and I opened with the same two questions. She answered the same, but I could tell she was uneasy. For a whole hour we talked. I cried, and she cried, too, but she didn't understand at all. She couldn't understand how I could find pleasure with a woman because she felt they only can do so much for you. That upset me, but inside I kind of laughed.

I remember getting kind of defensive and asking her what does it matter because relationships aren't all about the sexual aspect. I told her I loved her on a different level. I wanted to tell her that my girlfriend excited, enticed, and embraced me in ways most men hadn't. I was in love with her and our sex life was awesome. I didn't want to go into raw detail with my mom—I thought that would have been a little too much information, too intense. I didn't think she needed to know what we did behind closed doors. I told her if she was that curious she could watch lesbian porn, jokingly, but half serious.

Then my mom wanted to know if I was fully gay or if I was bisexual. I confirmed that I was bisexual, and she seemed relieved. I think she was afraid I might never give her grandchildren, or I'd be looked upon in a bad way—or, more importantly, she would. I didn't blame her for asking or possibly feeling like that. I wish I could have made it easier for her.

I never asked to be attracted to both sexes, but I'm not going to lie to myself or hide from the world because of it. I care about what others think—but more importantly, I care about how I feel and what I think.

It was hard, but it went better than I thought. It took my mom almost a year and a half to come to grips with it, but never once did she try to stop me from being with the one I love. Sometimes we'd talk about it, and sometimes I could tell she was acting differently around my girlfriend than she did before she knew. But I never forced her to accept it, just to accept and love me. She had to sort it out and I always told her you're never going to fully understand but just understand I'm happy. With my current girlfriend, I have tried to make it obvious so to lessen the blow.

Both my parents had a feeling that my first girlfriend was actually my girlfriend but they never asked me, and they never talked about it with each other. After I had broken up with a girlfriend after almost a year of being together, I confided in my mom. She didn't say she was glad because now I could be straight. Instead, she told me that she knew I was hurting and that sometimes people aren't meant to be. She told me to just relax and try to make myself happy. I knew then that my mother was accepting me of me.

I love both my parents with all my heart. I just hope that one day my mother will be okay enough to come out to her sisters and tell them that my girlfriend is my girlfriend and not just a friend, but I think most of them already have a clue.

My girlfriend and I are still together and it'll be two years very soon. I'm excited and I know she is, too. I love her with all of my heart and could honestly say I would love to spend the rest of my life with her and even start our own family. I'm aware of all the hardships I could possibly endure, but to me she's worth it. When I'm with her, it just feels right. All that matters is that we love each other with every fiber of our beings, and we want to keep moving forward.

Some people think that no one will love them or everyone will hate them if people found out they were gay. You have to make sure that the people who are in your life are going to support you no matter what and love you unconditionally. You can't force someone to understand or accept you—there will always be people who don't. If they don't, do you really want someone like that in your life?

When you first begin to tell others that you're not straight, some may be shocked, distant, or tell you things you don't want to hear. If they were meant to be in your life as a positive force they will come around. Sometimes those people are your parents, or siblings, or best friends, and it hurts but you are the one that matters the most. Love yourself before all others—that is the only way others can truly love you. Don't let the stigma of being homosexual stop you from being strong and being you. Just remember, it gets better.

Not a choice — Keith

Keith, 26
Georgia, U.S. Military
October 2010 - email

I am on active duty in the United States military. I grew up in a pretty typical conservative suburb in the South. I attended public schools and was involved with sports. I swam competitively for fourteen years until college, where I picked up playing other sports for four years. I was actively involved in my church youth group and other school activities beginning in middle school.

Socially, middle school was a strange time for me, as it is for most teens. By the end of 7th grade I had dated almost half of the cheerleading squad. I felt great about life and where things were headed. However, 8th grade rolled around and I felt strange. Something was different inside of me. I tried brushing it off by focusing on what I hoped to accomplish in high school. So began my dating dry spell.

I tried dating a girl in the 10th grade, but that didn't last very long—two weeks maybe. That experience reminded me that I liked caring for someone and doing special things for them, but I simply did not feel the chemistry. I had my hand in just about every club during high school and was student body president by my junior year. I worked hard in my classes and managed to get an appointment (which I gladly accepted) to one of the United States military academies.

Toward the end of my senior year, my thoughts and feelings grew even more complicated. I felt I could possibly be gay, but I didn't have any way to confirm my own suspicions. I continued to push myself and try to date girls before I graduated. I didn't want to leave high school feeling like an outcast or a statistic—the one gay guy at my school.

I started talking to two girls from local high schools in my final semester of high school. One, Eve, was the apple of my eye. Clearly talented (involved with the entertainment industry) and very personable, she quickly piqued my interest. We enjoyed random trips around town after school and slushies from the gas station. It was also fun being with her because of her spontaneity and celebrity.

The other girl, Mary, went to a different high school than Eve. I met Mary through a mutual friend on my swim team. She was cute and sweet—the girl next door. But after going on a few dates and buying her a few bundles of flowers, the flame fizzled away.

As prom grew closer, I asked Eve to accompany me. She gladly said, "Yes," which made me a very happy boy. These experiences in the final semester filled an emotional void—temporarily—as graduation approached. I felt more secure about my sexuality, even though Eve and I went our separate ways after high school.

Once boot camp commenced, I didn't think about much of anything. The whole experience was a haze and a precursor to my first semester of college. During my freshman year, I made the assumption that the military might help "make a man out of me"—up to that point in my life, my perception of gay was flamboyancy. I knew something was weird, but again, I didn't want to be a statistic. I assumed my chances of being gay were minuscule. It couldn't be me. I didn't have a lisp and I didn't want to wear makeup. I was an athlete and in the military—characteristics I understood as the makings of a man. But I had not gone beyond second base with a girl. That fact made me exceptionally insecure.

Before Christmas break that first year, my roommates made a pact to lose our virginity over leave. I felt trapped in a silly rip-off of an American Pie movie. I was already thinking up some fake story to tell when I returned in January. I could have just stuck to my story of waiting for marriage like I had always been taught in church. But, on New Year's Eve, the opportunity presented itself, and I lost the V-card to a fiery red-headed girl in her senior year of high school.

That experience solidified my assumptions about my sexuality—I completed the job, but I had to think about a guy. I returned to the academy triumphant, and didn't have to share a fake story with my guy friends. But on the inside, I hurt.

The next two years flew by. I found myself fooling around with girls at weekend parties or at hotel room hangouts on team road trips. I'm not really sure if I was actively trying to keep up a perception of "straightness," but it seemed to work. No one questioned my sexuality.

During my junior year, I experienced a terrible skiing accident. It was the most painful episode of my life. The recovery was long, and I wanted to give up on so many occasions. Because I was at the academy, I didn't have anyone taking care of me, keeping me on schedule for classes and appointments, or making sure I took my medicine. My roommate had a girlfriend, and I always longed to have someone that cared for me the way she cared for him. But I survived and tried to get back into my normal routine. Making it through the recovery gave me hope that even if I was gay, I possessed the inner strength to make it through the days of silence that lay ahead.

The summer going into senior year, I deployed overseas. I continued my physical rehabilitation while working alongside some amazing people. We performed numerous patrols and conducted countless night and day operations. In my down time, I managed to sneak off to a gay-friendly bar once or twice, and I kissed a guy for the first time.

After having such an awesome experience overseas, I returned to school with a positive attitude about life. I focused on school and kept a smile on my face. However, about midway through the fall semester of senior year, I started to get antsy. I had reached an intersection in my personal life. I could go about this on my own, or I could open up with my family and hope for support.

I figured I could go a little further on my own. I made a fake MySpace profile in an attempt to connect with local gays. I really just wanted to go to a gay bar, but not alone. I knew of one other guy in my school who was gay, but we were not close.

I chatted with a stranger from the local area via MySpace for a week or so, and he convinced me to come out to a gay club in a nearby city. He was one of the bartenders, so he would make sure I got in for free. On a weekend in September, I took off to the bar alone. I found the club, but sat in my car for a solid two hours before I summoned the courage to get my ass inside. Once I was in, I shot straight to the bar. The guy gave me a drink and I stood there for the rest of the night. I was too scared to move or talk to anyone else. Everything about the place seemed so alien and extravagant. The other patrons' mannerisms were confident and diverse, which confused and intimidated me. Even though I didn't tear down any walls that night, the experience definitely opened my eyes and forced me to assess my sexuality. I was uncomfortable, but I didn't run away from my feelings.

When the spring arrived, I was feeling more content with myself and started to visit the city on the weekends on a more frequent schedule. I had made some friends at one of the bars, and enjoyed just hanging out.

While visiting the city made me feel more whole, it also marked the beginning of my second life: the life of lies. I was making up stories at school and telling my classmates tall tales. It hurt and it still does today. But the reality is that I had no choice. The "Don't Ask, Don't Tell" policy was doing a great job of keeping me fearful of facing discharge and losing a dream.

Today, I do my best to replace lies with ambiguity. I know I have damaged strong bonds I developed through my time at the academy because of my second life. I distanced myself from people I cared about and from fellow soldiers I know would have my back in a sticky situation. From the outside, I would look at someone like myself and think, "What happened to him? He seems so sketchy these days."

Since committing to many years of service after graduation and commissioning, I now live in Florida. I am an officer and currently going through specialized training. My goal is to become a pilot. If I'm going to serve my country, I'm going to do something exciting, purposeful, and respectable. However, even since leaving the regimented academy environment, I continue to face bumps in the road with remaining closeted.

For example, upon reporting in, a superior officer (O-5) asked me, "Are you gay?" I replied, "No," while doing my best to conceal my shock. He clearly violated the "Don't Ask" part of "Don't Ask, Don't Tell."

I affirmed my commitment to honor and integrity when I joined the military, yet I have to break that oath every day in order to remain in the service. From a work perspective, it's extremely hard to go through a career without any type of support from the organization. Service men and women have to be strong in the service of our nation, but those individuals that live under the cloak of "Don't Ask, Don't Tell" have to be even stronger. Regardless, I have hope for the future and I know I will be okay. Many soldiers before me have gone through these same emotions and lived in silence to protect the lives of Americans and the silencers.

Understanding my commitment to the military, watching the debacle over "Don't Ask, Don't Tell" in Washington D.C., and living this second life certainly make me think about the choices I have made. Even if I wanted to, opening up about my sexuality is not an option in this profession. Staying closeted from my parents has become second nature.

It's kind of ironic, really—my dad always says, "Life is a series of choices." I have to make them and learn from them. But being gay was not a choice, and that seems to be complicating the ones I have made and the ones I wish I could make.

October 2011 Email

I came out to my family on February 4. It's been a long eight months. Things are not resolved, and we are not on good terms for various reasons. They cry every day. My dad is especially devastated.

In better news, I'm nine flights away from getting my wings. I just received orders for my post-flight school assignment. I'll be flying HH-65s for the Coast Guard out of Air Station New Orleans. I'm really excited about it!

Love,
Keith

Learn and move on — Kieran

Kieran's first email told me he had been attacked by two Marines because he was gay. I tried to follow his story online, but there were few details about the trial. After that he seemed to disappear.

It is frightening when I receive letters from troubled LGBTQ people and then never hear from them again. After a couple of years of emailing Kieran and looking for him on Facebook, I finally found him again. He told me what happened in his trial and the many changes in his life—including his new life with his partner and his beautiful twin boys.

Kieran, 27
Savannah, Georgia
October 2010 – email

I was born and raised in South Africa and moved to the U.S. at age 13. I came from a very strict family background, and even as a child I was constantly taught that being gay was wrong.

I began realizing that I was attracted to males very young, but was constantly reminded by my father that being gay was unacceptable. Through high school I denied my feelings for men and dated girls. I went through high school believing that my attraction to males was disgusting and was simply a phase—a phase that would pass with time if I simply chose the straight life. At 19, I married my best friend, and three years later we were blessed with twin boys.

In 2009 my mother, with whom I've always had a very close relationship, suffered two massive strokes. Both times she was on death's doorstep. It was only then I realized that I could no longer lie to myself and pretend to be happy. I could no longer be the person others wanted me to be—it was time to be myself.

In December 2009 my wife and I separated, and in January I came out to my friends and family. My father kicked me out of the house.

He later asked me to return home but was very vocal about his objection to my "sexuality choices."

In June 2010, I was attacked by two United States Marines, because they thought I was winking at them. The attack nearly cost me my life. I was revived by a friend performing CPR and was transported to a hospital, where I spent several days. I endured eight weeks off from work, medical bills galore, media attention, and a lengthy stay at a mental health facility. I haven't been able to walk into crowded areas or sit with my back towards a door since the attack.

My father has come to grips with the reality of his son being gay. While he still believes it's a choice, he at least treats me like he once did—like a son. My mom was not shocked by my coming out and has been accepting. But she is still searching for reasons to explain why I'm gay, and why I could never come out. The strokes left her with massive brain damage, and she hasn't been the same woman that raised me. That hurts more than anything. I am sorry I couldn't accept who I was until it was too late for my mom. She will never fully comprehend that she is not at fault for this. I feel like I never had a chance for the mother I once knew to have a relationship with the real me.

If I could tell my mother one thing, it would be this: You taught me never to regret, just to learn and move on. Regret is how I feel about never accepting who I am and having the chance to have a truthful, honest relationship with the real me and the old you. I love you, Mom. Thanks for all of your love and support.

November 2013 Email

Momma Traci,

The court proceeding lasted almost two years and was absolutely draining. The charges were dropped against both of the men who attacked me. I did receive a small settlement of $5,000 which did little to cover my medical bills of $34,000 and the mental health hospital bills.

In 2011 I met the man of my dreams, Chris, who was visiting Savannah from Los Angeles for a conference. He moved here six months later, and we have been together ever since.

Four months ago, my life changed drastically. Beth, my ex-wife and mother of our twin boys, passed away. My twins now live with Chris and me. While as a family we have risen to meet the daily challenges of life without Beth, I continue to grieve for what should have been. I miss my best friend and our twins miss their mommy, but it's usually coupled with talk of happy memories, and laughter. They are doing an amazing job at dealing with everything life has thrown our way. I am so fortunate.

Kieran

Jesus loves the Little children — Matt

Matt, 35
Memphis, Tennessee
November 2010 – email

I was raised as a Southern Baptist and the church condemned homosexuality. I wanted to serve God, but I was having trouble fighting my desires. To make matters worse, when my parents drove me to school every morning, I had to listen to *Love in Action* and *Focus on the Family*. They were Christian focus groups led by Pastor James Dobson that preached—among other things—that homosexuality was a choice.

I started getting picked on in school in about the 3rd grade. I think it was because I had such a gentle heart. When the other boys found out that it bothered me to get teased or picked on, it got worse. When I was in about the 7th grade I realized that I had sexual feeling for boys but I kept it a secret.

In high school the bullying centered on me appearing to be gay. If I talked to a new guy and tried to be friends then rumors would spread that I was attracted to him. The guy would freak out and never speak to me again and then join the bully wagon. The cruelty and humiliation made me want to die.

In 10th grade, I decided I could no longer fight myself. I was going to either come out or kill myself. I told my mother and stepdad about the feelings I was having, and they put me in therapy. After a while I came clean with my therapist. Then my therapist came on to me. I told my parents but they decided not to do anything about it aside from discontinuing the sessions. I called him and confronted him but he completed denied it. My parents sent me to a different therapist. My mother and stepdad and I continued to fight all through high school since being gay and being Baptist wasn't acceptable.

When I was 18 I decided to accept myself. I was beginning college and working at Wal-Mart, I started acting on my feelings in secret with adult men I felt comfortable with. A few of them went to my church—the largest church in Memphis. My new boss at work was gay, and once he talked about going to a local gay bar called Amnesia. A big group was going, and he asked if I wanted to join them. Curious, I went. About twenty-five people were there who I knew but had not spoken to about my feelings. I had a blast. I even had my first foot-popping kiss with a hottie that night.

About the same time, my parents got suspicious that I was sexually active. They overheard me talking on the phone to a guy I was interested in. They told me I had to quit living this lifestyle or move out. I was forced to move out. Thankfully, my dad had set up a college fund for me. My dad and step-mom were okay about me being gay, but they didn't live in the same town that I did.

I started going to the University of Memphis. I dated a lot of guys and learned a lot of lessons the hard way, but I matured. My first love lasted about a year, but he wasn't comfortable with who he was or being public with our relationship. We lived together but he insisted we called ourselves roommates. It caused many fights and finally we broke up.

I finished college and started working, many times two jobs to support myself. In 2009, I met Galvin and we have been together ever since. We have a home and a stable life together, complete with two precious dogs. My family's acceptance has been gradual. As my relationship with Galvin became more serious they eventually realized that by not accepting me and my partner they would see less of me. Now both sides of my family are loving, inclusive, and accepting.

It destroys my heart to see kids lost in this homophobic world. I had a hard time surviving growing up gay, and I hope LGBTQ youth realize that it does get better. Luckily now there is The Trevor Project and the local Gay and Lesbian Community Center for youth to go to. As someone who attempted to fight off his feelings with prayer and therapy, I can testify that embracing how you feel is the only way to go.

If I had a chance to give advice to parents who suspect their kid is LGBTQ, it would be to talk to their kid. This is the child God blessed you with. Love, accept, encourage, support them and fight for them. Your child needs to know that you are there for them 100-percent.

The hatred in this country makes me sick to even call myself an American, living in a country that is supposed to be one nation under God. I remember the song from Sunday School, "Jesus Loves the Little Children":

All the children of the world

Red and yellow, black and white,

They are precious in His sight.

Jesus loves the little children of the world.

This song is easy to sing, but when are these people going to start practicing it? I was raised Christian and raised to love Jesus Christ. I love Jesus, but not most Christians.

February 2013 Email

Momma Traci,

All is well! Galvin and I are doing great. Our fourth anniversary is in April. It is hard to believe, but it has been great. I have no idea where I would be if he wasn't here for me.

My twentieth high school reunion is in May. I am planning to go and to take my man with me. We are also singing in an all male chorus and having a good time doing so.

Matt

I'd been lying to myself — Anthony

Anthony, 50
New Jersey
October 2010 - email

Dear Momma Traci,

I come from a very conservative, traditional Italian family. My father was born in Italy and my mom was born here. My mom is extremely caring to an overbearing point. I was very attached to my mom growing up and not close to my dad at all. Being the youngest child of two and having a sister nine years older didn't really leave me with many people to talk to. Unfortunately, I did not have many friends growing up because I was picked on constantly. As a result I went to a private Catholic school that was not in my neighborhood. That did not allow me to have any type of a friend network even in high school.

I suspected that I was gay in my early 20s, but like many gay men I suppressed the feelings and didn't really admit it to myself until I was around 28. When I was 32, I finally came out because of a wonderful person I had met at work who I was attracted to. We became friends, and he was so caring and gentle. He knew that everything was my first time and he wanted to help me come out. He was going to graduate school majoring in social work, so I guess in a way I was a perfect "specimen"—although he NEVER made me feel that way. We had a relationship for a few months and then he moved to California to pursue his career. Things did not work out between us but we remain good friends.

Upon this breakup I was hurt and kind of went back into my shell. I did come out to the rest of my friends. Unfortunately I lost all my friends except one, and we are still friends today. I find it interesting that he was the one I thought I might lose. He was the one that was and still is the most naive about gay people, but to this day he stands by me, always trying to help in any way he can.

I met someone else a few years later and we started dating. It became very serious after only six months, and we even went shopping for wedding rings. Unfortunately he became very scared because someone at his job found out, and he broke it off. I was devastated. I felt so bad that I ended up in intense therapy and on medication for a long time.

My mom noticed something was not right because I resorted to staying in my room anytime I was home. Finally after a few weeks of this behavior, I was confronted by my sister who told me I really needed to sit down and talk to my mother because she was hurting so bad. I sat down to talk to her, and it was perhaps the most difficult thing I have ever had to do. She was understanding and said that she already knew. She had wished that this was not the case, but she did not love me any less. She just wanted me to be careful and to be happy.

I did not have any kind of a similar conversation with my father because he was not understanding, being old school and "right off the boat."

I was in my early thirties, and it was time for me to move out of my parents' home. It was awkward meeting people. I was never able to bring them home after a date or over to watch TV or whatever. I moved out and bought my own condo near an organization called the Gay Activist Alliance which I had recently joined.

The Gay Activist Alliance was extremely helpful in assisting me with understanding who I was, and getting me to understand that I was normal and like everyone else. I still hated the two years I lived in that condo because I am a very insecure person with a low self-esteem. I did not sleep nights and was totally miserable because I felt that the people in the complex never really accepted me. I do not know if it was because I was gay or because they were all part of the preppie yuppie crowd, but I definitely did not fit in.

My mom and dad were getting older, and my sister had an addition put on to her house for them to move into. In November 1997, I sold my condo and purchased my parents' home. I was able to completely remodel the house—it hadn't been updated in forty-five years. I worked like a dog trying to get as much work done myself and had some great friends to help. I continued teaching and working at a major hotel chain and had some relationships that never amounted to anything.

I am the kind of person who gets attached very quickly and only winds up getting hurt in the end. I was never into the casual sex scene and thought everyone was like me—very sincere and true to heart. I found out the hard way that everyone was not like me, but not until I was much older. It wasn't until a few years ago that I took the attitude of, "I really don't care which friends know I'm gay because I cannot change it, and if you love me for who I am then you will accept me for who I am."

I also was very reluctant to come out at school. I teach elementary school and although things today are much better than they were years ago, people still have many misconceptions about gay people. We are not child molesters.

For many years I went on working two jobs, never having a life. I had a few dates here and there but that was all. I was so tired of getting burned time and time again that I was afraid to get into another relationship. Every time I let down my wall, I would wind up getting hurt again. So for the next twelve to fifteen years all I did was go to school, the hotel, and home.

The only time I would socialize was when I went on vacation. I told myself that this was the way it was going to be, and that I would be fine with it. Besides, who would want to look at an overweight gay man who walked with a cane? My depression led me to pack on the pounds and an injury when I was moving left me somewhat disabled. This was not a good thing—in the gay world if you do not have every hair in place and every muscle toned, no one will even give you the time of day. So I threw myself into my work and that is where I stayed for many years.

This past summer I bought tickets to go see this show off Broadway with a few of my dear straight friends. It was called *My Big Gay Italian Wedding.* I thought the show was astonishing and absolutely unbelievable. I came out of that show saying, "I NEED to come see this show again."

I bought tickets for another performance a few weeks later, and I did some research on the actors. I found out that one of the grooms was the writer of the show and that this story was not all that farfetched. I went to see the show again with a couple of different friends and loved it more the second time. I came out saying, "Someone is trying to tell me something." I went back to see the show for a third time. This time some of the stars of *The Real Housewives of New Jersey* made an appearance on the stage.

After the show was over, a representative from Marriage Equality New York got up to speak about this organization and what it does. Then I KNEW someone was DEFINITELY trying to tell me something. I was interested in this organization, and working two jobs was not so important anymore.

A select group of people in premium seats were invited to an after party at Etcetera Etcetera, a few blocks from the theatre. After the show I stood outside to greet the cast and to tell them how unbelievably remarkable they all were and that the level of talent that comes off that stage is phenomenal. I walked over to the restaurant with my friends and into the after party. I was a bit nervous. I had the opportunity to mingle, but it was when the cast walked in that I knew something was about to change. The two grooms, Anthony and Daniel (your son), could not thank me enough for coming and had recognized how many times I had seen the show. They knew that I was there for them. Everyone from the show was so remarkable to me, taking the time to chat, take pictures, and thank me for coming.

I had the privilege of meeting Dina Manzo, one of the top producers of the show. As soon as I was introduced to her I started crying because I realized what had happened. I truly had an epiphany! If it wasn't for her and a few other key people, this show would have never made it. I realized I had been lying to myself. I have been telling myself that working so much was just fine. I had been teaching for twenty-five years and been employed at a hotel for twenty-six years. I thought never going out was okay. I thought I really didn't want to meet anyone because all I was going to do was get hurt and burned. I had been lying to myself for all these years.

I do enjoy going out. I do enjoy being with other gay people. I do want to meet someone because I am a good, loyal, trustworthy person and I have a lot to offer someone—I do not know who, but if I do not go out there I will never know!

I came home and was up till 3:00 a.m. sending emails to gay organizations trying to volunteer. I thought this might be a good way to get involved, and it was all because of the gentleman who got up to speak on behalf of Marriage Equality New York at *My Big Gay Italian Wedding.* I started taking days off from my second job and realized that work was not everything. All I did till now was socialize with my straight friends, and it was time to make a change. I NEEDED to be with people of my own kind, with similar interests and likes and dislikes.

Lo and behold, in spite of being somewhat disabled, I volunteered at the march in New York this year and assisted in registering over 900 people. I organized a team and raised over $300 as well. I even managed to walk in the march across the Brooklyn Bridge and was PROUD I was there even though I was with a bunch of strangers. The icing on the cake was that one of the acts performing as part of the entertainment in the park on the Brooklyn side was the cast from *My Big Gay Italian Wedding.* I was so thrilled to see them and ALL of them recognized me sitting there on the grass in the front row!

I have been going out more and spending more time with people just like ME! I have not met anyone yet, but that will come someday too.

    Love ya'
    Anthony

How things should be — Luca, Italy

Luca, 36
Italy
October 2010 - email

Momma Traci,

I am 36 and live in Florence, Italy. When I was a child, almost everyone used to call me queer and sissy, and it made me touchy. I hardly had any friends—only a few female friends. When I played with the girls, they used to say I was a girl because I didn't want to play with the boys.

My first attraction to a man was when I was six, but I didn't understand what sexual attraction was. In my first year at elementary school, there were two kids I was charmed by. One of them was a neighbor who was blonde, and the other was his friend who was dark-haired and light-skinned with light blue or green eyes—he still represents my perfect guy.

My whole teenage experience was really bad. When I was 11 I felt a strong attraction to boys and men. My fantasies were about them. I was curious but I felt lonely. My first experiences were in the bathrooms of the train station; but just touches and kisses and caresses. I was really afraid because it was also the time people started to talk about AIDS.

At the age of about 19, I started to hang out with someone who was five years older than me. I told him about my experiences. I don't know whether it was for curiosity or something else, but once we were joking and he touched me. I found I really liked it. After that happened, we had some fun together and sometimes were intimate. He was gay, though he had some experiences with girls. We had been hanging out together for about ten years. We were more than friends but less than lovers. People called us the married men, the couple. I was gay, but I didn't admit it because I wanted to protect him.

In 2002, he told me that we were not married but that I acted like were. He said he didn't want to hang out with me anymore. He didn't want to be my friend. He told me he had to find a girl and get married, but he is still single today. He was cruel and my world seemed to come to an end. I felt abandoned.

After that I decided to officially come out to my friends and family. I have been lucky that my parents accepted me. I was adopted when I was one month old, and I know my biological mother. When I told my biological mom I was gay, I was kind of anxious because she has struggled a lot in her life. She is strong but she tends to get drunk when she is nervous or blue. She suffered when she had to give me to my adopting family though they "adopted" her as well. She is more open-minded than other people, maybe because her life was hard.

I think my adopting mom would accept me even if I brought someone home and introduced him as my boyfriend. She has never mentioned my homosexuality after I told her. I think she already knew. I don't remember my father's reaction, but we talked about it easily. Even though we hardly ever talk about it, I know they accept me. I also told some of my female friends and my sister who told me that she knew.

In 1997, I had met a young man who was five years older. I was really attracted to him. I made the first step and introduced myself when I was on the train going home from Florence. He lived in a small village two hours by train from my place and was going to the university. I would go to Florence on Thursday almost every week just for the pleasure of talking to him. I could say we were friends but I should be more honest and say I was trying to be more than his friend.

I do not know what I was to him—I suppose not a close friend. He never called or visited me or invited me to his house. He never let me know his world, and I am almost sure he sometime told me things that were not completely true. He told me that he was selfish, an asshole, and thinks about great things, tries to get the best but doesn't treat others well. I was glad he was open-minded about me and gays. I thought he was gay but he didn't tell me that he was. He told me he used to have a girlfriend but they weren't together anymore.

When it ended I received a message: He confessed he was gay and was dating someone. He told me that when we used to go to Florence together, he was sure I was in love with him. I was in love with him and had been for about seven years, though nothing ever happened between us. He said he wouldn't keep in touch with me. I still wanted him to be in my life even though I knew he wasn't good for me. In 2003, he came to Florence. We spent a whole day together just walking around and talking. The next day he told me his boyfriend had read a message of mine and threatened to leave. He told me we couldn't be friends anymore, but we sometimes still communicate by email.

In 2006, I decided to see a psychotherapist. I have been seeing him for four years and I feel better now in general. The "gay thing" is something we have discussed, but that is not the main thing. We focus more on my childhood and teenage problems. I hardly had friends. My doctor says the first thing I need to do is to learn to deal with people, make friends, and establish and understand relationships. When I am able to do that I will be ready to experience a relationship based on love and all the things connected to it.

I wish I could meet someone, but it seems hopeless because most gays are worse than straight people—you have to be special for them to talk to you. You have to be good-looking, have good fashion, and be skinny. Not everyone thinks this way, but most.

Since I have been working here in Florence I realized there is a world outside that I wish I could discover. I have met lots of gay people who talk to me, who I get along with and have fun with. All of these people were non-Italian—English, American, Irish, French—and some were really hot. When I was in New York visiting a friend, he took me to a gay bar. I met someone whom I talked to and we shared a kiss. I really had fun. It felt good to be with non-Italian men!

In Florence, there are lots of gays who still hide in the closet. Most of them are married. The Church is against homosexuality.

There are some people who claim their beliefs with such hatred that it is astonishing they are living in 2010. In Italy, there is a strong homophobia. When some young gay boys come out of gay bars or are together, they are beaten up by bunches of young people. This is very frequent in Rome and in Florence. Italy is a strictly religious-based country and a macho society. Even among gays there is kind of "racism," especially if you are submissive or feminine—then you are seen as a woman. You hardly meet people who talk about people who love each other.

I would like to move to another country. But I have a long-term job and at my age it's not easy to find another job. Lots of Americans have told me that I could find a job quite easily if I decided to move to the USA. I wish I could move to New York but I know it's hard now especially because of the world economic crisis.

Now I am in love with a younger man. He is straight, he likes women, but I think he could fall in love with a man. I guess just not me. I am someone that doesn't like categories. I am tired of hearing words such as straight, gay, and bisexual.

I feel lonely and I wish I could talk to someone or hang out with someone. I wish I had someone to share a life with. I need a boyfriend. I really liked watching your son in *The Big Gay Musical*. I would like to have a friend like Paul from that movie. Paul helps Eddie, loves Eddie as a friend, and jokes with him but not badly. That's how I think things should be.

February 2013 email

Dear Momma Traci,

This last year has been great for me. On my last trip to the U.S., I went to Los Angeles, Hollywood, and I have felt much better. I had the chance to meet great people and go to a gay club. It was a blast. I really felt comfortable, more than I do in Florence. It felt like home because people were really friendly to me.

My social life has become better. I am in touch with other gays who make me feel appreciated. I owe this change to my interest in movies and music and my participation in some Kickstarter Campaigns, which is a funding platform for creative projects. *The Big Gay Musical* has given me the chance to know your name and your work. That's why I am sitting here at work writing this story, dear Momma Traci. All these cool things—meeting other people, gay and not, visiting a great city, the gay life—have made me feel stronger and more secure both with myself and with others. I would say this is kind of a happy end to my old "sad" story. Well, this is not the end—I hope it is the start of great new things to come.

Love,
Luca

April 2014 email

Dear Momma Traci,

This last year I have tried to be more positive about myself thanks to the great people I am in touch with through Facebook and those who share the common interest of music, movies, and LGBTQ projects. Those connections have helped me to relate to other people and be more comfortable with myself. Sometimes I still feel lonely because I am still searching for a "soulmate." Sometimes I wish I could be straight because I tend to blame homosexuality for my bad times and my insecurites. It's a continual fight between good times and bad times. All in all I feel better and I KNOW I am gay, that my attractiveness to men is not only physical.

Love,
Luca

Twin brothers — The Netherlands

Samuel first emailed me in 2010 when he was just shy of his 18th birthday. He told me his coming out story but didn't tell me he had a twin brother or that his twin was gay. In 2011, I received an email from his brother, Adrian, telling me his coming out story. They are very different young men with very different outlooks on life.

Coming out on my 18th birthday
Samuel, 17
The Netherlands
September 2010 - email

Momma Traci,

I'm 17 and from the Netherlands. I think there's a bit of a different situation here, because the Netherlands is a much more homosexual-tolerating country. The Netherlands is quite liberal when it comes to homosexuality and is considered to be one of the gay-friendliest countries by far in the world. The Netherlands has a reputation of being the first country to recognize same-sex marriage, and openly displaying your orientation wouldn't cause much upset in the Netherlands.

However, even a gay friendly country like the Netherlands has room for some criticisms of homosexuality. This varies depending on where one travels. This country is considered to be a gay utopia and safe for gays and lesbians, except in Muslim neighborhoods in the major Dutch cities.

The Netherlands has been referred to as the best country in the world for gays to live. A lot of people think coming out in the Netherlands is as easy as being straight. That is not true because the Netherlands has a small minority of gay-haters. You could draw one straight line through the Netherlands and on one side you can find the so-called "De Bijbelgordel"—a line of villages which is the very conservative Bible belt. Of course there are gays born in those villages, so they're still facing that problem. The Netherlands is slowly getting more influence from the Islamic world. With a huge integration problem in the big cities in the last few years, the confrontation between gay people and Muslims often goes with violence. Lucky as I am, I was born in a gay-friendly neighborhood in the Netherlands.

I'm not out to my parents, but since last June I am out to my sisters. One of them isn't totally straight, but only has had boyfriends. She tells me that she can imagine that someday she will fall in love with a girl. Once she told me she had suspected I was gay. My parents were both Christian, but they don't practice it anymore. They are very open-minded, but I don't know how they are going to react about gays especially if their son is one.

I knew I was gay since I was 13 or 14 years old. For a few years I ignored the feelings for boys, thinking, "Well, it will disappear one day, so I can live as a straight boy." But it didn't. I always looked at boys and men instead of girls and women. When some gay boys became my friends, I realized I was like them.

When I was 15 years old, I started to tell people. After a few months I told a girl I knew from school. It was a turning point, because from that moment someone in my daily life knew I was gay. Since last summer I started telling more people. There are some people I don't even trust that already know. I guess it will be time to tell my parents in a few weeks or months.

I'm doing fine. I even have two gay friends at school. One of them is out to everyone, and one of them isn't. My parents are very progressive people. My mother worked for twenty years in the musical-industry, so she knows a lot of gay people. One of my parents' friends is a gay man. He became a really good friend of the family in the last few years.

I think my father will react in silence. I think he will see me differently for a short time, and he won't know how to react. I'm planning to come out soon. I will write to you about how it all went when I come out to them as I celebrate my 18th birthday in December.

Greetings,
Samuel the Netherlands

December 2010 email

Dear Momma Traci,

I once promised myself I'd come out for my family before I became 18. I told them a few days before the holiday. I told my mother while she was driving me home from school. I was very nervous, but I knew that this should be the moment to tell her. She couldn't walk away and we were totally alone. So, when we were almost home I told her I prefer men. Her reaction was very relaxing. She asked me how and when I first noticed that I'm gay, and she told me it wouldn't change anything in our relationship.

When we were home she asked if I had already told my father. I told her no, but I'd do that in a few days. As spontaneous as my mother was she walked inside to my father and told him I had something to say. She said she did this because it shouldn't be any problem. I told my father. He immediately said that he was not happy with the fact that I'm gay, but that it shouldn't change anything.

After a few days with a tense atmosphere he told me that he loves me. He said all he wants is for me to be happy with my life and accept myself. The only thing my parents didn't like was the fact that I had waited so long to tell them. My mom has talked to me about being careful. At the moment I am out to everyone in my family except my grandmother. She's from Russia and is very conservative in her thoughts about gay people.

I was very glad to read on Facebook that you were happy for me. I will need a few months before I'm out to all the people I know, but I'm sure that will happen in 2011.

Thanks again,
Love
Samuel

December 2013 email

Dear Momma Traci,

I'm now living in Amsterdam. I wrote my first e-mail to you while I still lived in a village with my parents. A lot has changed since then. I'm more in the gay scene of Amsterdam, which is still the most liberal city in the world. I made a lot of new friends. My life has changed in a very good way. I live on my own now with three other students and enjoy everything as before. Living in a city is really something else than living in a quiet village in the south of the country.

I never wrote you about my brother, because he wasn't out. I didn't think it was fair to write with other people about it. He came out about a year ago. My brother lives in London now with his boyfriend. I told him about you and your book.

Since my coming out my brother has been a great support, but I think that I have also been a support for him. At high school I hadn't told him yet about myself, but he understood that something was going on with me because of my changing relations to boys and girls. I talked a lot about it with my best friend. He must have noticed something. And so I noticed something about him, but I waited to talk about it with him until he told my parents.

My parents are very happy for us. And they really made the words true. They told my brother, my sisters, and me since we were young: "If any of you are gay, don't hesitate to tell us, because of course it won't be a problem and it won't change anything for us."

Love,
Samuel

We never spoke about being gay
Adrian, 19
The Netherlands
June 2012 - email

Samuel and I are twin brothers. We were born in the Netherlands on the Dutch 2nd Christmas day/Boxing Day, December 26th, in 1992.

I think I first knew I was gay when I was about 10. I noticed I was physically more attracted to boys. Boys from the last elementary grade (about 12 years old in the Netherlands) started to fall in love with girls, but I didn't feel anything for them other than a friendly interest. I thought that the feeling for girls would come later as I would get older, but when time passed by I got more and more attracted to boys/guys/men.

When I was about 14 years old I was sure that I was gay, but I didn't acknowledge it let alone accept it. It would be so much easier to live a straight life, no complicated situations: I would get a girlfriend, get married, have children, a house, and a job and live my life. I thought it would work. Of course it didn't, but I still believed that for many years while all the time I was looking at guys/men and not at girls/women.

I started acknowledging I was gay to myself when I made a trip through the States last summer. I travelled through the States on my own for six weeks and I felt like I could be whoever I wanted to be. I didn't tell others that I was gay, but I felt more open to express myself the way I wanted to. I went to a language school in San Francisco and stayed with a host family. There I met a girl from Italy, Alex—another student who was staying there for three months. We became very good friends. We contact each other daily and she visited me in the Netherlands last January.

When I returned from America, I didn't know how to deal with the situation. I accepted that I was gay but I postponed the moment of telling the truth to the rest of the world. The first person I ever told was Alex. We were talking on Facebook, and she actually asked me so I told her about my sexuality. I knew Alex would accept it, since she describes herself as not gay, not bisexual nor straight. She doesn't really like choosing. She was the perfect person to tell.

I feel stupid for not accepting it or telling someone sooner, but I feel relaxed with it now. It was never a sorrow for me. It was more like a complicated worry in my life that I would think about for hours.

I met a guy in London, out of the blue, and I feel very comfortable with him. Edmundo is a super hard-working, highly educated, and very intelligent Mexican man who lived in the Netherlands for many years and has now moved to London for his career. He travels a lot. When he has the chance to see me I go to London so we can enjoy a weekend together. We talk a lot, take walks through central London, go out for dinner, see his friends, go out to parties, go for a drink, visit the gym, and really just enjoy being together. Edmundo is a very good guy who makes me feel very safe and special. I miss him when I'm not with him.

When I came back from a trip to London recently I did not feel comfortable with my family. I decided it was time to come out to them. I stayed in my room in the evening for two days, racking my brain over how to tell them. I wanted my mom to ask me what the matter was, so I waited for her to come upstairs. She noticed I wasn't behaving as usual, and she came upstairs to ask me. I burst out in tears and cried in her arms. Still she had to pull it out of me. I couldn't tell her. She asked me if I was attracted to men. I said yes, and a big load fell off my shoulders. She told my dad who of course reacted very well and would always have accepted anything like that. He joked it would be such a pity not to get another woman at home.

The first three days after I told them I was gay, I felt a little bit awkward but relieved. I have now have come out to my family and close friends. If people ask me if I'm straight or gay, I'll be completely honest with them. It took much energy, and so much time—years—to get myself out of the closet but I'm feeling relaxed now. I have nothing to hide. I'm proud of who I am, and I don't feel uncomfortable anymore. My family is a loving and caring family, and we all respect and love each other for who we are.

Samuel and I never spoke to each other about being gay. A bit weird, though—I have always known about Samuel and I don't know why. When he came out, it wasn't a surprise for me at all, not even a small one. When I came out, he was very surprised. I told him at first that I wasn't sure about my sexuality. Later, I fully came out. The first couple of weeks, I don't think he really believed it. Maybe he thought I wasn't sure, but he knows I am gay now.

I told my closest friends. They deserved to know. I knew they wouldn't react negatively—that's why they are good friends. Most of them didn't see it coming, but some of them expected it. I think since I always behaved very manly that made many people think I was straight, although there were a few people who still questioned my sexuality. It seems funny that all my close friends are girls,—such a stereotypical thing if you'd ask me.

Even though Samuel and I now know that we are both gay, we haven't really spoken about it. Since Samuel moved to Amsterdam last summer, he has become much closer to me in some ways, but he still doesn't share anything about his life in Amsterdam or any personal things even though I share with him. Our relationship has become a bit superficial, but we're having fun joking with each other daily. I tried a couple of times to talk about being gay and gay life, but he did not seem to be in the mood for it. To him it is very personal, even though he is very open with his friends. I hope that time will help him be more open with me since I think we can be great support for each other. Maybe he just needs a little bit more time to get used to the fact that we are both gay.

A big hug from Holland.
Adrian

December 2013 email

Hello Traci,

Half a year ago I moved to London, and I am very happy with my life here. After a while I gave up the room that I was renting and I now live with Edmundo. We are together and deeply in love. Since the moment I moved to London our relationship seems to be very serious. When I lived in the Netherlands he didn't see the possibility of something long-term. We live in central London. He works for a bank and I study at the University of West London.

It is great to live here and be together with him. I have an amazing life and we make each other very happy. He took me to Mexico two months ago so I could meet his family and friends. It was a wonderful trip. I've met many people since my move to the UK and I am never bored.

Last summer Samuel came to visit me in London. I hadn't seen him for 2 months, which is the longest time we have been apart. Then he came to visit in October and I have seen him about three times in the Netherlands. Now we both live our lives out of the closet in different countries, but we seem to have more contact than ever before. We speak to each other via WhatsApp, Facebook Chat, or FaceTime/Skype. We laugh a lot with the same kind of humor. It's a lot of fun to have this much contact with him. It's also good to know that he is busy and is happy living in Amsterdam.

There has been some stress between the two of us during the last few years, which maybe had to do with our age, but I think we're getting more mature towards each other and we always look forward to seeing each other. Also, we both developed completely different interests and hobbies. Where before we used to be identical, we now very often go our own way but the brothership—if there is such a word—is still as strong as before.

Adrian

Part Eight

Unspoken Words

Unspoken Words — Momma Traci

Over the course of four years, I interviewed and received letters from people of all shades of the rainbow. Some have been embraced by their families; some have not. All have struggled with acceptance, both of themselves and by others. These interviews and letters have been cathartic and healing, but many are still holding onto unspoken words.

The interviews in this chapter mirror my own wounded spirit and its impact on my life. Unspoken words damage us and leave us feeling empty, alone, and defeated. Feelings about our parents are confusing, and no matter how old we are we still long for their love and acceptance.

In 2010, I received an email from a handsome young gay man who told me he could never come out to his parents. He was working on writing a letter to his parents—the letter he wished he could send them. Recently I received this from him:

Momma Traci,

I really never wrote that letter to my parents—I talked to YOU about it—but I never did!

It was too hard a task, to even start.

I had no words.

The letters to parents in this chapter are ones they wish they could write but most still remain, unspoken words.

Don't want to hide the truth — Wilfredo,

Wilfredo, 19
Venezuela

September 2010 - email

Momma Traci,

I want to thank you for the opportunity to open my heart and deal with my feelings by writing this letter. It feels good and makes me feel better. Thank you.

I am 19 years old and I am going to college. I am from Venezuela where we only speak Spanish. There might be some mistakes in the letter. I study English but I don't know everything about writing.

When I was growing up people called me names like "queer" and "faggot." I tried to ignore them, but it hurt. I couldn't understand why they were so mean. Now when I hear those words it takes me back to those times.

I am sending you the letter that I wish I could write my parents. I hope it might help you with your book.

Love,

Wilfredo

Dear Mom and Dad,

First, I want to tell you that you are the most important people in my life, and that is the reason why I need to share this with you. There is something that I realized when I was 12 or 13 years old, but it's been really hard for me to open myself to you about it. I feel like I'm lying to you by not telling you and I want to share all the things that are happening to me now. I don't want to hide the truth anymore.

I'm gay.

I'm sorry I couldn't tell you this before, but I just wasn't ready. I know this probably isn't easy for you, but it hasn't been easy for me either. I've been scared for many years, and I still am. Every single day I think about you hating me for being the way I am, not ever being completely happy, not ever finding someone to share my life with, and not ever having children. I am afraid I might die alone. Sometimes I wish I were straight because everything would be easier, but I'm not.

Please, don't ask me why, because I just don't know. What I do know is that it is not your fault. You've been great parents. I was born this way. I love you both and I know you love me, too. I've finally accepted myself for who I am, and I'm happy and comfortable with that. I want to share my happiness with you both.

I know you're worried about me, but I'm still the son I've always been. I wish I could tell you that everything is going to be okay, although to be honest I don't have a clue. I do know that as long as I have your love I will be fine and happy.

I've told some of my friends, and they've been really supportive with me. They have helped me feel less lonely and to trust people. They have given me the strength to finally share this with you, and I'm truly grateful to God because I've got you and them in my life.

Now more than ever I need your love, support, understanding, and respect. This would mean the world to me. I just want to be myself in this world, and being honest with you is going to help me to achieve that. Thank you for all of your love and for always being there when I need you. No matter what, I will always love you.

Love,
Wilfredo

March 2013 email

Dear Momma Traci

I just turned 22. So many things have changed in the past couple of years—events that have changed my life. When I first wrote you I was learning English, but now I am at an advanced level. Even though some things have remained the same, I think that it is about to change.

Two years ago, my grandmother was told by someone—I believe it was my aunt on my mother's side—that I was gay. One Friday, during a family reunion, my grandmother and my mom—who had been drinking alcohol—got into that rumor or gossip mode, as I choose to call it. She told my mom about it, and after we got back home, my mom started asking me if I was gay.

I was really upset about people talking behind my back, especially to my grandmother. Deep inside, I always believed my mom knew I was gay, but I denied it the first four times she asked. She refused to take no for an answer and kept pushing. She told me she would love me even if I was gay.

Then, I said yes—I told the truth to her, nothing but the truth. She burst into tears and then asked me why I was that way. I responded that I just felt a natural attraction towards men that I had never felt towards women. She told me she was hurt by it and that it made her sad. I started to cry as well. After she mentioned she was disappointed in me, she went to bed.

Saturday and Sunday passed and we barely spoke. I could tell she was feeling really sad. Then, she told me she had talked about our conversation to my aunt on my father's side, since we are really close. On Monday, my mother invited my aunt over and we talked about it. My aunt was really supportive. She just wanted to make sure I was okay and was being emotionally and sexually responsible.

My mom asked if I wanted to see a psychologist. I said that it would not help me because this is just the way I am. Nothing could change me. After some more talking, she said she was okay with that, and she expressed that she would like me to get married some day and have children—and that if I wanted to be sexually involved with men, I could do it behind my wife's back. I refused this nonsense idea. I let her know I would never do that. My aunt left and my mom went into a denial stage. We never talked about it anymore. She sometimes mentioned that she would like certain girl friend of mine to be my girl-friend.

A little more than a year ago, I got involved in my first romantic relationship. I had had sex before, but I had never had a boyfriend. I always dreamed for the day that he would come along, and fortunately he did. It was not a good relationship. It lasted almost four months, and it ended when I found out he was cheating on me with another guy.

I believe everything happens for a reason, and this was not an exception. There was a reason I did not want to have sex with him until I was sure we were going somewhere, which we did not. He was nice and he got to meet my aunt, which I felt was a step forward. I felt I could trust her with these sort of things. We broke up and it hurt, but it was easy to let go. That made me want to tell the rest of my closest friends that I was gay and what was going on. They were all really supportive and I got to educate some of them by answering their questions since they did not have any gay friends. That break-up pulled us closer.

Sadly, I cannot say that it brought me closer to my mom—I did not feel I could tell her about it.

My ex-boyfriend tried to make his way back to my life. I shut the door in his face for good and did not let him in at all. He had served his purpose in my life.

In November 2011, I applied for a scholarship through the U.S. Embassy in my country. After a long selection process, I got news in May 2012 that I had gotten it and that I would travel to the U.S. in August. So I left home. I am currently a full-time student at Augustana College in Sioux Falls, South Dakota, and I am loving the whole studying abroad experience.

I Skype with my mom once a week. She misses me a lot. I am the oldest son, and we are very close. She always asks me if I liked any of the girls I had met here. Last week was my birthday. She messaged me and said she loved me and she was proud of me. I decided to break her denial since I have been feeling that I need to educate her. I told her that I have met a lot of girls from different parts of the world and I had not liked any, because I am only attracted to men. I reminded her it is not her fault—it is just who I am. I also told her that I was hoping she would still be proud of me even though I was gay. She finally said that she was okay with it, that there was nothing she could do about it, and that she would love me no matter what.

I am not close to my dad, and he doesn't know anything about me being gay. I haven't told him and neither has my mom.

I am coming back home next June, and I am determined to educate my mom. I want us to talk about it face to face and answer all of her questions. I am hoping she will not be too uncomfortable, that she will keep an open mind, and that she will let me fully trust her. I have a positive attitude about it. The time I have been away has made her appreciate me more, and I am planning to use that to my advantage.

Love,
Wilfredo

Feel like a caged bird — M.C., London

M.C., 27
London

September 2010 - email

Momma Traci,

I knew I was gay from a very young age—I would say around the age of 12 or 13. Looking back now, I would say I was more confused than anything. I fancied girls and guys. Into my teenage years, I thought I was more bisexual than gay. When I was about 18, I finally accepted that I was gay and no longer said I was bisexual.

I have only told one of my sisters, one of my cousins, and two of my close friends that I am gay. They all reacted quite well, and they were all very supportive. I thought it would end my relationship with them but in fact it hasn't. It was very hard coming out to them, but I felt pleased that I did.

In the last year I have met my best friend, and I feel I can talk to her about everything in my life. I can tell her about the issues I'm facing and have faced in life with my sexuality. We have a lot of fun together making jokes and laughing, which has helped me to accept who I am. Before this last year I didn't really have anyone to talk to. When I came out to my sister, we didn't talk about it very much—not because I can't, but because I didn't feel comfortable.

I have not told my parents I am gay, and the reasons why are because I come from a Muslim background. My parents' upbringing was very different to mine. I wouldn't say they are very strict religious people, but they still have beliefs and values of being Muslim. Being brought up in a Muslim family, there is no room to be gay. It's just unacceptable.

Another reason I have not come out is because I would hate to disappoint my parents. I feel like they would be disappointed in me more than anything and not accept me for being gay. I live at home and I feel that if I come out now, even though I don't think my parents would throw me out, I don't want to take the chance. Apart from being thrown out with nowhere to go, I feel that if I told them while still living at home the tension between us would not be good. I don't think I could live like that.

I feel like I will one day be able to tell my mum, but I don't think I will be able to tell my dad. I think it will disappoint him too much and he won't ever understand. I say this because of his reactions when there is a gay couple on TV. I can see the different reactions from both my parents, and my dad's reaction is never a good one.

My secrecy affects my life when the conversation of marriage and kids come up with my parents or family. It is hard to always come up with excuses as to why I don't want to get married. It also affects my life when I'm dating someone—I have to be discrete. If my boyfriend buys me a gift, I have to say it's a present from my friend or I try to hide it away. I would like my parents one day to meet someone I am dating when I know I have found the right guy, but for now I know that is impossible.

I think once I move out of the house, it will be the right time to tell my family that I am gay. I will finally be living my own life away from my family. Once I have come out to them, it will make things easier in terms of introducing them to someone I am dating, and when I go out to gay places I won't have to lie anymore. Once I am out it will give me the freedom to accept myself, and if my family accepts me for who I am then I think it will make it a lot easier to come out to other people. If I could write my parents this is what I would say:

M.C.

Dear Dad and Mum,

Writing this letter has to be one of the hardest things I will ever have to do in my life. There is so much I would like to tell you about who I am as a person but I've been too afraid I will disappoint you. I hope by reading this letter you will understand the things I have been through in my life and ultimately accept me for who I am.

There has been so much in my life that I have been through, and now at the age of 23 I'm happy to still be alive and say that I've made it through those dark times. There are still a lot of issues I have to work on within myself, but I now realize that with time and patience things can improve in my life.

I say I'm happy to be alive because there have been many times when committing suicide seemed like the only option for me. I know that this may come as a surprise to you, because from the outside I hide my emotions and feelings. For the last ten years I have felt trapped within my own feelings and thoughts. I feel like a caged bird that no one can hear. Not being able to talk about my issues with you has led to a life where I have felt so alone. If there is one thing that scares me the most it is that I will end up being and feeling alone for the rest of my life.

Over the last ten years I have had to deal with being depressed. It has been one of the hardest and toughest things to get through every day of my life all alone. Every day is still a struggle for me. I've had to deal with a lot of confidence issues that have led to body, weight, self-esteem, and many other issues over the years. Having to deal with so much at such a young age by myself has made me have to grow up a lot faster.

I know that everything I have been through has made me a stronger person. It hasn't been an easy journey to get here, and at 23 I feel more like 43 because I feel like I've lived a lifetime of pain.

You might be asking yourself why I have gone through so much and what has caused so my pain. Well, this letter is to tell you all that I am gay, and my sexuality has affected my life in so many ways.

This letter is about three things: It is about an ending in my life because I no longer have to lie and hide being gay; a beginning to a brighter and much happier life now that I have come out to you; and to tell you a bit about who I am. I hope you can accept me for who I am and still love me the same, because I'm still the same person that I was five minutes before you read this letter.

I love you.
M

December 2013 email

Momma Traci,

I have not come out to my parents yet. I do feel like I've grown a lot as a person and learned a lot over the last couple of years. I do feel a lot more comfortable with who I am and in my own skin.

However, I do still feel alone at times as it has been difficult to meet people and find new friends. But I am in a much better place now than I was back then. I do feel and see the growth in my progress, and I just wish to continue with it.

M.C.

Remaining closeted — Stan

Stan, 42
Chicago, Illinois
September 2010 - email

Momma Traci,

I'm working on a letter to my parents—the one I wish I could write to them—but it is difficult because the thought of actually writing a letter like this had never crossed my mind. I am not a miserable person. I have a strong support system, and I am happy in every aspect of life. But, to my parents, I have decided to remain closeted.

My father was a great athlete and received a full-ride football scholarship at a prominent university. To make extra money during the summer, the team ran a youth football camp. One year my father shared a tent with another player. One night, my father woke up to discover his roommate was gone. He thought something was wrong, and he went looking for him. He looked all over the place, finally ending up at the beach—where he found his roommate holding one of the young kids from the camp and anally penetrating him. My father told me that the kid had a look of horror that he had never seen before and has never seen since. The kid was ghostly white and too shocked to even speak. Dad ran down the beach and punched his roommate in the face, grabbed the kid, and took him back to the campground. That roommate filed a complaint against my dad—and as much as my dad tried to explain the situation, there was "no excuse for violence." Plus, I'm not sure the administration believed him. Not only was he kicked off the football team, but he lost his scholarship and ended up going to a different university.

I have heard him tell this story over and over. I think he used the term "corn-holing the kid." Needless to say, he wasn't exactly pro-gay. He'd always say, "If any of you kids even thinks about becoming a wooden nickel…" This became a sort of a barrier to any kind of coming out. Once, I had my mouth washed with soap for calling my brother a fag. It was the worst thing you could call anyone.

Luckily for me—or not—I played football and soccer and ran track, and my sexuality was never questioned. I have been in a relationship for 17 years. No one in my family has met my partner. I just can't come out to my family. I'm out at work, and of course all my social networks are gay-friendly. I work for AIDS charities and support gay initiatives. Still, I'm not out to my family. I wish I could be as out and open as your son is, but some things are just not to be. Thank you for letting me get that out.

Stan

Felt like a coward—Jeff

Jeff, 19
New York, New York
November 2010 - email

Momma Traci,

I'm writing to you because I am still "in the closet." I am a coward and afraid of coming out. I am struggling with coming out to my parents, especially my mother.

My upbringing is an enormous part of it because my family raised me to be a "man." Coming out for me is hard because I am afraid of the way my family and close friends will perceive me as a gay man. I really care about my family and I don't want them to pity me.

My mother will not be happy, and she is the main reason why I still haven't come out. I know she will really be disappointed and the last thing I want to do is upset her. I know I should do it for me and she should be proud of me, but she's close-minded. She mimics and repeats what I say if I talk girly, which really bothers me. Recently she has been asking me questions about not having girlfriends. Maybe she is curious? She is not dumb and probably suspects, but she also might be in denial.

I am ashamed because I am still living a lie. I am pretending to be somebody I am not and it is hurting me inside. I am so stressed out and confused and I don't know what to do anymore. I wish I could just liberate myself and be who "god" made me. I guess I'm just afraid of the consequences.

Here is the letter I wish I could give my mother:

Dear Mum,

I haven't been quite honest with you. I can't stand lying to you any longer. It is hurting me inside. I have been lying to you my whole life because of my fear of rejection. I am sorry for not telling you earlier but it is important I finally share something about me: I am gay.

I am constantly hiding my natural feelings and living a lie that is tearing me apart. I want to be myself, and be free. This isn't a phase. I did not choose to be gay. I have been attracted to the same sex since a young age.

You probably knew my whole life that I was different but denied it because it was wrong in your eyes. There is nothing wrong with me. Even if you reject me, just know that I love you. I've spent nights crying myself to sleep, wishing things were different. I always feared losing you.

Even though we have a hard time communicating and we are constantly fighting, I really care about you and need you in my life. I need you now more than ever. I want to share my experiences with you. I want to open up and tell you everything about me without you judging me. I want you to be the best friend I never had. Even though I want this, it probably won't work because you don't accept me the way I am.

So now that I told you my deepest darkest secret, I hope you will think this through. I can give you time but I really need you.

Love,
Jeff

February 2014 email

Hello, Momma Traci,

I'm doing well, and I feel really confident and comfortable with my sexual orientation. I did come out to my family in 2011. My mom has been very accepting, and she has been there for me. My dad, on the other hand, does not accept it and will not tolerate it. He says that he does not agree with the lifestyle I "choose" to live and that he will not be there for me until I change. We are currently not talking with each other. I hope things turn around.

Jeff

The way God made me — Gregory

Gregory's story unfolded through email over the course of several years. I was saddened and deeply touched by his feelings and his situation. I know how religion can hurt people who just want to be who God made them to be.

I encouraged Gregory to write a letter to his parents in order to express his feelings, his fears, and his hopes about how his family might react. I urged him to write this letter without fear in his heart. Even if his parents would never read his letter, his words here might help someone else feel less alone. I told Gregory that he might change someone's life for the better. I reminded Gregory that I was listening, that I am here, and that I care.

These are Gregory's emails to me.

Gregory, 22
New Jersey
September 2010 - email

Momma Traci,

I was raised in a Baptist pastor's home, which probably says enough right there. I am 22 and the second oldest of five children. My oldest sister is a missionary. There has been a lot of pressure for me to live up to the religious standard they have set for me.

Since I was 10, I knew I was different. As a boy, I was drawn to more feminine things. My father found me looking at gay porn when I was in 8th grade and immediately asked if I was gay. He then proceeded to pull out the Bible and have me read it. Then he talked and prayed with me. When I was 16 my sister, brother, dad, and I were all sitting around the kitchen, and my dad asked my sister—who was 18 at the time—what she would do if one of her brothers was gay. She said she would disown him and never talk to him again. I still remember her words.

It wasn't until I graduated from high school in 2010 that I tried to tell my father I was a homosexual before I went to Baptist Bible College. It was one of the most awkward conversations I have ever had with him. The conversation ended with him believing I was only struggling with being gay and that I would get over it with the help of God. As if my father's response wasn't good enough, I then proceeded to get kicked out of Baptist Bible College for acting on my feelings with one of my guy friends.

I refuse to completely come out at this point because I know the rejection I will feel from my family. Despite people feeling like their family has come around after their coming out, I know for a fact that my family will never accept this lifestyle. Although they will always love me, if they do not accept me it will hurt just as bad as if they did not love me at all since this is such a big part of who I am as a person.

Gregory

October 11, 2010 email

Momma Traci,

Thank you so much for thinking of me. It is nice to know I'm not alone out here in Indiana.

I'm a mess. I'm going through a constant roller coaster of emotions. One day I'm encouraged and the next I'm down again trying to pull myself up. I've tried to get the words across for a letter to my parents on being afraid to come out, but I just can't to do it. I'll work up the courage to—it is just rough.

I've been meeting with a counselor here. She's wonderful. I just sit down and pour things out to her. It's nice to not have her pressuring me about religion and God.

I've come to a fork in the road in my life. Now is when I'll be making the important decisions in my life, and it stresses me out. This "issue" of being gay is always on my mind, and it's not going anywhere. I can barely focus on schoolwork and it is affecting my social and physical well-being. Although I might dress up and look like I have it all together, I'm bleeding on the inside and I just want it all to go away. I feel at any moment I could just burst into tears, but I try to hold back. I know if someone here at school knew who I really was, I'd be rejected.

Gregory

October 25, 2010 email

Momma Traci,

Here is what I could get out. It is always on my mind. I hope I didn't ramble too much. Thank you for listening.

~~~~~~

Dear Mom and Dad,

I'm done. I can't do it anymore.

For so long, I've been trying to be the son you would be proud to have. The son you couldn't wait to brag to your friends about, tell them how successful I am, and what a great life I've started. It's no secret that I got kicked out of school. I wish you would stop pretending I have some sickness that I will overcome. This is no disease that will go away no matter how many Christian schools I go to or how many church services I attend. I know secretly you are hoping that the more I go the more likely it is that I will hear the one sermon that will speak to my heart and change me from my feelings of homosexuality.

Yes, I said it. No beating around the bush about it, acting as if it never happened. I need to stop trying to please people. Living life for other people, even the ones you love the most, is not a way to live at all.

Mom, I have felt more lost and alone dealing with this than at any other time in my life. All I want is to be comforted. Let me know that it will be okay. It hurts.

The one time I have felt anything for anyone was broken up for the sake of my family, and neither of you knew what was going on. The whole time I was with him all I wanted to do was tell you all how happy I was so you could share in my excitement. Now it's over and you still have no idea. To be out of that intimate, passionate relationship knowing my family would never approve tore at me.

You don't even realize how broken up I've felt inside. I can't tell you why I have these feelings. I do. It doesn't have to make sense to you but it does to me.

Dad, you get up on Sundays and preach on love, acceptance, forgiveness, and moving on. Where is the love for your son? You can lead a congregation but you can't even see the hurt in your son's life caused by the people he loves the most, all in the name of "God."

I have never been at a lower point in my life because of the religious pressure. This is always on my mind, and it is starting to affect everything about me. I hope one day you will see me for the person I am, not the person you want me to be, and accept me for as I am.

I love you with my whole heart,

Gregory

~~~~~~

October 26, 2010 email

Momma Traci,

It was good to get things off my chest. I hope to one day show them and let them know the pain they're causing me. Just makes it so much harder for me to accept myself in this situation. Thanks for listening to me. I really hope it speaks to someone someday going through the same things.

Gregory

January 11, 2011 email

Momma Traci,

I have transferred to a school in Ohio—was a little crazy for me. I felt like I stuck out like a sore thumb. This school is a little stricter—it is Baptist-affiliated.

I've just been in such a weird state lately. I have people in two areas of my life that have expectations of me: My family and church friends expect me to be one way, and my non-church friends and people at work expect me to be another. It's very frustrating and lonely. This makes me mad.

I've grown up being taught that being gay is wrong and I don't even know where to start thinking for myself. It's hard. I love my family and friends so much, but I hate being a disappointment. They'll never understand.

You asked me what I felt about the change in the military policy of "Don't Ask Don't Tell." I had a chance to ask someone in the military about his feelings and thoughts. It is not going to change anything for him. He's a pilot of a C-17 and has been in the military for eighteen years. He isn't going to have a huge "coming out" party or anything because this policy is changing. He is out to the people he knows and trusts, and he said that is how it'll stay.

As for my feelings, I think it is a great step towards equality, but it will always be something that will be there, much like the issue of race—we'd like to think it is no longer an issue, but in parts of the U.S. it is still a hard topic.

Gregory

February 2011 email

Momma Traci,

I'm doing really well. I really like the school here. There is a group of gays here. Although we're forced underground, it's nice to have that support. Even though it is a very conservative school, there are professors that are not trying to change us. I'm falling for someone, and that is tough because I do not know exactly where he stands but I am getting vibes. I'm trying not to read too much into it. I am learning that you can have God and religion and still be gay. It is very encouraging. I know my family will never understand, but eventually I'm sure they will come to grips with it.

I know that my decision one day to tell my parents will be less of a "forget you, I'm gay" attitude and more of an intellectual sit down to dinner and discuss what really happened in my life the past couple of years leading up to this point.

I am talking to someone right now who came out to me this past weekend. I never felt so challenged to become a better person. Momma Traci, I don't know how to explain it. All I can say is that I have a huge smile on my face right now. For someone to tell me that what I'm feeling isn't "natural" or "the way God made me" is garbage. This is real and it makes me want to draw closer to God.

Gregory

March 2013 email

Momma Traci,

One reason I transferred to this school was their underground LGBTQ organization, *Out.* I say it's underground because it's a group of mostly alumni and a few current students. It exists only on the Internet. There's a website and a private Facebook group.

In my first semester, spring 2011, after about three weeks of lone-liness and isolation, I reached out to the group leader and he intro-duced me to a few accepting faculty and a students. It gave me hope as a student and I didn't feel so alone.

About a month before spring break two years ago I met the student body president, Grant. My gaydar went off with him way before we ever found out each other's "struggle." We got talking and it started off as an amazing connection. We could relate on a lot of the past, while each offering something new to the relationship. After a couple weeks of intense friendship/relationship we added the physical com-ponent. It was ecstasy. Everything felt right.

In the beginning, I was okay with being this "chameleon couple," knowing when to be friends and when to be "friends" depending on our environment. He was very shut off to opening up to anyone about me. After being openly gay, aside from my family, I began to grow discontent in the way he viewed me, so I asked him to start telling his closest friends. He did, which showed me he cared. We never made anything official and continued to still like each other.

He had an internship in D.C. and I was in Jersey. We got to see each other every two weeks. He met my family as strictly a friend—deceiving on my end but I did what I had to do. That summer was the worst and the best of my life. Although my external actions were say-ing one thing, my internal self was suffocating. I was lying, I was de-pendent on him, and I didn't know who I was or wanted to be aside from the emotional feelings I had.

The semester started again and I didn't feel okay with where the re-lationship was. I ended things two days before my 23rd birthday. I needed to regain clarity and establish who I was apart from him. Looking at it now, we were both drowning, existing in a suffocating environment and using each other to remain afloat. Didn't work. Ob-viously. After a six-week break we talked and tried to figure out what it may look like going forward. We tried again and it really didn't work. We didn't talk for three months. We had a huge falling out, and he is completely out of my life now. The emotions are too deep for me to revisit anytime soon. He lives out in Arizona now and is working with Teach for America. That chapter is over.

I worked and lived in Ohio all last summer while digging into me—who I wanted to be and what I valued. I desire authentic, genuine relationships. I want the pain I've experienced to ease some of the pain for others I may meet in my life. I am no longer consumed by the thought or idea of an orgasm. I value openness in friendship.

I had a friend accept a job in Miami, and she asked me to come live with her, knowing I was taking off a semester of school. I drove down towards the end of August. It was amazing—the climate, the people, the culture, everything! Incredible. I met so many influential people in my life, and I'm hoping I made some sort of impact with my time there.

I met an older man, a publicist, who I had an amazing connection with. He flew me out to L.A. for a weekend. I met a girl whom I hit it off with! Turns out she was a victim of rape at the age of 16, and we sat and shared our stories for over three hours over brunch. Amazing. I met a friend who was HIV-positive and was able to love him in a way that not many people love him once they find out his status. I got into my art, the creative side of me that has been suppressed by so much pressure and negativity. I read, I sketched, and I journaled which was therapeutic.

People didn't bother to ask if I was gay. It didn't matter. I was Gregory. Around the end of October I met a guy, Matt. This is the craziest story of my life. We sang in district choir together back in high school, and he now works at the same school as my roommate! It was insane. We started to build a relationship and seeing where it would go. Miami with him was incredible.

Then when we were both home over Christmas. We were able to be together and do NYC and Philly together. The day he left to go back to Miami and me back to Ohio, we made it official. It was going well for about a month. Then the distance really hit us. It wasn't easy. He accepted a fellowship through the Luce Scholars Program—I'm so incredibly proud of him—and he will be in Asia for a year starting in July.

Momma Traci, I really like this guy. But we ended things, and it was one of the hardest things. Neither of us wanted to but we knew it was inevitable. Distance was difficult. I needed more than he could give me.

I'm finishing my last semester now. I'm so excited. Who knows where I'll go from there? Yes, I'm back in this conservative town but I have to tell you this: I started a meeting group for current students at my place every Monday night! It's incredible. I love getting all these kids together and just talking—letting them know that although an educational institution may not legitimize them, they can find legitimacy and worth in a group of like-minded, loving people. I'm hoping to leave an impact in their lives as I look to move on come May.

I dove into a lot of what makes me who I am in a paper I wrote for my Bible class, of all things—got an A! For the longest time, I merely existed in a numb state, letting my sexuality define every part of my life. I live now in light, and not defined by my past. I don't live according to my parents' religion—it places unneeded shame in my life.

I'm starting to truly accept myself, and it's been wonderful. Of course, I have people that don't agree with my lifestyle decision, but I still love them and we find other common ground. I've come a long way since I first wrote you.

Gregory

April 2014 email

Momma Traci

In the conservative evangelical world, being gay had to be presented as a "struggle"—as if you were continuing to sin, such as lying, porn, pride, etc. After I opened up to a guy I knew through church about my "struggle" and he encouraged me to talk to my earthly father about it. It took me over a year to talk with my dad. Upon telling him I had an attraction to men, he was dumbfounded. Had no idea what to say. Tried to relate to an extent but failed.

After three different Christian schools, and a Christian bachelors degree later, I am living peacefully at home. After a rocky road with my parents I have come to a place where I can talk with dad openly. He doesn't agree with lifestyle decisions but he assures me he will always love and support me throughout my life.

Gregory

Hoping not to disappoint—Trevor

Trevor, 21
Ohio
September 2010 - email

~~~~~~

Mom,

I'm gay.

I know I told you before when I was about 14, but you denied it and told me that I wasn't. I tried to deny it myself because of the way you reacted, but that only made me hate myself. I would lie in bed at night and get extremely depressed because I couldn't be me.

I knew I was different in middle school. I couldn't relate to the other boys in my grade, and because I couldn't relate to them I spent my entire life developing this persona—we'll call him "Straight Trevor." Straight Trevor had ladies he could have easily taken advantage of but he didn't because that wasn't the real Trevor.

By coming out to you, I don't change as a person. I'm still me. I just refuse to deny who I really am. When I found God, I let everyone tell me that being gay was wrong, so I denied myself even more. Although I found the happiness that God could give me, I was still sad inside. It wasn't until just recently that I realized that even when I gave my heart completely to God, I still had those feelings, and I had the epiphany that God made me this way.

I don't feel comfortable telling Dad. I feel like if I told him, he would make the same jokes he makes about my aunt, and cannot take being a joke. It will be easier when I move out, but not while I still live with him. I trust that you won't make those simple-minded jokes as he does.

I've only told a couple of my closest friends because they've gone through the same thing as me. They've trusted in me and opened up to me and shared every small detail of their life. I've done the same and they still accept me. They know that being gay doesn't change who I am as a person.

I want you to know that I'm not doing this for attention, and I'm not doing it as a way of "getting back at you." I just can't hide who I am anymore. I hope you can still accept me, because I'm still the same Trevor that you raised these past twenty years.

This doesn't change who I am. I still love you.

Trevor

*****

Dad,

This isn't easy to say for many reasons. I already feel like I've failed you many times as a son, and I don't feel like you look at me like I am your son anymore. To tell you that I'm gay only makes things much more difficult. You have another son now, so the whole "carrying on your name" thing isn't a big deal, really. But I still feel like it's my obligation to do so, and it makes me not want to be gay because I don't want to continue to let you down. But this is me, and I have to accept it and only hope that I don't let you down.

I struggle to tell you because I see the way you treat your sisters who are openly members of the LGBTQ community. They are the punch lines to your jokes, and I don't want to be the punch line. You talk about the neighbor being gay, and it just seems like you're not accepting.

I feel like you won't be accepting to me. You talk about how I should be with these "hottie girls" and I laugh, but it's my uncomfortable laugh. I just can't seem to find it in myself to tell you that, yes, I find them beautiful but I don't want to be with them.

I want you to see me as your son, not as your gay son. That label doesn't change me, if anything it just makes me stronger. Don't look at it like I'm changing. See me as the same person, but who trusts you enough to finally tell you that I'm gay.

Hoping to not to disappoint you.

Trevor

April 2013 email

Momma Traci,

I still have not come out to my dad. I don't see him much and when I do, my personal life to that extent isn't really discussed. I think my dad and stepmom know, and that is why it never comes up in the conversation. And if it does, I don't think much would be said.

As for my personal life, I really don't have one. With work I really don't have much free time. I have been talking to a guy for quite some time but it doesn't seem like there are enough hours to consider a relationship right now.

Trevor

So many lost years — Bear, Canada

My correspondence with Bear began in October 2010. He has a lot of medical problems, and he has occasionally given me a scare when I don't hear from him for a while. Bear is a sweet man who has never been able to live his life to the fullest. He has slowly been able to meet new people in the gay community, which has brought much happiness.

Bear, 58
Ontario, Canada
October 2010 - email

Ms. Traci,

I was amazed when I watched *The Big Gay Musical*, that there was so much of my personal life in it. I would first like to thank you for listening to me. As much as I loved my mom and dad and the rest of the family, no one would ever listen to me. If they did, it was to tell me that I was wrong and things should be done their way, not mine.

I just came out last January. So at 58, I'm starting my life again. I wish that I could say I was one of those people who had family support while coming out, but I wasn't. I knew I was gay in high school, but my best friend—who I was in love with—didn't really accept gays and never knew how I felt. He kept pushing me to be straight.

Mom and Dad silently knew about me but we didn't speak of such things out loud. Later, when I lived with my brother for a year in Calgary, I knew they knew because they went through all my stuff including gay magazines I had. They still didn't want to talk about it, but at least the jokes and comments about gays stopped.

At this time of my life, I was working three jobs and my parents were coming to an age when they were beginning to need care. It only got worse as time went on. I never got any help from my sister and my brother in Calgary, which really threw a wrench into our family because it took all my time to do my job and keep our family from falling apart.

I was always taught that family came first, never say I don't like it until I've tried it, always be a gentleman, and no matter what happens, never quit or give up. Dad and particularly Mom taught me to be very strong. With the family problems we have had, being strong has been very useful.

My mom and I grew very close when Dad died in 2005. She started opening up to me about some of the hell she had gone through with Dad and his family. I put my life on hold until July 2009, when I lost Mom. My mom was always my best friend, and there isn't a day goes by that I don't miss her. In fact, I think I miss her more everyday than I did before.

I came out this January to my family and friends. My friends were great but my sister told me it was okay as long as I didn't talk about it or do anything about it. I've stopped going to dinner at my sister's for things like Thanksgiving and Christmas because I might say something in front of her friends that she would not approve of. I am being told that I'm not worth it by my family, that I'm not to look for love let alone sex or companionship. I wish my sister could be a quarter of who and what you are. Then maybe my life wouldn't have crumbled in some of the places it did.

So here I am 58 and alone. I wish I could have come out when I was young, and I could have been loved and accepted for who I am. Perhaps my life could have been different. I have never had a relationship. It is getting harder all the time physically and emotionally, and I am running out of strength.

I am working hard to make myself a better person, emotionally and physically. I joined a gym club and I'm currently working with a trainer three times a week as well as going there on days in between my booked sessions. Hopefully it will make me better, so that somebody will take notice of me. I would like to meet a good person to share my life with.

Respectfully,
Bear

~~~~~~

Dear Mom and Dad:

Well, another year has just about passed, and once again I sit alone in the dark trying to make sense of my life, or lack thereof. I wonder if this hole in my heart and darkness in my soul will ever be cured.

I needed for you guys to know who I was, but I was afraid to tell you. I gave you ample opportunity to learn about me by telling you that you could ask me anything about my life and that I would give you an honest answer. There was a most pressing question which you should have asked me but you didn't. Since you didn't ask when you could have heard the answer, I will tell you now: Mom and Dad, I am gay.

Yes, you heard right—your youngest son is gay. I know you must have known. When I came home from Calgary you had been through my room, straightened it up, and put all of my gay magazines in a box in my nightstand. Why couldn't you have asked me instead of leaving me to live in a quiet torture of not knowing what was going to happen if it just happened to stumble out and had not really been addressed? If you were afraid that, like my older brother and sister, I wouldn't stay and love you and take care of you two when you were old and sick, then you never really knew me. I was there because I loved both of you more than my own life.

It would have been wonderful if I could have found someone to love me. If they ever turned their back on you two then I wouldn't have wanted them in my life. Now it's too late for me. I'm 58, and nobody out there wants me and my dog. You don't know how many times I wanted to be hugged and kissed and made to feel that I'm not just taking up space and air.

Being gay isn't just about sex—it's about someone to share your world with. So here we go towards another new year, and I'm still waiting for my life to start, which it should have done forty years ago. I am now so old that no one wants me. I have to sit and watch the world pass me by and wonder what it might have been like.

Your gay son still loves you with all of his heart.

I love you and miss you.

Bear

Part Nine

Now I'm Really Confused

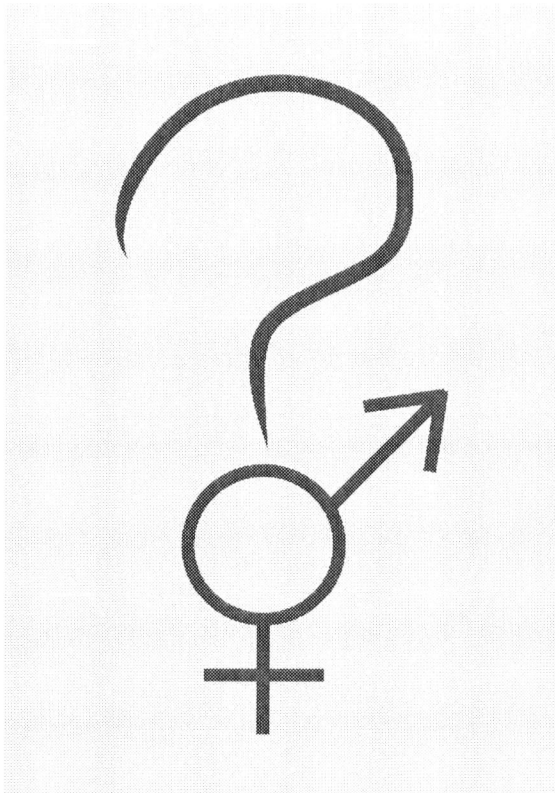

Now I'm really confused — Lee and Marie

I became reacquainted with Marie, one of my closest girlfriends, at our 40-year high school reunion. Soon my husband and I become friends with her and her husband, Lee. They surprised me when they came to the opening of The Big Gay Musical *in Portland. A couple of months later they visited my husband and me at our coast home in Depoe Bay.*

I told them about this project and about my interview with a transgender friend in New York. Lee handed me his business card, and I did a double take—the card had a picture of Lee dressed as a woman.

Lee is a cross-dresser. He does not feel like he was born in the wrong body. He does not wish to be a woman or want to have a sexual relationship with a man. He just likes to dress like a woman.

Lee invited me to go with him to a meeting of the Northwest Gender Alliance in Portland. I had asked if he would be dressed as a woman and when he said yes, I teased that he couldn't look better than me. When I arrived, I spotted Lee with his hair down and wearing a dress with red high heels and carrying a red purse.

There were about a dozen people between the ages of 40 and 70 at the meeting. All were born male. I was the only biologically born female, and the only one not wearing a dress. Two or three were married to women and just liked to cross-dress. Several liked expressing their femininity in the way they dressed but preferred relationships with men. Some felt like they were women and had transitioned to the gender they identified with—by hormones and/or surgery—and some had not. Some of these ladies really looked like they could pass as women, and it felt like I was talking to women.

One of the ladies looked at me and said, "You need to have a chapter in your book called 'Now I'm Completely Confused.'" I flashed back to the family movie night when Daniel picked the movie, The Bird Cage—with Robin Williams in his white pants, open shirt, and gold chains, and his partner Nathan Lane, a drag queen.

I have talked to many people who are accepting of my son, but some of these same people make fun of transgenders, transsexuals, and cross-dressers. I didn't stand up for them in the way I should have. I apologize for that. You don't have to understand why a person is the way they are to accept them. Everyone wants to love and be loved.

One lady at the meeting told me she is a grandmother—her children consider her a grandfather—and she is not allowed to see her grandchildren. She loves them and, given the chance, they would love her. Perhaps when they are older they will seek her out and discover what a wonderful grandmother she is.

We started talking about clothes, and they agreed that most women today don't wear dresses very often. I admit I probably don't own a dozen dresses—I prefer jeans. Lee considers herself a "clothes whore"—her closet is filled with at least a hundred pairs of women's shoes and dresses.

Do I feel uncomfortable with Lee dressed as a woman? No. I have been with him dressed as a man and when "she" expressed herself as woman. Either way, it feels right.

In touch with feminine and masculine side
Lee, 62
Portland, Oregon
March 2011

I am a 62-year-old male, biologically. I consider myself transgender.

A transgender thinks of who they are on three axes:

One is who they are biologically: genetically male, female, or androgynous (i.e. our anatomy).

The second part is sexual preference or sexual orientation: who they prefer to have as a sexual partner.

Then there is gender identity, which is how they view themselves: feminine or masculine.

This is a social construct, what society defines as gender—what society defines as masculine and feminine, dominant or submissive, and the gender roles in society, which is different in different countries.

Most cultures are male-dominated cultures. If you look back in anthropology in the early Native American and Pacific Ocean cultures, there are roles for people that are "two spirits"—those who are in touch with both their feminine and masculine persona and identity.

Transgender is beyond gender. It is basically transcending the gender that you were born with and grew up with. Transgenders adopt a dimension that is outside generally accepted gender roles and embrace an image of what they want to look like.

It gets complicated. It's a rainbow, a continuum. On each end, there are people that identify with a biological sex that is in harmony with sexual orientation and gender identity. On one end is a male who is masculine, who is comfortable with that role, and who moves very little down the continuum toward the feminine side. On the other end is the female who is feminine and who moves very little down the continuum toward masculine. Then you have of a lot of people in between with different combinations.

But society still dictates certain things like clothing. At one time in our culture men wore more feminine frilly things and wigs. At that time women only wore dresses. Then culture changed and pants have become acceptable for women.

Over the last thirty or forty years, there's been a general movement where people have been expressing more fluidity in their gender roles or identity. Many people are now are choosing a gender role that is opposite of the one they grew up with.

That's where the confusion comes in. People get biological (or anatomical) sex, sexual preference, gender identity, and gender presentation confused. Some people assume that just because you want a partner of the same sex as who you are biologically, then you are gay.

That is true if your biological sex and your gender identity is the same—but not if your mental image of who you really are is the opposite gender.

The word "transgender" has become an umbrella term for both transsexual and transgender. A transgender individual presents themselves as the opposite of the sex they were assigned at birth. But to transsexuals, their body looks wrong. They identify with the opposite sex, not the sex that they were assigned at birth. Transsexuals feels like they have the wrong anatomical body and are extremely uncomfortable in that body.

I am married to a woman. I am biologically a male. I consider myself heterosexual because I prefer a woman as a sexual partner but I am equally comfortable in either gender presentation. I am transgender or gender non-conforming. If I present myself as a female, I present myself as feminine and wearing women's clothing. If I present myself as male, I present myself in a suit or jeans—in masculine clothing.

It started before junior high, but I really wasn't aware of it until high school. In high school I remember being interested in nylons, lingerie, and dressing up. It was like a fetish, or a sexual turn-on to wear women's clothing. But I was very masculine. I didn't play with dolls when I was growing up. In high school I rode a motorcycle, wrestled, and played football.

There was something about the exploration of the feminine body and style that was part of me, but no one else knew. I would find women's clothing at thrift shops. I became involved in the Northwest Gender Alliance (NWGA) in the mid-80s. I had occasionally been going out in public dressed in female clothing, and I found a club that embraced that. At that time I had been married about fifteen years, but my wife was unaware.

At first, my wife had problem with my cross-dressing. She didn't want to see it. We had good communication, and I told her I needed to explore this. We went to a NWGA club meeting together. There were about forty people, some with their spouses, and I presented myself there as a man. She told me she thought that the people were nice. It wasn't like she had been afraid it would be.

She talked to one of the wives, and later they had coffee together. They talked about the reasons they were attracted to their spouses, and part of that was our feminine side. They both felt if we didn't have those traits they wouldn't have been attracted to us. My wife realized she still loved me even though she didn't understand some of my dimensions. It has been a slow evolution to understanding but now she doesn't mind seeing me dressed feminine because that is part of who I am.

Originally NWGA was mostly cross-dressing, but now the club includes transgender and transsexuals. There is a group called The Society for the Second Self (Tri-ESS) which is one of the first national organizations focused exclusively on heterosexual cross-dressers. When the NWGA was founded, they felt uncomfortable being restrictive in their membership. It was basically for cross-dressers but they aligned themselves with the Gateway Gender Alliance (GGA) in San Francisco, which was more open.

Although NWGA was a cross-dressing club, there were members who were homophobic and were not comfortable going to gay clubs. It was more acceptable to be a cross-dresser at a drag show than other public places. It was easy to tell the cross-dressers from drag queens because cross-dressers are usually not as flamboyant as those dressing in drag. Most drag queens (men dressed as women) and drag kings (females dressed like men) are in the gay and lesbian community, but this is a grey area.

There has been tension between the trans community and the gay and lesbian community. Part of the reason is political. Gays and lesbians have been fighting for many years for human rights. The majority of people accept or at least understand sexual orientation and are becoming less threatened by it. But when it comes to transgender identity issues there seems to be a problem. When you are talking about children who have identity issues, it becomes emotional. When you are in the bathroom and someone comes in that looks like the opposite sex it can be upsetting.

There are other issues. If you are a white male, you have the power. If you are a white trans male and are going to transition to female you will lose power. Some people don't understand why you would want to lose that power. Also there are the fear issues. If a straight male becomes attracted to a trans woman and finds out she is really a male, that makes the man angry—it insults his masculinity, and he is afraid he might be gay.

One of my friends in Seattle is in a cross-dressing club. He and his friends dress very well and often go to high-class straight bars. One night an intoxicated straight man was making negative comments and becoming increasing aggressive. One of the club members told him that if he felt uncomfortable he should leave. The drunk man told him that they all should leave or he'd make them. The club member said he might want to reconsider. He pointed to the other members sitting at the bar and said, "He is in Special Forces. Next to him is a SEAL. Next to him is an Army Ranger. The last guy won't tell us what he is in, but he taught the others."

I have been involved in the community volunteering for a long time. I got involved with the Portland police department in '95 with the Sexual Minority Roundtable. Portland is one of the few cities to have an agreement between the sexual minority community and the Portland Police Bureau that sets relationship parameters and tries to build a better relationship. There are five or six community roundtables which meet with the police once a month to normalize the relationship between the community and police department, to get to know each other, to have dialogue, and to build a community that co-operates and is not antagonistic.

For a long time, the gay community and the police department were targets for each other. Look at Stonewall in New York and police raiding the gay bars. There was some persecution by the Portland police and a lack of understanding, awareness and sensitivity. A few years ago we had a police chief in Portland who had a lesbian daughter on the police force who is well-liked and active in the community—this helped.

I am also on the Crisis Response Team, which are volunteers who respond in cases of a homicide, suicide, major assault, officer-involved shooting, or some mental health crisis. We explain what the police are doing, or translate. I am called if it involves a sexual minority, to help the loved ones or partner, to help follow through with victim assistance, and go to the funeral. We are there for support for several weeks or longer if necessary. I am also on the Use of Force Review Board—we determine if the police have used extreme force, and we participate in performance reviews and as part of hiring panels.

Since I've retired I've also become more active in Parents, Families, & Friends of Lesbians and Gays (PFLAG), Gay, Lesbian & Straight Education Network (GLSEN), and Oregon Safe Schools & Communities Coalition (OSSCC).

I'd always been part of the corporate world but since I've retired I have become less confined. I was always concerned about whether my immediate management was going to be biased against me. I was concerned about conforming to the corporate image. As far as hair, earrings, and nails there are expectations and dress codes. The last few years I worked, I crossed the line. I went from being fairly conservative to having hair past my shoulders and long manicured nails. My performance reviews became critical. I was more of a target.

I would like to see a change but I feel we have two generations before we have that hope. We now have young people in their late teens, 20s, and 30s who are aware and knowledgeable of the sexual minority community. Unless there is a backlash, their children will be more attuned to diversity.

There are still many countries with zero tolerance for anything that's outside their idea of conformity and many where the punishment may be death. I think we are way ahead of the rest of the world in embracing diversity.

Part of the problem is young people who have gender or sexuality issues and who don't have the skills to articulate who they are and what they feel. It takes an adult who pays attention and listens to what the child is really saying. If you're willing to hear what they really have to say, they will tell you. Instead of following our expectations for our children, we have to be willing to open up and hear the answers we might not like and follow up with questions.

Most importantly, we need to stop putting labels on people. We need to learn who people are as individuals.

What would that mean for our family?
Marie, 64
Portland, Oregon
November 2013

Lee and I met right after high school through a mutual friend. I was attracted to him right away because of the dichotomy of his personality. I'd heard about this wild guy who rode motorcycles and wore black leather boots with chains around them, but when he took off his helmet he was a clean-cut young man wearing a big smile and a button down shirt.

We dated about six months before we married. We had a baby right away. After we'd been married for about seven years, he came home with a pair of pink high heels and a matching purse for me that he found in a second-hand store. Somehow that felt odd. There must have been a suspicion in my mind. Then occasionally I would find a pair of women's underwear or women's clothing I didn't remember buying, but I would dismiss it—my life was very busy with a young child. I was sure he wasn't having an affair. I never asked where the clothes came from. I must have not really wanted to know.

We had been married about fourteen years and things were not going very well in our marriage. We were fighting a lot, about everything. He started to drink to excess, and he would become extremely short tempered. I didn't want people at my house anymore, because he wouldn't be nice. It finally got bad enough that I took our daughter and moved out. I left in the middle of the night with nothing and stayed at a motel down the street. Then I moved into an apartment in Forest Grove after sneaking into our house and getting our things while he was at work.

After about three months, Lee and I decided to get some counseling. The counselor told my husband that he could change himself but he could not change me or our daughter. He needed to live with us the way we were, change himself, or move on.

My daughter and I moved back in and things seem to be better. Lee was drinking less and he was keeping his temper under control. I think that's when he came to a realization of who he really was, and he decided he would have to tell me.

My fifteen-year-old daughter and I were sitting on the couch, and he told us both at the same time: He liked to wear women's clothes—he was a cross-dresser. He said he was going to cross-dress more and not hide it. He was very clear that he was still heterosexual. He just liked wearing women's clothes, and he hoped we would accept him. My daughter told me later that she wondered what that meant for our life as a family, but she hoped he would be nicer now.

I was relieved. Big secrets between spouses are not healthy for a marriage. Now it was out in the open. We could deal with this. All the things that happened in the past came together. He had an office upstairs, and that is where he kept his women's clothes—but I was never a snoop.

I don't remember the first time I saw him dressed as a woman, or how I felt. I think I have deliberately forgotten because I didn't want to think about it. I loved the man. I wanted to stay married. If this is who he was, I could accept him.

In the beginning, seeing him dressed in women's clothes was weird, because I'd never thought of him as anything else than a man. The first time I went with him to a Northwest Gender Alliance

(NWGA) meeting was the Valentines party. Lee told me that if it made me uncomfortable he wouldn't go dressed in women's clothing. All the other men at the party were in women's clothing which actually made me more uncomfortable. But it was kind of him to dress like a man to make it easier on me.

Some men dressed like women but were sitting on a couch with their knees apart watching a football game—acting like men in dresses. Other men in dresses looked more refined and were acting like women at a party. I imagined if my husband had worn women's clothes he would have been with the second group. When he does things, he doesn't dabble around the edges—he does it all the way. That seems better to me. I feel if you're going to dress like a woman, you should act like one.

There were also wives and girlfriends there, and I got to know a few. I went to a conference with Lee, and I got to know an older woman—one of the wives I had met before. At a lunch break, she asked me to join her at a restaurant around the corner. We spent the rest of the afternoon together. She told me about her husband, who called himself Ellen when he dressed as a woman.

We talked about cross-dressing and what that meant to a marriage. When she was with her husband and they would visit neighbors, he would be dressed as a man. When he was Ellen, he was still her husband—they still had that connection, regardless of how he dressed. When he went out as Ellen, he would get into the car in the garage. He didn't want to flaunt it to the neighbors.

The children had known since they were young and were fine with it. One of their sons was at a business meeting at a restaurant in Portland. His father was dressed as Ellen and was at the same restaurant with her friends. He saw his dad and excused himself, went over and greeted Ellen, and then returned to his group. It didn't occur to him there was anything wrong with it.

One of the best pieces of advice this other wife gave me was that I have the right to boundaries, to say this does not enter certain parts of my life. In my case, Lee dressed as a woman does not belong in our bed.

It was hard for me at times, mostly because we decided not to tell our families. Keeping this a secret has been difficult. The biggest problem is that she is a clothes whore and has more dresses, shoes, and purses than me. She has trouble learning restraint—just because she likes it doesn't mean she has to have it.

It took about five years before I truly felt comfortable being with Lee dressed as a woman. One result is that if I am getting ready to go somewhere with Lee dressed as a woman, I tend to dress nicer. We even go shopping together now.

It's kind of strange that older people don't seem to recognize that Lee is a man dressed as a woman, but teenage girls and younger women do. As soon as they walk past us I catch them looking and talking about her.

If I had a chance to go back, I still would have married Lee. He is a good man, a good husband, a good father, and a good provider. Despite all the problems, I still love him.

Didn't have a name for it — Kim

After I went to the NWGA meeting with Lee, he suggested I interview Kim Peterson, founding member and training director for Trans-Youth Family Allies—a national organization that empowers transgender children and families by partnering with educators, service providers, and communities to develop supportive environments in which gender may be expressed and respected. TYFA works to create a society free of suicide and violence in which all children are respected and celebrated.

Kim Pearson
Training Director, TransYouth Family Allies
Arizona
December 2010

I knew something was significantly different by the time our daughter was three. She told me she didn't "do" dresses. She didn't say she didn't like dresses or that they were uncomfortable. It was a statement of fact. I remember telling my child, "You will wear dresses if I tell you to wear dresses. I'm the adult I'm in charge." But when I realized how miserable dresses made my child feel, it wasn't worth it. Every time I put our bubbly, happy child in a dress, she became a miserable, sulking, angry monster. What was point? It was just clothes. I let her wear jeans.

We had a call from her preschool when she was three or so—she had cut off her eyelashes. I asked her why, and she told me it was because people said they were pretty. I asked her if that was a bad thing. She said, "I can be cute, but I can't be pretty."

I told my husband that our daughter was really having a hard time. I suggested that we steer away from the word "pretty," use the word "cute" instead, and run some interference because we didn't want our child cutting off anything else.

She didn't like to be hugged or touched by people she didn't know—she was adamant about that. Her dad could hug her. I could hug her, and her brother and sister could hug her. But other people could not hug or touch her.

We had a pretty good idea that she was a tomboy, but in my heart I knew there was something more. I had no point of reference for what was really going on. My best girlfriend at the time had two little boys. They were my daughter's best friends—they played together, took baths together, and had sleepovers. When my daughter was four, my girlfriend asked what I would I do if my daughter grew up to be gay. I told her that you actually don't have to do anything if your kids are gay. You just keep doing what you've always done—it doesn't require a paradigm shift. She asked me if I would be okay with that, and I told her yes. My biggest desire for my kids is that they are happy, contributing members of society. If they partner with someone who makes them a better person, it doesn't matter what sex they are. But during that conversation I was very disturbed that we were talking about the sexuality of a four-year-old. I didn't think of a four-year-old as a sexual being, that it came later.

My daughter started asking for a flat-top haircut. We knew our child had a lot of hero worship for her older brother who always wore a military buzz and was always going to be an Army man, but we thought this was a little too much. I used the standard mother response, "We'll see," but she asked for the haircut a couple times a week for months. Finally we sat her down and told her that we knew she wanted this haircut but she would probably get teased or bullied, and that kids might even hurt her. We warned her most people think it's a boy's haircut and that sometimes people get upset when girls act like boys. She didn't care. We took her to the barber shop, and she got a buzz cut. She wore that that haircut to the age of 10 or 11.

She started school looking that way and if anyone ever said anything, she never told us. I have found with the families we work with that when a child is bullied for this reason they usually don't tell their parents—because their parents might make them change their haircut or the way they dress. Our daughter went to private school where they wore school uniforms—she had her choice of slacks, shorts, or a skort with white polo shirts. We bought all three, but the skorts were always hidden behind the bed or the dresser. I never saw them on her.

There is a picture of her taken when she was showing the first signs of puberty. She had on her sister's bathing suit which she never liked—she liked swim trunks. Up until that time she would wear her brother's hand-me-down swim trunks with no shirt. I told her she had to start wearing a top. She needed a girl's bathing suit. The picture is of the kids on the block, but she is standing at arm's length from everybody else with a weird look on her face. At the time nobody noticed, but you look at it now and it is disturbing.

When she was eight or nine and really started to develop, we started losing her. We didn't see her body anymore. She covered up, wore layers in hot Arizona weather—long pants and shirts, trying to hide her form. The more she feminized, the more she hid in clothes.

When she was 10, her older sister asked her to be a bridesmaid in her wedding. She would do anything for her sister. She grew her hair out and wore a gown. They put makeup on her and she cried. She started her period. This was probably the worst day of her life. As soon as the wedding was over, I found the dress in the waste bin. I remember looking at the dress and thinking this wasn't worth it.

I didn't know she had started her period. She had some supplies and didn't tell me until she ran out a couple months later. I bought her underwear—I bought her panties and bras and guessed on the sizes since she wouldn't let me check to see how they fit. She would just tell me she didn't care, just buy it.

Her grades were going down. She was sick all the time—headaches, stomachaches and pains. Finally I had to get a note from the doctor saying she was suffering from clinical depression.

She went to a counselor a couple times a week but it was hard to get her to talk. I would have to go with her. When we went to a restaurant, she would whisper what she wanted in my ear—she didn't want to talk out loud. She had been so incredibly gender-variant for so long that by the time she started experiencing significant distress we were not connecting the dots. She had been accepted for so long the way she was—short hair and wearing boy's clothes. She did everything that boys did—she played soccer, baseball (not softball), basketball, skateboarding. She was just one of the boys.

She was kind of a loner at school and didn't invite people home. I didn't realize at the time that she was so isolated because she had such a good neighborhood group of friends. Plus she and her brother did everything together. It was like I had two little boys. Looking back at their activities, it was definitely the relationship of two brothers.

When she was 12, she came out as a lesbian. It wasn't a declaration of who she was attracted to. She had felt masculine and wanted a masculine role, but the only way she thought she might fit in was as a masculine lesbian. For several months she seemed to be feeling better, but about six months later she began to decline. It was hard to understand, because everybody accepted it. She had the support of her family. She had realized that wasn't it. It wasn't enough. Homosexuality wasn't her source of her distress.

By middle school, she was really struggling. When kids were talking about dating and girls were talking about their bras and periods, she was just disappearing. It was like she became an invisible person. When she would come out of her room, she was completely shut down. For about six months we were on suicide watch. It was a really scary time.

The counselor couldn't understand the source of her depression. She wasn't ashamed, but she did not own it either. She wouldn't say she was a lesbian out loud, but she would do things artistically. She had even written me a letter, but she wouldn't talk about it. I told the counselor about her body issues—covering up and not caring about the bras and panties—and the extreme secrecy. All my kids were private, but this was so much more intense.

Finally, I decided to push. I told my daughter that someday having a relationship means sometimes you get naked and have skin-to-skin contact. I told her I hadn't even seen her body since she was a little kid and I wanted to know how that was going to work. She told me she just wouldn't do it.

I told the counselor. She looked confused—here was a 14-year-old who said she would never have sex if being naked was what was required. The counselor said she wasn't sure what the problem was, but we were close to getting to the heart of the matter.

The next session, the counselor asked her what she saw when she looked in the mirror.

She said, "I don't."

"You don't look in mirrors, or you don't see anything?"

"I don't look in mirrors."

Puzzled, the counselor asked, "You don't look in mirrors when you brush your hair or teeth?"

"No".

"Honey, I think there are some body image issues here. Everyone looks in mirrors."

"That's just bull."

The counselor asked her how she felt about her body, but she refused to talk about it. We knew this was it—something about her body image. But my daughter was finished talking and wanted to leave.

The very next week we went to see the movie, Transamerica, about a man who transitioned to be a woman. My daughter told me that if a man could become a woman, then maybe a woman can become a man. She got on the Internet and did the research.

At our next counseling appointment, she told us she didn't want to be a lesbian. She wasn't a girl—she was a guy. She was in the wrong body. I did a replay in my mind of all that had happened and wondered, "Holy hell, how did we miss that?" Once you know what you are looking at, it is as plain as the nose on your face.

My daughter went on to say, "How could you know? I didn't even know." She didn't have a name for what she felt. She thought people would think she was crazy and she would be locked up. She didn't think there was any place for someone who felt like she did.

So he came out as a transgender at 14 and had a named picked out: Shawn. He had a mental list of things he needed to do. He wanted a legal name change, hormones, and someday surgery. He said he wanted new clothes and new underwear from the men's store.

I just about disintegrated. I didn't know how to do those things, or if it was even possible. But shopping was something I could do. We went shopping that day. It was the first time in years that we had gone shopping where he wasn't totally impossible, disagreeable, and obnoxious. We bought a lot of stuff.

We didn't know what we were going to do when we got home because my husband had no idea what had happened. I told Shawn that his dad was going to need some time and not to take what he says personally. We didn't expect it to take a month. When Shawn was getting the bags out of the car I ran into the house and told my husband we'd had a major breakthrough in counseling. I told him whatever you see in the next fifteen minutes, just roll with it until I have time to explain. Please don't burst our child's bubble because our child is really happy right now.

Then Shawn came out modeling men's clothing—the most masculine things he could get. He would say, "What you think, Dad?" And his father would reply, "Wow, you look good in blue." He didn't really know what to say. After Shawn was done and went to his room, I told my husband that our daughter wasn't a lesbian—she was, in fact, a boy.

My husband needed some time. He needed to think about it. It was really hard for him. He admitted later that he'd had a distorted mental image of a transgender—he envisioned a 6-foot-7 drag queen with false eyelashes, big hair, too much makeup, long nails, platform shoes, and big boobs. Really strange, because our child was born a girl and identifies as a boy, but that was the image my husband identified with transgender.

His reaction was, "Hell no, not my child." He wouldn't comment. He wouldn't talk about it. He didn't ask questions. There was no conversation.

Shawn expected me to have everything lined up for him to start his freshman year in high school as a boy, but it was only 60 days away. I met with the school principal, school counselor, and the nurse and got things lined up—and then promptly went out to the parking lot and lost my lunch because I had been so nervous about what was going to happen.

I applied for a legal name change and showed the school the paperwork. They told me to come back when it was completed. I tried to explain how difficult it was going to be for them to wait. If they put Shawn in the computer now under her birth name and as female, then they would have to change everything when I got the paperwork back. I explained what problems they would have that if the test records were not changed by the time Shawn became a senior. It seemed like it could be a nightmare. They decided to put him in the computer as Shawn and as male. Maybe it wasn't legal, but they didn't want to deal with any of the other scenarios so they just did it.

The biggest problem was going to be Physical Education. The PE teacher said there were other kids with medical releases and that there was a online PE course, so that is what Shawn was enrolled in.

The only thing they would not let him do was use the boys' bathroom—they said they wanted him to use the nurse's bathroom. But Shawn just went to the boys' bathroom during class and no one noticed. He told me he had never used the bathrooms at school before because if he went into the girls' bathroom and they didn't know him, they would tell him to get out because he was a boy.

I talked to other mothers of transgender kids about how difficult it was to transition your kid into school as a different gender. I told them how I got the school to agree with the name change and the gender change. Some mothers told me they had been working with the school for three years and still were not able to do it. That's when I realized that not all parents were equipped to do this. We were moms looking for resources and information and we found it difficult, if not impossible to find the information we needed for our children. I talked to two mothers who had successfully transitioned their children, and we began talking about forming an organization to help others in the same situation.

TransYouth Family Allies was founded January 1, 2007—six months after Shawn came out as a transgender male. We found experts and parents who had transitioned their children successfully in schools, the names of the counselors, and what we needed to pull it all together in an organized fashion.

I live in Arizona. Our board president lives in Indiana, and our board treasurer lives in Michigan. We formed this organization by working together on the Internet. We are the three original founders— just three moms trying to figure out what we could do for our kids and how to share our information with others.

We use the term "gender variant" because it does not lock a child into a long-term outcome. People are worried that if you allow kids to transition early and call them transgender that they will feel obligated to continue on that path.

Gender-variant means kids have run into resistance because of the way they express themselves—girls who are more masculine and boys who are more feminine. A boy who wants to wear pink tennis shoes and nail polish will run into resistance. Boys run into resistance at a very young age for any kind of behavior or preferences that seem feminine. A seventeen-month-old baby boy was beaten to death by his stepfather for being a "sissy"—that is what we are up against. If you don't conform to these unwritten rules in society, people will come down on you like a ton of bricks.

Girls can be tomboys and people think nothing of it. Their struggle seems to come later and can be more pronounced.

We don't just work with children in schools where they need to transition to live as the opposite gender, but also in all schools to create a safer environment for kids to have more latitude to be who they are. We want people to be aware and accepting of kids who vary from regular sex gender roles. Typically when I go into a school, it's because there is a child there who is transitioning from their biological sex to their identified gender—whether it is a boy living full-time as a girl or a girl who is going to live full-time as a boy.

Sexual preference and gender identification are two completely separate issues. Sexual preference is the gender of the person you are sexually attracted to. Gender identification is what gender they identify with, and gender variant is behavior which is different than what is considered gender appropriate. We work with families with children under 18 years of age who are gender variant and with those who are considered transgender—transitioning from living with their biological gender to their identified gender.

According to the American Academy of Pediatrics, gender identification is not fixed and stable until the age of five or six. We do not work with children younger than five because they could be just going through a stage of trying on different roles and gender activities. You also don't transition children who are doing fabulously the way they are. A little boy with a lot of feminine traits and could be bumping into some resistance, but if he is happy healthy, interacting well, doing well in school, he is not a child that would be transitioned.

Eighty-percent of the families in our organization have children under the age of 12—pre-puberty—with strong cross-gender identification. We do not deal with medical procedures, as these aren't available to young children.

We have found commonalities in the stories of kids that end up transitioning. Usually a family has been working with their child's variance for three to five years before they come to us—three to five years of the child and parents grappling with these issues. They are running into resistance in the schools, with other families, and with their extended family. The parents are trying to get their child to conform but it's just not working. The parents have consulted their pediatrician and a counselor or two. They may have gotten some advice that they have tried, but basically nothing is working.

The family of a six-year-old may come to us, hysterical, because their son was found in the bathroom trying to remove his penis. The boy has been told repeatedly that he is not a girl, that they know he is a boy because he has a penis. In his young mind if he does not have a penis then he will be a girl. Some trans-boys (born girls) going through puberty cut themselves in the breast area. We have children in distress, who only want to bathe with their undergarments on because they don't want to see their body parts—they look down and they know those are not the body parts that should be there.

Education is so important. Some people think transitioning is just permissive parenting—they don't know how acutely distressed the child can be. People don't believe that five-year-olds can be suicidal. One child living in a fourth-floor apartment told his parents that if he couldn't be a girl he was going to fly out the window and never come back. That is a suicidal five-year-old.

We find that there are just as many transgender girls as boys—in fact we probably see more girls. My theory is that the social stigma of boys transitioning to female is so much more stringent, and that parents just don't want to go there. They may instead try to ignore it or even try to beat it out of their kids. This may account for the huge population of trans youth who are homeless.

Usually mothers are more accepting than fathers. It is really difficult for dads especially if it's their only son or their only daughter. But some of the dads really surprise me. A lot depends on how much the parents have invested in what that relationship looks like and how much they have projected into the future of what it will be like. The greater that investment, the harder it is to accept a transgender child.

For me it was easy. It was a choice between a dead daughter or a live son. It took me two seconds to make that decision. For my husband, it was more difficult since he had a mental image of "transgender" that was not in any way connected to the reality of what our child's life would be.

So when we are in schools, we try to stay away from terms like transgender because people can have these erroneous mental images. My husband was invested in walking down the aisle with his daughter. I already knew our child was never going to be in a long white dress.

Our organization hopes for social acceptance for all children. In a perfect world, gender variance would be accepted and we wouldn't have to work so hard to transition kids into schools, but that is not the world we live in.

For more information on TransYouth Family Allies:
http://imatyfa.org

Crawling under bus seats —
Rev. David Weekley

When I first met Reverend David Weekley, I would have never guessed that he had transitioned (F to M) over thirty years before. I was nervous asking him for intimate details about his life and surgery, but his sincere demeanor made me feel as though it was natural to ask.

As he spoke I could only see him as a man—gentle, and soft-spoken with a great sense of humor and a strong dedication to his faith. He gave me a copy of his book, In from the Wilderness. It would be a shame for such a genuine person not to be able to continue as a pastor.

Rev. David Weekley, 60
Oregon
March 2011

I was born and raised as a biological female, but from my youngest memories (age three or four) I saw myself as a little boy. I grew up in a small rural town in Ohio, outside of Cleveland, in the mid-'50s. There were just a few kids on my street and we all played together, boys and girls. I had a best friend, Gary, and I thought I was just like him.

I used to love watching my grandfather shave while I played with the shaving cream. I remember asking him when I would start shaving. He tried to explain to me that I wouldn't, but I was sure that someday I would.

In my family, there wasn't a lot of pressure as far as clothing or gender roles. I wore jeans and my brother's hand-me-downs. We used to watch the TV show Leave it to Beaver—I would call him Wally, and he would call me "The Beav." I always saw myself as his little brother.

I was unaware that I didn't match the rest of the world until I started kindergarten and experienced kids divided by gender. The struggle began because the school dress code required me to wear a dress. Wearing a dress to me felt wrong. When I was on the bus I would crawl under the seats and hide. The bus driver would sometimes stop the bus to try to make me stay in my seat. I just didn't know any other way to express how upset I was. By the time I got to school, I would be filthy and would get in a lot of trouble.

My kindergarten teacher would come out on the playground and try to make me play with girls. I don't think she was aware that she was picking on me by trying to get me to conform to accepted gender roles, but seeing her do this made the other kids feel safe to ridicule me. By the fifth and sixth grade, I didn't have any friends in my classroom. No one would talk to me.

Middle school brought puberty. The other kids started to date, but I couldn't date. I was openly laughed at, ridiculed, and ostracized. Those were the worst years of my life. I hated my body—having breasts and a period felt wrong. I wore my hair short and tried to dress as masculine as I could. I kept my body completely covered, even in the summer.

In seventh grade, we were studying human reproduction and human sexuality in science class. My teacher told us about intersex babies—babies born with ambiguous genitalia. He told a story about a kid who was in middle school and started having a period, and they realized he wasn't biologically a male but a female.

I decided that was probably what was wrong with me—they just hadn't figured it out yet. I thought about finding medical help. I wanted to talk to my parents about it, but I was afraid they would be mad at me.

Then I saw an article in The Inquirer about Christine Jorgensen who was born male and was drafted into the Army but identified herself as a female. After "he" got out of the service, he went to Denmark for sexual reassignment surgery, went through the transition, and returned to the United States in 1952—where she was greeted by hundreds of people from the press and became an instant, scandalous celebrity. She lived a very public life as a transsexual woman and wrote *Christine Jorgensen: A Personal-Autobiography*—a great autobiography that was made into a film, *The Christine Jorgensen Story*.

After finding out about Christine, I searched the library for information on transsexuals. It was hard to find but it helped me understand what I was feeling. Just imagine waking up one morning and finding yourself in the wrong body, the wrong gender. In high school, people openly laughed at me and picked on me, accusing me of being on drugs or being a "queer." Sometimes when I would enter a classroom, I could hear everyone snicker. I liked girls but never considered myself a lesbian—I considered myself a guy.

I've talked to other transgender people who felt the same way I did, but just as many others have told me that they started out thinking they were gay or lesbian, not transgender.

Luckily I had five friends—two males and three females. They knew me, accepted me, and encouraged me to stay in school when I wanted to drop out. Their friendship kept me alive. My best friend, Scott, used to say how neat it would be when we both had beards.

My tenth grade English teacher is the one who finally picked up on how I was very different. She stayed after school sometimes and talked with the kids. One time, when everyone else had left, she asked if I was "all girl," and I told her no. I wasn't completely sure what she meant and I'm not sure if she knew what I was saying, but that was a turning point in my life.

She arranged for me to meet with the school counselor, who was a psychologist. He became my support during high school and helped me through those times when I was depressed and on the brink of giving up. I told him I was a transsexual. I felt like I was a male with physical problems. He had never met with anyone that identified as a transsexual—the word they used at that time.

We talked about what was going on in my life, my feelings, and my most pressing issues, one of which was self-image. I continued seeing him all through high school and even saw him during the summer. My parents never came in to see him even though they knew I was talking to him. He wrote a letter to my parents requesting that I have a full medical evaluation. Instead they took me to our family doctor. It was a short visit, and we didn't talk about it. I couldn't stand him. My parents were supportive in their own way, but it was just too much for them.

When I was 17, I was friends with a family who were part of my small support group with whom I had discussed being transsexual. They suggested I talk to their doctor. He told me he really didn't know what to do, but he told me whenever I felt I was ready he would do his best to help me find medical help someplace in the U.S.

After high school I got a job in a factory, rented a room, dressed like a man, and went by the name Sherman—but legally, I had to put my female name on my taxes. I'd gotten the nickname Sherman in seventh grade after giving a history report on General Sherman. When starting to write my book manuscript I looked at that name and realized Sherman was "She-R-Man."

After about a year, I had saved some money. I went back to my friends' doctor and asked him to start looking for medical help for me. After six months he called and told me he had good news. He found a doctor in Cleveland—just ten miles from me—who was part of a team that did these kinds of surgeries. Back then, insurance paid for the surgeries because the insurance companies had not figured out how to exclude them. I made an appointment to meet with the doctor.

There were only three or four places in the U.S. at that time that dealt with transgender people. They were modeled after the Harry Benjamin Standards of Care, a process of working with someone who was trying to figure out their gender and go through transition. Harry Benjamin was one of the early pioneers working with transgender people.

Then, there was only one way to transition. It is different now—there are more options, and it is easier. Now they can get medications prescribed to stop you from going through the wrong puberty. I would have done anything to have not had to go through that. Now it is much easier to get the hormones and find surgeons, because you pay for it yourself and don't have to jump through any hoops. I think insurance should pay for it like they did for me—I have heard some larger companies do provide this coverage. I also think it may be too easy now. People should make sure they realize what a serious step it is to undergo transition.

The doctor connected me with this program at the Cleveland Metropolitan General Hospital. They had a whole team of people: social worker, psychologist, two psychiatrists, sociologist, urologist, plastic surgeon, endocrinologist, and others. There were about nine people on the team, and I had to have an initial interview with each of them. Then I took medical, psychiatric, and psychological tests. They were very scared back then. This process was new and they didn't want to make a mistake.

For the next three years my life was working, medical and counseling appointments, plus going to school—majoring in psychology to try to understand what was happening with me, and also taking a lot of classes on different religions to try to understand the religious dimension.

After six months of tests, I met with the review committee to hear their verdict. They decided to keep me as a candidate and would allow me to start hormones, but I had to wait on the surgery. They felt I was too young because the surgery was irreversible—so were hormones, depending how long you have taken them.

The first things I noticed with the hormones was my period stopped, my voice started to change, and a little chin hair appeared. I was going to the gym, and I started to build muscle. My clothes began to fit me differently. I was in a relationship with a woman, and we were hoping to marry after the surgeries and the transition were complete. She was straight and considered me a man with sexual issues. I did have sexual climaxes but to me it felt like it was from my penis.

In 1975, after a year and a half of hormones, I had my first surgery. They chose to do the phalloplasty surgery first—the construction of the penis. This kind of surgery was originally developed because of men in the military with war injuries. It was the most complicated and riskiest but they still wanted to do it first. The skin graft came from my thigh and muscle and skin grafts from my abdomen. The scrotum was made from the labia lips with silicone implants—I had a lot of excess skin there—and the ovaries were removed. I had a prosthesis for erections, but they did not know if I would ever be able to climax or have any sensations—though there are many things available now for erections.

I was one of the very first female-to-male transitions done in the U.S., and the first one by this particular surgeon. Unfortunately, the next surgery like mine was not successful. The skin graft did not take and the surgeon was sued.

The healing took about three months. I couldn't work or go to school. I had to take three baths a day, and for first three months my penis was attached bottom and top to my abdomen so the blood flow could build up.

I still didn't know until the next step if the surgery was a success. With the next surgery, they detached my penis from my abdomen and removed the breasts. My surgery was a success. I urinated out of the penis and I have had a successful sex life for the last thirty-six years. There was an additional outpatient surgery for touch-ups. Information on my surgery is in a textbook but I have never seen it. There are some video interviews with me for teaching purposes. I was 24 when the surgeries were complete.

As far as my parents, they were happy for me and were supportive verbally, but they only came once during the major surgery because my mom said it was too hard to see me in pain. That's the only time they visited me in the hospital. Once I was home, life went on. My parents and my brother were okay with the new me. My girlfriend stayed with me through all the surgeries and my transition, but a couple of years later we broke up. We tried to get back together but after she told her parents, things got worse and we just couldn't make it.

I finished college with a degree in psychology and religion. I had planned on taking a year off and then going back to get my masters. I got a job at a small private psychiatric hospital working with clients.

I'd always had a strong spirituality in my life, even though my religious upbringing was sporadic. My mother was Roman Catholic. I have early memories of going to Mass but as I got older we really didn't go to church much. By the time I was 13 or so, I knew that some of the churches were saying that God hated people like me, that we were an abomination, doing something that was disrespectful and rebellious and that God doesn't make mistakes. They also said we were going to go to Hell if we didn't straighten up. That is when Anita Bryant and the whole Moral Majority thing started. But I always loved being in a church. I would go on weekdays when no one was there, by myself or with a friend, to talk about God and spirituality. Back then they didn't keep churches locked.

I moved to the other side of Cleveland and worked at a different clinic. I moved into an apartment with a straight guy I worked with who didn't know about my transition. I was stepping out into a whole new world. I felt led to graduate school in phenomenology of religion—studying the categories of religion and what the different spiritualities have in common. All my friends up to that point knew my story, but now no one knew.

I legally changed my name halfway through the surgeries. I chose the name David, which means, "Beloved of God." I wanted a name with personal meaning. I didn't want the name Sherman because it was just a nickname given to me by friends.

It was relatively easy to legally change my name, but in Ohio they would not change my gender on my driver's license because you have to have your birth certificate changed. The first time I was pulled over by the police, the officer looked at my driver's license and he started joking with me, asking me what sex I was. I told him male and he said, "I thought so but look what it says has here. You better have that corrected."

I knew there was nothing I could do, so I took a knife and marred that place on my license. I went to the DMV and told them that it had gone though a ringer. They made me a new license with my sex as male. Since 2009, the law has been changed in Ohio. You now can change the gender on your driver's license, but it is different from state to state.

I have a friend who is a transgender woman (M to F). She is in a relationship with another woman, and she identifies as a lesbian. Before I transitioned, some people might have considered me a lesbian. But I considered myself a male. As far as I was concerned, I was in a heterosexual relationship.

I met women and they didn't know my history, but I was not sexually active. I knew they would know I worked a little differently. I was trying to date and get to know what it felt like to be a guy. I was out there like anybody else in the world, and it was scary. What took me the longest time to understand was that I had lost a certain kind of intimacy with women I didn't even know I'd had. Before, friendship with women was open and unguarded but now there was a fear that I was hitting on them. That easy kind of friendship with women was now lost and I missed it.

If I did date someone and it started to get romantic, I wondered what to do. When and how did I say something? Do I not say something? There was a lot of hit-and-miss and a lot of experimenting but I never went in for one-night stands. What was most difficult was learning how to create a relationship and when to share that part of me.

Twice I shared and I was turned away, and it hurt. The first time, it was how I brought the subject up with the woman I was dating. It was too much of a surprise for her. We talked about it again later, and maybe we could've started dating again but I didn't go down that road. The next time I was rejected but we really weren't compatible. The chemistry wasn't there, plus she was a single mother with little kids. I was too immature and not ready to be a dad. There was another woman I was interested in. I asked her out but she said she was a lesbian. I told her that it was okay because I am trans but she said no, I was a guy. The irony of it all.

I finished the academic program I was in and I started to rethink church. I joined the United Methodists Church, and I was in the choir. I felt called to explore seminary school. I was accepted at Boston University School of Theology and moved to Boston. While I was there I met my first wife. We were very different but liked some of the same things. There were no fireworks, but I felt that was what mature love was. I thought since we liked each other and could work together, we should get married. I was 28 and had one more year to go in seminary.

In 1982, we moved to rural Idaho where I was a pastor. It was kind of scary because that part of the country was very conservative. I didn't have medical care there because I didn't feel safe. I was afraid I might have to go to the hospital, but there was no one I could trust. I got my hormones from my doctor in Boston. I even flew back to Boston for my physical. My wife really wanted to have children. I didn't think I really wanted to but we talked and talked. Finally I agreed and she conceived with artificial insemination. We had our son.

We moved to Salem, Oregon, where our daughter was born. We were busy being a family. I was a pastor of a church, my wife was working as a physical therapist, and the kids were little. I stayed in contact in the trans world with people in other states but not in my area. I was active in advocacy for gay and lesbians in the church, but no one thought anything of that.

The United Methodists Church has had this kind of schizophrenic attitude towards gays and lesbians, but they didn't even talk about trans back then. They are starting to now because there is more awareness and education going on. When I was ordained, they wouldn't ordain gay or lesbian people. There were and have always has been a lot of gay and lesbian people in the church as clergy, but it was the hiding thing: "Don't ask, don't tell."

Over the years I wrote legislation and tried to do a lot to support the full inclusivity of gay and lesbian people in the church. The church started to talk about including bisexual and transgender people, but they still do not officially ordain gays or lesbians.

As far as preaching against these groups in my denomination, it is different from church to church. I have examined many times over the years whether I should stay or go, but I felt led to stay because I wanted to create change. In the in the late '60s and '70s there were these bumper stickers on cars that said, "America: love it or leave it." I thought back then, "Hell, no. This is my country, too, and I'm not leaving it to you."

I feel the same way about my church—it is my church, too. I have stuck it out even when some of my colleagues have left to go to more progressive churches. I want change and I want the church to be what it is called to be and is not yet. This became increasingly difficult after I was moved to a more conservative church in Forest Grove, Oregon, in 1992.

In 1994, my first wife and I split. Things had not been going well. It's very difficult with all the moves and being a pastor's wife. My wife and I never talked about me being transgender even though she knew. As time went on, I became more and more active as an advocate. We both realized we had a friendship but not a romantic relationship. We talked to counselors and tried to work it out, but it was more difficult to stay together as a couple than to be apart. Our marriage was not an example for our children as a loving, healthy relationship. Even though I really don't believe in divorce I do believe that sometimes it is best for everyone involved.

A year later I started seeing my present wife, Debra. We got engaged and married. That also led to some conflict. Some people in our congregation thought clergy getting divorced was one thing, but that I shouldn't have remarried. I decided to leave the church in Forest Grove, even though some of the congregation was supportive. The kids stayed with their mom, and we continued to have a good relationship.

We moved. I worked in a youth group, in a homeless center, and as a walking messenger.

Then in 2000 I took a church position on the east side of Portland. Debra and I talked about how we could be more supportive of LGBTQ people. We also continued to discuss when it would be the right time to tell our blended family that I was transgender—even my kids didn't know.

In 2008, it was beginning to seem like it was almost time to tell them. Our youngest son had graduated from college and our youngest daughter was almost out of college. Our oldest son came to me one day and said he had some friends whose child was identifying as a little boy but his birth gender was female. He wanted to know if there was anything I could say to the parents to help. So we sat him down and told him we understand because I am a transgender male.

It was funny because he is Debra's son and the one that I was most afraid to tell—he's a big guy and likes trucks and guns—but he was very accepting. We met with each of our children and told them. Each of the children reacted differently. For our two oldest—Debra's kids—it was simple and they were excited because they had so many friends in the community that were trans. The most difficult were my children, because I had to tell them I wasn't their biological father—but I'm Dad. I assured my kids that they are full brother and sister from the same donor. That was actually the hardest thing, telling the kids.

By this time I was the pastor of a largely Japanese congregation. Debra and I went on a trip with them to one of the internment camps in Idaho where so many of them had lived as prisoners during WWII. We were there for five days and heard some incredible stories. One lady had not told her 60-year-old son about being in the camp.

It was during that time I felt I should tell them my story. These people had been oppressed. They knew what it was to be called names and be a minority. We felt they would understand. Debra and I started talking about what was the right procedure for me to tell the congregation my story. I had started writing my book about four years earlier and when members of my congregation would ask what it was about, I would tease them and say I would tell them sometime.

The morning I told my congregation, I called my sermon my "book report." I told them what my book was about. As I was talking, I saw many shocked looks on people's faces but the acceptance and support was incredible. Initially, the response was great. After I gave the sermon people applauded, and after church many hugged me and my wife. But within four months, there was a small group that was causing problems. It became clear I was going to have to leave. I had to move to another church.

A church appointment is decided by our bishop and the cabinet. I was hoping to be sent to one of the more accepting congregations, but I was told I had only one choice. The reasons they gave me were about everything but me being transgender. The moment my colleagues knew I was a transgender man, I was treated horrifically. After twenty-nine years as clergy, I was at the bottom of the pay scale with two part-time churches. I would live in the parsonage on a busy street in Portland. I couldn't afford to keep our house. They took away my power because they could. It was gender politics.

February 2013 email

Hi, Traci,

My last meeting with the church and district superintendents is a long and complex story. Briefly, despite my congregation doubling in size, my district superintendent and bishop's cabinet were unwilling to allow the Sellwood church to use its own funds to have me serve there one more year and see what might happen if my time was focused on just one congregation. So the church closed and all the people (largely LGBTQ) were left high and dry.

The new appointment they offered me was another two-point charge of two churches—again dying congregations and again minimum salary. I declined.

We have moved to Boston where I begin doctoral studies next week at Boston University.

David

Making holes in fences—Darcelle XV

Darcelle is the drag alter-ego of Walter Cole, and his documentary Queen of Hearts—a psychological study of drag performance that takes viewers behind the scenes—left me spellbound.

After reading Darcelle's book, Just Call Me Darcelle, and watching his DVD of the same name, I arrived at Darcelle XV Showplace for a performance and was given the honor of sitting with Roxy, Darcelle's partner. Roxy talked about growing up, his love of dance, and the support of his mother. He told me about his days in Las Vegas and his move to Portland where he entertained at the elegant Hoyt Hotel, which has since been torn down. As he spoke about his forty-four-year romantic and business partnership with Darcelle, he described how dangerously difficult a relationship between two people in show business can be—especially with two male egos in play.

Now in his eighties, Darcelle is still performing to Rhinestone Cowboy. Onstage, Darcelle is larger than life, a sharp-witted, funny, spirited, and gutsy woman—the kind of person many women wished they could be.

Darcelle, 83
Portland, Oregon
March 2012

I was born November 16, 1930, and have been alive for 83 precious years. I am a gay man and the proprietor and headline performer at Darcelle XV in Old Town Portland. It's the longest running female impersonation show in the United States, now over 40 years. I do not consider our show a drag show, because a drag show is a drag—and we are entertainment. I put on a dress for entertainment reasons, but never in my personal life.

When I was growing up, I didn't know I was gay because back then nobody knew what "gay" was. There were no gay slurs like "faggot" or "queer." I lived in Linnton, a little town in Oregon. I was very shy and introverted. I was picked on. I never played sports because other boys hardly picked me for their teams. I was never very good at baseball—if I did play, I was picked last and they would put me way out in the outfield. If I threw the ball, it was always in the wrong direction. I liked to play with the girls. We played hopscotch, and I was really good at jacks. The boys called me a sissy, but back then that just meant I wasn't very butch.

I lost my mother when I was about six. My father was abusive, but I still survived. My aunt was my caregiver after my mother died. My father molested me for about two years after I reached puberty, but it didn't mean anything to me except that it was pleasurable. No one would've ever said my father was gay, because he was a man's man—one who hunted and fished and worked at the mill. He told me to not tell anyone, and I didn't—until I did my one-man show a few years ago.

During high school, I did act on my feelings toward men, but I still ended up getting married to a woman when I was 20. I didn't realize then that two men could live together and have a family. It was different back then—the streets were not filled with fairies like now. I think I survived because of the love of my aunt and because I have always surrounded myself with supportive people, like my friends.

After I got married, I went into the military and had a couple of sexual encounters there, though I never started anything or looked for it. After I got home from the service, my wife and I had two children, built a house, and had a very happy situation—but I was cheating at regular intervals. It wasn't anything binding—a little trick here and a little trick there. I wasn't cheating with anyone I would ever see again, mostly in bath houses.

I was a manager of a Fred Meyer, and I owned a coffee shop. I would go to work at seven in the morning, get off at three, take a nap, and then open my coffee house at seven in the evening. I did this five days a week. When I started my business, my wife said we were going to go to the poor house. She said I couldn't make it, but I have. In my life there is no "can't"—don't tell me I can't, because it will be done one way or another. I have started four businesses since the 1950s.

I sold the coffee house and bought the Demas Tavern in NW Portland. I stood in the middle of the space and cried thinking, "Look what I've done! It's such a mess!"

So, I had this place, but I knew my gay friends who came to my coffee house wouldn't come over to this side of town. All I had here were winos who were drunk and sitting under the trees by nine in the morning, and I wasn't getting any business from them.

I hired a lesbian bartender, and we opened the doors as a lesbian bar. It was a rough dyke bar. The lesbians then were not like the lesbians now. They were mad and they were evil. They took the worst part of a man and made it worse, and they loved to fight. I had to change the glasses and pitchers from glass to plastic because they kept throwing and breaking them.

Then I met Roxy and fell in love. I'd had the bar for about two years, and I met him in a gay bar. He tapped my knee, we introduced ourselves, and he asked me to come to his show at the Hoyt Hotel where he did choreography and danced. We didn't have sex for three or four months after we met. He must have thought I was a kinky queer or a young man kept by some old fart—he didn't know then that I was married.

Finally we started dating and going together, and I made up my mind that I wanted a different lifestyle—I wanted this lifestyle. I wasn't being fair to my wife by cheating and lying, but I didn't want to tell her I wanted to leave her because of Roxy. I also imagined how horrible it would be for Roxy if later I blamed him for my decision to leave my wife. I didn't want to be married to a woman, and I didn't want to call it quits with Roxy. After much soul-searching and much consideration, I made my decision on my own, without input from anyone else.

One evening in 1968, I sat down with my wife, Jean, and told her that I was gay. I told her that I liked men. Her first response was to ask me to go to a doctor. She didn't know anything about it and I really didn't either. Then we went to a bar in our neighborhood and drank margaritas until we were stone drunk. My wife was the first person I told. I had been hanging around some really flamboyant people, but I didn't have to tell them.

Soon after I told my wife I was gay, I told Roxy that I was married, but I continued to stay at home for a while. Eventually, it just wasn't working. Jean told an interviewer once that our marriage had just become unraveled. I moved out, and Roxy and I moved in together. At the time, one of my children was in high school and the other was starting. I didn't tell them. I didn't have the guts. One day my son overheard my wife when she called my aunt to tell her about me, and my aunt disowned me immediately.

My life just had to change. If I hadn't made that change, I wouldn't have made the decisions I have with my outside businesses. I probably would have become a fat slob on the couch, living in SE Portland, retired from Fred Meyer—or even dead.

I am still legally married to Jean, and I have continued to support my wife and children. My father had deserted me and I didn't want to do the same to my kids. I wanted to be truthful to Jean, and now we are good friends. I am also very close to my children. We all get along. In fact, my son has been working at Darcelle XV for twenty-three years.

Roxy and I decided to have entertainment at the bar. He had seen a female impersonation show in San Francisco, and then we both went and to see it. We thought it was just wild. The Hoyt Hotel had closed by then, so Roxy came over to the bar. He had experience putting on shows, and I had been in theatre for about ten years, so we decided to give it a try. We didn't have costumes, so I got a sewing machine. Every week, I made a new costume, and every week we would add a new song to the line-up. Some of the first songs were by Barbra Streisand or Tina Turner. At first it was just on weekends, with Roxy, our friend Tina, and a guest entertainer or two. The audience loved it. We didn't have a stage, either, so we danced on a table. Then, one day, a writer from Willamette Week came in, saw the show, and wrote an article about it—that was the turning point.

When we started this, I didn't really have a plan. Things evolved—that's our forte. We didn't have any idea that it would last this long—forty-five years—and I'm not sure back then if we cared. We weren't making any money. We didn't have a cover charge, and a beer cost a quarter. But we entertained the guests and they enjoyed it.

As we invited more guest stars and as Roxy put more production numbers together, the show evolved and it has continued to this day. These days, the place is bigger. We used to have a cement wall down the middle of the building, but we picked away at it and now it's gone. Since we didn't have much money, we had to put the remains of the wall in trash bins all over town. We also have a real stage now, not just a table, and we have great lighting. I have learned the craft doing stand-up and making people feel comfortable. Tina worked with us for twenty-seven years and helped to make Darcelle's what it is today, but now she is gone.

If we would have tried to plan this, we couldn't have. If a fortune-teller had told me back then we would still have this show, I would have told her, "I won't keep tucking my dick away for forty-five years!"

A few years ago, I was making a documentary about Darcelle's called *Queens of Hearts*. I was talking to the director about being called a transvestite, a drag queen, a faggot, and a queer. I told him I didn't want to be fenced in or be just whatever. If I am fenced in, I will make some holes in that fence.

I'm proud to say that we have made a difference. Ever since the early years, when were asked to help with a charity, we have—I can't begin to tell you how many. All of that work has helped us to build a foundation of who we are. We're not just silly faggots. We are people trying to make a difference.

For some, coming to our show is a rite of passage—they might bring their families and friends; they celebrate weddings, birthdays, and divorces. Our audience is a mix. We have straight men that come in, sometimes practically kicking and screaming, but within few minutes they calm down and enjoy the show. Some of the straight men are turned on by our beautiful girls. I think it opens their minds to be more tolerant of feminine men. Some straight men have told me they were afraid to see the show, but afterwards they liked it. They say they didn't know that it was like this. I've wanted to ask them what were they are afraid of. Did they think we were going to masturbate on stage?

Straight women come in to see this show and feel safe. I always have a woman come up to me afterwards to say, "God, I wish I could wear those earrings or gussy up like that," and I tell them to do it. They would love to emulate what we do.

I have a theory that men don't really like women. I don't think they treat a woman the way she should be treated. If they liked them, they would have fewer nights out with the boys, and they would treat them with respect and caring—that is what they get from us. When I'm on stage and I say to a woman, "Those are really good lookin' hum-bas, darling," they beam. Men are always thinking, "Let me play with them," in a sexual way. But when it comes from me, it's a compliment. Here, they don't have to deal with a man with a hard-on—which, incidentally, would look terrible in a dress.

Our audience has changed a lot through the years. Today we are more inclusive of the general public, not just the thrill-seekers. People tell me that their aunt or their neighbor came here ten years ago and had a great time, so they decided to come. We have actually had several women priests that have come to our show, and they loved it. When people come to our show we just want to make them smile.

We started with three entertainers, and now we have eight. Most of our entertainers are gay men who dress up to entertain, but after the show they take off their costumes and makeup and go home. Our show has also changed our entertainers' lives—they have gained confidence and gone on to do other things and to other venues.

Darcelle has made an impact on Portland, too. A few years ago, The Oregonian newspaper had a familiar name contest, and the most recognized names were Mayor Vera Katz and Darcelle's.

The biggest change I have seen in the gay world in the last forty-five years would be all the initials that are now used to represent gay and lesbian people, like LGBTQ. I can't even memorize all of them—if you held a gun to my head I couldn't tell you what they are. I won't use a set of initials to identify anyone as gay or lesbian or whatever. People are more precious than a bunch of letters grouped together.

I love what I do. I am not ready to retire. I love Darcelle's—it's a part of me.

Part Ten

Over the Rainbow

The bully and steps to respect—Jennifer

Sometimes, when you are in the grasp of a bully, you don't even recognize it. I recognized it when my son was in junior high, when he was pushed into his locker and the word "FAG" was scrawled on it. I could identify it in story after story told by my LGBTQ friends, but somehow I didn't see it when it happened to me.

A few years ago, I was working for a local school district as a substitute teacher assistant for children with special needs. I worked in a high school as a substitute for several months with five others. It was a difficult job, working with teens who had extreme learning, emotional, and behavioral disabilities.

One of the teacher assistants decided she didn't like me. When we were walking to the cafeteria to get breakfasts for the kids, she would brag about beating up kids that got in her way when she was in high school. She peppered me with negative comments that no one else could hear, and she gave me nasty looks.

I was in charge of one particular boy who could be violent. This other woman took over while I was on lunch break. Even though the boy and I would have a good morning, after lunch I would often find him sitting under the table with a wild look in his eye. Also, this other assistant would often comment—loud enough for the other assistants to hear—that I was late coming back from lunch, even when I wasn't.

At the end of the day, she would tell me that the dirty job of mopping the kitchen floor or cleaning up a mess from one of the students was mine—and then harass me for doing it wrong. There even came a time when I began to fear she would be waiting for me in the parking lot when I left to go home.

I told my daughter about my co-worker. She told me simply, "Mom, that woman is bullying you." I was astounded. I had felt depressed and paralyzed by fear. It was staring me in the face, and I didn't even see it.

As the bully takes hold of his victim, the target becomes weaker and the bully becomes stronger. I began standing up to my bully and taking back my power.

When I worked as a teacher assistant in a third-grade classroom, the school counselor came in to teach a program called Steps to Respect. She described different scenarios and asked the kids to identify whether statements were compliments or putdowns. One example:

Dan often played basketball at recess with his friend, Eli. One week, he played Frisbee with some other students instead. Eli said, "Frisbee is a sissy game. You are a wimp." When Dan got upset, Eli asked, "Can't you take a joke, Danny boy?"

As the students discussed the story and whether words like "sissy," "wimp," and "Danny boy" were putdowns, I found myself in tears as I remembered when Daniel was in grade school. I decided to find out more about this program, and I interviewed the counselor who taught it.

Jennifer
Elementary School Counselor
Oregon
January 2011

Steps to Respect Bullying Prevention Program is a research program taught in the classroom. It starts in third grade. Its purpose is to educate students who are witnessing their peers not being respectful to each other—specifically bullying. It is also meant to give strength to the victims of harassment or bullying so they can learn to stand up for themselves.

The lessons teach the kids about the differences between being passive, aggressive, and assertive. We teach the kids that being strong doesn't mean that you are aggressive—you can be a strong person by speaking up and being assertive. We try to give the kids the language they need and help them believe in themselves so they can be strong. The program also speaks to those who are bullying, so they can understand how it feels and so they can build empathy.

Similar lessons are taught in the younger grades. At that age, disrespect may even look like playing, but it is a minor version of harassment and bullying which can get worse as the kids get older.

Bullying is unfair, not respectful, and not equal. It is one-sided. One side has a problem with the other, they have some sort of power, and they are not using that power in a positive way. It's a misuse of power to hurt or threaten another person. The power could come from one kid having large group of friends, while another kid doesn't have as many friends. Or this power can come from simply being taller or older.

Kids can be bullied because of nationality, religion, strength, or size, or simply because they are different—and power is used to hurt, threaten, and frighten them. It happens a lot with girls with what's known as relational aggression—when they say things about each other behind their backs, spreading rumors and secrets, or not letting them play with them or be in their group. Boys tend to be a more physical in their bullying, but girls can be physical too.

The program starts with finding and building relationships, but the most important part is having respect. If you don't have respect, you don't have a foundation for a relationship. I tell the kids to think of the relationship like a house—if you don't have a foundation, it will collapse. We also talk about learning to treat other people respectfully and how to identify what harassment and bullying are.

Three steps—Recognize, Refuse, and Report—are the foundation for identifying and stopping bullying and harassment. We try to empower the kids not to be victims. We teach them what to do, to use the right language, repeating the words and talking about what different choices mean.

The first step, Recognize, is to understand that uncomfortable feelings are a signal. We explain that bullying is when someone is threatening or scaring another person. A child might feel sick, get a stomachache, or be nervous and scared. When it keeps happening, and there is one particular person that comes to mind, the child might be the target of harassment or bullying by that person. We teach them first to say, "Stop"—the Refuse step—and if that's too scary for them, to tell their teacher or counselor—Report.

That can be scary for kids. I don't have the statistics, but I believe only fifty-percent of bullying is reported due to the fear of revenge or of being labeled a tattletale. We teach that there's a difference between tattling and reporting: Tattling is trying to get someone in trouble and not trying to solve a problem; reporting is when there's a real need for intervention because you are feeling unsafe or scared, or because something is dangerous.

I always tell the kids to err on the side of reporting, because a teacher can help them distinguish whether or not it is something that needs to be reported. I would rather they tell a teacher than have it keep happening.

We teach a lesson where we paint a scenario, and the students tell me whether they think it is tattling or reporting. If someone calls you a name one time and then you tell, then it is tattling because you could have ignored them, walked away, or told them to stop. If you have tried two of these ways to deal with the problem and it keeps happening, then you should report it to an adult.

When I was in elementary school, we didn't have programs like this. We didn't even have a counselor. I remember being on the bus with my younger brother, and some kids got off the bus and followed us. I used the power I had of being older and I told them to go home, but by that time my brother was crying because he had been bothered by these kids all the way home.

I have another brother who is ten years younger. He was a quiet kid, and because he didn't speak up he became a target. He was bullied and even had pencils stabbed in his arms. He is bothered to this day by the way he was treated by other kids. I think everybody has either been picked on or has picked on someone in their lifetime—but there is a difference when it is continual.

This program is in many of the Forest Grove and Hillsboro schools, and I have been presenting this program for about ten years. I collect data on the kids for the program before and after the class, and I have seen how it has increased their knowledge. We have referral forms in our schools that are written up if someone has been harassed or bullied, but we do not have a huge number of those incidents. I believe a lot of that has to do with this program and how we continually talk with our students about being kind and respectful citizens.

To learn more about Steps to Respect, visit:
http://www.cfchildren.org/

Making it better for the next generation — Aaron

Lee invited me to an Oregon Safe Schools and Communities Coalition (OSSCC) meeting in 2011, where I met Aaron—a kind and sincere young man who is deeply involved with causes for the gay community.

When Aaron spoke about how his life might have been different if there had been an anti-bulling law when he was in school, I remembered that day when my son was on stage singing and a student yelled "Fag!" No one said or did a thing. I hope for a better world where LGBTQ kids feel safe in school.

Aaron Ridings, 32
Oregon Safe Schools and Communities Coalition
Portland, Oregon
April 2011

I work for Multnomah County as a staff assistant to a Multnomah County Commissioner. I also serve on the Board of Directors for the Oregon School Safe Schools and Communities Coalition.

I have been out to everyone as a gay man since I was 18. This is my fourteenth year of being out of the closet.

I grew up in Clackamas County, Oregon, splitting my time between my mother's, father's, and grandparents' households. I knew I was different. When I was in the second grade, a French foreign exchange student was visiting a woman that my dad was dating. I thought he was just gorgeous and I loved his accent. I didn't know what these feelings meant.

I was always considered one of the girly guys—a sissy—and was always teased, bullied, and harassed in school. In second grade, they put me in a group of other "misfit kids." A counselor worked with us and tried to get us to stand up for ourselves, and this gave us time away from the classrooms where we were bullied by as many as fifteen other students and even some of the teachers who passively observed and did not intervene.

I knew in sixth-grade that I was different when they started sex education classes. At about the same time my mother's brother came out of the closet. He was the first in our family that ever came out as gay. He did the hardest work, basically educating our entire extended family—a large number of people. He took the time to talk with everyone and explain what it meant. He told them it was not a psychological disorder. My family is generally open and accepting, but it wasn't easy for them. He was in his late 30s at the time, nearly 40, when he started coming to family gatherings with his partner. I knew he was different before that, but until he came out I didn't have a good understanding of how to think about it.

Once I was in junior high and reached puberty, I knew that my feelings were considered inappropriate and the harassment became worse. This was during the peak activity of the Oregon Citizens Alliance that was working to pass Measure 9—which would have prevented any mention of gay or lesbian subject matter in schools and would likely have banned people who were out of the closet from working in government.

Junior high was the most painful because I had low self-esteem. I was jabbed with rulers, whispered about, screamed at, and attacked in the classrooms, the lunchroom, gym class, choir practice, and on the bus. The teachers and other adults watched and did nothing. They just allowed it to continue. Sometimes they would say something passive like, "It's time to quiet down," but they never directly addressed it. I felt absolutely miserable. I was completely detached from my environment and had difficulty confiding in my family or anyone else.

I was a good student, but I never wanted to be in school. I always just wanted to leave. It was so bad during the Measure 9 campaign that my junior high school set aside a time for me and other misfits to meet with counselors away from other students. The school counselor and I discussed my family and being unhappy in school, but not being bullied and harassed. I didn't feel comfortable talking about it because bullying was accepted and was considered normal. We were just separated from our peers while those who harassed and bullied were never punished. Most of the other misfits in that group later came out like I did.

I stayed busy in school. I had a couple of teachers who I connected with, which is what sustained me during those years. I knew two of these teachers were lesbian and had partners, but it wasn't discussed openly. They couldn't discuss the issue with any students, but everyone knew. One of my teachers did address bullying and harassment in her classroom. She confronted the bullies and sent them out of the room. She sent the ring leaders to the office. She just didn't tolerate it.

In high school, people made comments up and down the hall. I knew a couple of men who had come out of the closet and had to move because they were chased in cars and beat up. I was never injured in high school, even though I was constantly threatened.

Before I came out, I did what was expected. I would go on dates with girls, but we would just become study or shopping buddies. I knew my parents accepted my uncle, but it was hard for them and I knew it would be even harder for them to accept me because I was their son.

I tried to be "normal" in order to be accepted and have a good life. But I had trouble sleeping, became very depressed, and considered suicide many times. My parents were concerned about me. I filled up my time with lots of work. I was the editor of the school newspaper and president of the speech team. I started the Young Democrats, went to Stanford summer school, sang in two different choirs, and volunteered for many nonprofit organizations. Keeping busy was my way of coping—it kept me away from that place where I considered suicide.

At the end of my senior year when I was looking at colleges, I knew that things were going to come to a breaking point. I knew I only wanted to be with men even though I hadn't yet. I found what I thought would be the "gayest college" in the U.S.: Macalester College in St. Paul, Minnesota. The reviews of the school said one quarter of the students were gay or lesbian.

I applied and was admitted. While I was there, I pretended I was dating a woman who was on the soccer team. We were hanging out one night. I looked at her and she looked at me, and we both shook our heads and said good night. A month later she started dating the captain of the women's soccer team.

A month after that I was visiting a friend in rural Minnesota. I told her that I had to start telling people that I was gay. There was nothing I could do about it. I cried for a couple days. I felt awful afterwards because I gave her no warning. I can't remember what she said except that she was very comforting. I think she already knew because I have always been perceived as gay or feminine.

I told a couple of my friends on campus and then went home to Oregon for winter break, which I was really dreading. I was procrastinating. It was the day after Christmas and it was almost time to go back. I was sitting on the couch next to my mother and instead of coming out directly, I said, "I don't know how to tell my dad that I am gay."

She had a hard time with it. She was worried about my safety and wanted me to be sure. The next day I left to visit my father, and she was crying as I drove away. I told my father I really needed to talk to him. He folded his arms and just looked at me. I just said I was gay. He got up from the table and put his arms around me and hugged me. He said that he loved me, but he had to go lie down. He went to bed, and I left for the airport. His wife, my stepmother, had a gay brother who died of AIDS a few years before and they had been there for him. That was my dad's first exposure to someone who was gay, so it was especially hard for him when I came out.

I have a huge extended family, and I was very close to my grandparents who were like a third set of parents to me. I told my grandfather (on my mom's side), "I am just like my uncle." He said, "No, you aren't." I said, "Yes, I am." Like my father, he gave me hug and then lay down in his bedroom.

My grandmother told me, "He loves you, but it just hurts him. That may not be the right way to say it but that is the way it is. He will always love you, and you will always be his grandson."

It was a sweet interaction because it made me realize how close I was with both of them. I think my grandfather felt hurt because I wasn't going to have the life or be the person that he thought of and he could be proud of or be more like him. My grandfather was in his 70s, and after that things were different between us. It was easier for my grandmother. It seems to be easier for women to accept. For men, it is more threatening for another man to be more like a woman and date other men.

I wasn't comfortable talking to the rest my family, including my uncle who was out even though I knew he was gay and would be supportive.

I went back to Macalester. I was kind of quiet and kept to myself at first. Then I went to my best friend Sheridan's place for my birthday party. She and I worked at the Cultural House and we were both members of the Native American student association (PIPE). At the party, someone was talking about a guy in school. I said I thought he was really cute and I would like to date him. Everyone turned their head and screamed, "I knew it! I knew it!" Since then I have been out to every single person in my life.

I got my father and my stepmother the book *Now That You Know: A Parent's Guide to Understanding Their Gay and Lesbian Children*, by Betty Fairchild and Nancy Hayward, and they talked to a lot of their friends. I think they went to counseling. My mom talked to a lot of her friends and she went to counseling, too. It's hard to describe the intensity of it because of all those years in junior high and high school, relating to my peers and trying so hard to not be gay. When I finally started telling everyone, it was so intense that I only remember the highlights. It was such a rush.

At the end of the school year, I went back to Oregon for the summer and dated a guy I went to high school with but hadn't known there. It was exciting. We had lots of fun. He was my first "boyfriend." I was 19. He passed as straight better than I did. We really grew up together during our twenties. It was an exciting relationship to start, but it became mostly damaging and eventually needed to end.

Since then I have had one long-term relationship for almost seven years. Right now I am single.

I have not been back to any of my high school reunions, but I've seen many of my friends from back then. Everyone pretty much knew I was gay and weren't surprised in the least.

I've been volunteering in the community since 1992, when I was a youth activist in Clackamas. I have been involved with the gay community working with Basic Rights Oregon, Cascade AIDS Project, Equity Foundation, Q Center, and other organizations. My interests in public service led me to work for Multnomah County.

When I was working in the Multnomah County Commissioner's Office I saw an announcement for the annual Oregon Safe Schools and Communities Coalition meeting. The OSSCC is a state-wide coalition of individuals and organizations working together for the common purpose of keeping students safe in schools. I found out later that Multnomah County had been a founding body.

I brought up the announcement at our staff meeting and promised to report back about how we could support the effort. At the OSSCC meeting, I listened to presentations about the projects they were working on and the phone calls they were receiving from across the state from kids who had a hard time in school, as well as from their parents and teachers. This small group of volunteers routinely drove to schools across the state to advocate for youth, sometimes enlisting the help of counselors, lawyers, and educators.

After that meeting I became a member because I felt the mission was very important. I have always struggled with health and substance abuse issues. Many of the gay and transgender people I know have had similar struggles. Improving life for a few young people in school is the most important thing we can do for our community—to make it better for the next generation.

In the fall of 2010, I had the opportunity to participate in the National Safe Schools Roundtable, and that was really inspiring. The roundtable of advocates meets on a regular basis with the purpose of strengthening their own organizations and supporting emerging efforts like OSSCC. I learned a lot about the work being done in Washington, D.C., and by other state-based organizations that conduct research. Not a lot of research has been done on school climate compared to other issues.

In 2009, Basic Rights Oregon convened a Safe Schools for All Coalition to pass the *Oregon Safe Schools Act*, which requires school districts to adopt policies and set up procedures that address bullying and harassment. Our law specifically lists sexual orientation and gender identity in the enumeration of protected classes. This law protects all students—it is not okay to be bullied or harassed for any reason.

The law passed in 2009, but the process of implementation has been slow. OSSCC's task is to conduct research to support the full implementation of the law in all schools in our state, which is a big job. Forty-one states have anti-bullying laws, but only a handful of states—including Oregon—have statutes that specifically include sexual orientation and gender identity.

The significance of a school board's willingness to adopt a policy in alignment with the *Oregon Safe Schools Act* is symbolic. It is a recognition of the problem and a promise to do more. It sets an expectation that educators and communities must address bullying and harassment.

I wonder how different my gay and transgender generation's experience would have been if teachers and principals in our schools had been required to abide by an anti-bullying law. Would they have interrupted a classroom of students ganging up on one gay or transgender classmate when they heard the words like "fag" or witnessed other kinds of harassment or assault?

December 2012 email

I have confidence that things are getting better now and that we can make an even bigger difference for the next generation. OSSCC received funding from the Oregon Public Health Division to conduct follow-up research to the 2012 report about the implementation of the amended *Oregon Safe Schools Act*. We found that 142 of 197 school districts in Oregon either failed to update their policies or provide notice to the public as required. I'll be working as a consultant/independent contractor over the next few months on behalf of OSSCC with the division and the LGBTQ Bar Association of Oregon (OGALLA) to create a second report that will help with our broader efforts to advocate for anyone who is bullied or harassed in school.

April 2014 email

In 2013, the coalition was excited to publish the second annual report and announce that 127 districts had up-to-date anti-bullying policies that promise to make schools safer for everyone. There are fewer than 70 of 197 districts in Oregon that still have not updated their policies, but many are in the process of doing so. The second report received local media coverage throughout the summer. In the fall OSSCC and the Q Center were jointly awarded grants to hire staff who will continue to publish the annual report and build a pilot Safe School Certification program in Oregon.

Currently, certification staff from Iowa are working with the new Safe Schools and Training Institute Program Manager housed at the Q Center and OSSCC to focus on supporting individual schools in Oregon. I am back working at Multnomah County as a Policy Advisor in the Chair's Office and volunteering my time to this effort as part of the final project for my graduate studies.

This work still matters. Preliminary data from the 2013 Oregon Healthy Teens Survey indicates that LGBTQ youth continue to be bullied at persistently high rates. For eighth graders, 72 percent of gay and lesbian-identified students and 68 percent of bisexual-identified students reported they were bullied in the previous 30 days. For eleventh graders, 43 percent of gay and lesbian-identified students and 52 percent of bisexual-identified students reported they were bullied in the previous 30 days. There is no data available for transgender-identified youth.

http://www.oregonsafeschools.org/wp-content/uploads/ safeschoolsreport_2013_pages_v5.pdf

http://www.safeschoolcertification.org

The Indian way — mother and son

"Two-spirit" is a Native American term for people who identify as gay, lesbian, bisexual, or transgender—to reflect that these people have both the spirit of a man and a woman.

According to the Two-Spirited People presentation given by Raven Heavy Runner at the University of Portland in 2011, two-spirits were often revered and honored in their tribes and were regularly placed in positions of leadership. This practice was lost as Native Americans were forced onto reservations and their ceremonies banned.

I traveled to Seattle to interview Raven, a member of the Blackfeet tribe of Montana. In our conversation, I felt like I had found the answer to the hate and prejudice against LGBTQ people—not just coexistence with and acceptance of those who were different, but appreciation and even celebration of our two-spirits.

Telling the story that would keep my secret
Raven Heavy Runner, 47
Seattle, Washington
April 2011

I studied social work at the University of Washington, and now I am a supervisor for the Indian Child Welfare office for the State of Washington. My legal name is Raven Heavy Runner but my Blackfeet name is Ah Stoh Yoh Gatsi, which translates to "Sees-in-both-directions."

I knew I was gay around the age of five or six because I enjoyed "girl things." I had a Barbie doll and carried it everywhere. My grandmother—not my biological grandmother, but a white woman from Kentucky—let me play with it.

When I was in first grade, I was sent away to the Indian boarding school, and I realized I was different. The other boys told me I acted like a girl, but I really didn't understand what they meant until I started being attracted to guys. Soon enough, I learned the roles of each gender and the rules concerning what was supposed to be feminine or masculine.

Some other kids and I were sent to see a psychologist, and I thought that everyone must have known that I was different. First, the psychologist asked me to describe a woman. The most feminine person I could think of was my teacher, so that's what I told her. She then asked me to describe a man, and to me a logger was a masculine person, so I told her that. Then she asked me what happens in a relationship between a man and a woman, and I told her that they get married. I knew I was telling her a story that would keep my secret. As far back as first grade, I knew what society wanted.

My mother's younger brother, Steven, was gay, and that helped me and my brother. When I was about eight years old, we stayed with my maternal grandmother during school breaks because our boarding school and her home were on the same reservation. Her home was out in the country up near the mountains. My brothers, sisters, cousins, and I would go there and spend time with our grandmother. When grandma went to town for the day, she would ask my uncle Steven to take care of us.

He would watch out the window for my grandma to drive away and once she left, he would ask, "Okay kids, do you want a show?" We would all yell, "Yeah!" We didn't have bedroom doors, only drapes to allow heat from the wood stove to get to the other rooms on cold days—and Uncle Steven used them as stage curtains. We would hear the sound of the needle as it touched the record, then Diana Ross singing, "Stop in the Name of Love" as Steven's gloved hand reached through the curtain. His drag show began. At the end of the song, he would tell us all to dance, and the room was full of us native kids dancing around a big, tall drag queen, singing and laughing.

As early as third grade I had sexual encounters with other boys in boarding school, knowing it wasn't considered acceptable. After each of these encounters, I would ask God for forgiveness. I would tell Him that I wouldn't do it again—at least not for a couple of months. I knew I was gay, but I didn't tell anyone.

When I was 14, I ran away to Seattle to find my mother. She had just gotten a divorce and was having a problem with alcohol. For a while I was living on the street, and I got involved with the sex industry to be able to feed myself. One day, my sister-in law and I were standing in front of a restaurant looking in as people ate. A man asked if we were hungry. We told him we were. He told us to go into the restaurant and order anything we wanted. He would pay for it. He said he would be in the adjacent bar, and to tell the waiter to bring him the bill. We both ordered a hamburger, fries, and a drink, and after I took my second bite, the waiter brought the bill to us. I told him the man in the bar in the red shirt would pay for our food. He came back and told us there was no man in a red shirt. I went to the doorway and looked in—he wasn't there. I went back to the table and told my sister-in-law to eat fast, and I started shoving food in my mouth. The manager came over, took our plates, took our jackets, and pushed us outside.

It was winter and it was cold. We sat down outside and my sister-in-law started to cry, telling me that she was still hungry. I still had a lightweight jacket, so I gave it to her and went down the street to steal some food. She said it was sad that we had to live on the streets, and I remember telling her that one day we would look back at these times and laugh. And we have.

A lady named Edith Wildshoe took me in for a while. We went to the grocery store on one occasion, and when we got back in the car I pulled a candy bar out of my pocket. She asked me where I got it, and I told her, "I got it in the store." She said she knew I stole it, and that I was to never steal when I was with her. She told me that I was a naughty raven.

She explained that in her village, when the women would dry strips of meat or fish, the ravens swept down, stole the food, and flew off to eat it in the trees. When the women ran with sticks yelling at them, the little kids would run up to steal more meat and the women called them Tah Nah Lah (in the spoken language). That is how I got my name:

Raven. My mom's family name is Heavy Runner. I legally changed my name to Raven Heavy Runner.

When I first got to Seattle, I told others that I was bisexual even though I knew I was gay. My mom wasn't doing well—she sometimes lived on the street or in a shelter. For a whole year, eight of us lived in one room. My mother wanted me to go to school. I registered in a native school and got interested in native culture, especially dancing. Eventually mom found a more permanent place in the housing projects in West Seattle and I stayed there until I was eighteen.

Then I went back to Montana and lived with my grandmother. I was going to the University of Montana. I started going back to church and decided I was going to be a minister. My mom was also going to church to become a minister herself. I stopped identifying myself as gay, and for the next five years I attended church—and struggled constantly with my sexuality. I even dated women. I fasted and prayed that God would take away my feelings of being attracted to men.

At times, I just wanted to die. I would walk a lot by myself. When I would see a car, truck, or semi approaching, I would hope it would swerve off and kill me. It wouldn't be suicide—that was a sin. If it killed me accidentally, I could die in a state of grace. My struggle would be over, and I would go to Heaven.

I had become angry at God. Because I had prayed to Him, I felt hurt and betrayed. It took years for the anger toward the church to go away.

I didn't have enough money to finish college, so I went into the Army. After about nine months in the military, I stopped going to church. I started going to bars and met another guy in the military. We started dating. It seemed so wrong to me that the other guys in the service could talk about their girlfriends or wives, but I couldn't talk about my boyfriend.

My mother used to hang out in the gay community with my uncle and my older brother, who are both gay, until she went back to church.

It didn't bother me that she went back to the church—anything was better than her drinking. But soon we began to have problems.

I brought my first boyfriend to Thanksgiving dinner when I was 27. When she served dinner, she asked me if my "friend" wanted this or that, but she wouldn't talk to him directly. When I got home, I called and asked her why she acted that way. She told me she didn't know what I was talking about. She was dismissive to my friend. I didn't understand, because she was one of most loving people I knew. She had always been kind to the gay people in our lives, but not anymore.

I had friends who never told their parents about their sexuality and who didn't go home anymore. I didn't want that. I wanted my mother to be part of my life. I told her that if she treated my partner like that again, I would stop coming to visit. She started crying, saying things like "the Devil is taking my son," and that she wasn't going to give up on me. She said she was going to keep praying for me. Then, she hung up on me, and I felt bad because had I made her cry.

I called my older sister to explain what happened, and I asked her to call our mother. My sister called me back, saying Mom was fine and was sorry for acting like that. She had to learn to deal with it.

At that time, a lot of gay people were dying of AIDS. I had a good friend who hadn't told his parents that he was gay. When he was dying, his parents came to visit and they wouldn't allow his partner to say goodbye. I asked my sister to keep anything like that from happening to me or my partner.

Two weeks later, my partner and I went to my mother's for dinner again, and my mother treated him well. Since then, she has always treated anyone I brought home with love and respect.

I told my mother that I was no longer a Christian, and that I tried to live a good life. I believe that wherever I go will be a good place, and I hoped she would be there, too. We have a few cousins who are very religious and have told her that she should pray for her sons. They said we're going to Hell. She told them to never talk about her sons that way again—and those cousins stopped coming around.

By 1989, I got out of the service and decided to get into gay activism. I went back to school, and I took a class called Social Change Skills. At first, I thought the class was about learning how to behave in certain social situations, kind of a finishing school. But the teacher started talking about injustice and I wondered if I was in the right class. I looked in my syllabus—I was in the right room. I was too embarrassed to leave, so I listened to the professor and I liked what she had to say. We were each supposed to get involved in an organization for political or social change, and then come back to write a paper. I decided on Queer Nation, an organization that creates more visibility for homosexuals in our society. Queer Nation sponsored activities, like forty of us getting on a bus and pairing up—two guys or two girls—holding hands with each other. Sometimes we walked around downtown, took the ferry across the water, or went dancing at straight clubs. The people in the bars downtown freaked out when they saw us, because they thought they had accidentally ended up in a gay club.

One night when I was dancing with my 6-ft-5 boyfriend, the bouncer tried to make us quit dancing. He threatened to call the police, but first he called his manager. The manager told the bouncer that he was in Seattle, and if he didn't like men dancing together that he should go work at another bar. We were safe because we always stayed in a large group.

There were some gay bashings happening up in Seattle's Capitol Hill district, some of which put people in the hospital. We thought about calling the Guardian Angels—a volunteer organization of citizen crime patrollers—to protect us. Instead, we asked them to train us, so we could protect ourselves. They trained us not to beat people up but to hold aggressors down to the ground until the police got there.

I stayed in Queer Nation for about two years. We were up against skinheads and gang members. At first, the police didn't like us. They were afraid we would be a liability. But finally we got some credibility because we weren't hurting anyone, and there was a lot of violent stuff happening.

In 1993, I went to my first Native American two-spirit group. It was very informal then. These days we have presentations, sweat lodges, information sessions, even a talent show. Every year there is one national event, hosted in a different area each time. We plan two years ahead because it takes that long to raise funds.

I started going to Haskell Indian Nations University in Lawrence, Kansas, in 1995. I wrote an article in the school newspaper on two-spirit people in the post-colonial world and what it means to be two-spirit today. Some of the students and faculty—who were almost all native—didn't like it. They didn't know anything about the history of two-spirit people. I tried to start a two-spirit group at the school but it didn't go over well. Gay students were afraid to go to meetings because they might be seen and get beat up. I felt that when these people stayed in the closet, it was worse for everyone else, but I couldn't force them if they weren't ready. People need to come out when they are ready.

If I had lived hundreds of years ago, being gay or two-spirit would have been accepted in my tribe. There is a documented history of people in our villages who were two-spirit. Our people didn't look at genders in a physical way, since sexual preference was considered a gender by itself. There were more women than men in our tribe, and the men would have more than one wife. The chiefs loved to have one of their wives be a two-spirit since they were very strong and could do a lot of physical labor. When women would be "on their moon" (menstruating), they had to go away from the camp, leaving work undone. When several women live together they usually cycle together—but the two-spirit wife didn't and therefore could stay and do the chores. The dowry was quite high for a two-spirit wife.

Two-spirit is difficult to translate into other languages. It encapsulates gender fluidity, sexuality, and spirituality into one being. Traditionally, it may have pertained just to transgenders and not gays or lesbians, but culture is fluid and not static. It evolves. A two-spirit person is one who is both indigenous to the Americas and lesbian, gay, bisexual, or transgender.

In our history, whether people were called two-spirits or not, they were accepted. Each person had their role. All roles were important, and sexuality wasn't considered sinful. Today, we concentrate too much on sexuality and not the roles we play or other parts of who we are.

Through the years there have been many marches on Washington, D.C., and in 1987, the LGBTQ community had their turn. At that time, a national LGBTQ Native American group didn't exist. But—as happens with many large gatherings where people of color come together—the Native Americans in attendance came together as a critical mass. This newly founded group of indigenous LGBTQ people made plans to have a national gathering. In 1988, they gathered for the first time in Minneapolis.

For the next couple years, they batted around a name for this new group. In Ojibway country, they called our kind of people niizh manidoowag, which is best translated into English as "two spirits." We have the spirit of both a male and female. It is readily visible—a person may look like a man but express female energy, or vice versa.

During the early 1990s we were really pushing this term. We wanted to empower ourselves. We were having difficulties with the American Anthropological Society using the term berdache, a Portuguese word meaning, roughly, a captive boy or girl kept for sex. That isn't who we are, and it's not the role we play. We petitioned the AAS to stop using the word. If they didn't want to use two-spirit, they could use words from each tribe to describe our roles. The Lakota people call their two-spirited people *winkte*, the person who talks to the above people for those of us down here. The name *nadlé* was used by the Navajo people—it came from a myth in which the men and women were fighting and went to live on separate sides of the river. The *nadlé* knew they had to get back together to survive so they negotiated between the men and the women to get them back together on the same side of the river.

The people in our organization took the term "two-spirit" back to the reservations. They asked their elders if they identified them as a two-spirit, and what a two-spirit's role was. The term didn't translate well into all of their languages. Thus, not all people in our organization describe themselves two-spirit people—they use the name given by their tribe. In any case, our organization is very inclusive and we welcome all LGBTQ Native Americans.

I have read some research done by two-spirited people and by non-Native American LGBTQ academics. They found a lot of information in historical records, mostly in the Library of Congress, which were packed away and forgotten—including notes from anthropologists, ethnographers, and priests who came through and visited many tribes between the seventeenth and nineteenth centuries. Though priests documented their travels, if they thought whatever they were documenting was immoral, they would leave it out. A lot of tribes that had social roles for two-spirit people were not written about. These people were given roles within the tribe—institutionalized roles like teachers, healers, historians, and treaty negotiators. Two-spirit people were often well regarded and honored. We are still discovering the names and roles given to the two-spirit people in many tribes.

A lot of cultures worldwide had similar understandings. Even though a lot of people now say it's a new phenomenon, it has been a part of all sorts of different cultures, even in early Europe before the advent of Christianity.

When the Conquistadors came in the sixteenth century to what is now Mexico, they asked to meet the two-spirit people in native villages. The tribes thought the Spanish conquerors wanted to honor the two-spirits, but Captain Vasco Nunez de Balboa set his dogs on them and killed them. The Conquistadors felt homosexuality was an abomination—they were doing the work of God. The Conquistadors documented these slaughters as the killing of sodomites. But they also knew that two-spirit people were given civic responsibilities and influential roles in their tribes, and that they were killing some of the more powerful indigenous people. When the tribes caught on to this practice, they started hiding their two-spirit people to protect them.

The spiritual part of being a man, a woman, or a two-spirit person in a tribe meant fasting and praying to the spirit helper that would guide them in their role. Men, women and two-spirit people each had certain spiritual powers. Two-spirit people in my tribe, the Blackfeet people, were called *Ah Who Wah Ki*, which translates as "those who cross over."

When white people first landed at Plymouth Rock, treaties were established with native people. The first were treaties of peace. As more of them came, there were treaties of commerce. Then began the treaties that took our land. With the growing population of settlers and the shrinking population of natives due to disease and the Indian wars, the natives were placed on reservations. After the Civil War, old forts were turned into boarding schools where Indian children were sent when they were five or six years old. They didn't return home until they were teenagers. The Indians felt it would be very positive for the children to learn to read and write. They thought their children would be able to help their people understand the treaties and negotiate better terms. No one was aware of the devastation the boarding schools would have.

The native social roles and responsibilities the tribes had — for young women, young men, and two-spirit people—were wiped out. Their rites of passage were taken away. All the domains of who these children were and who they were to become in their tribe were gone. They were taught that their traditional cultures were evil and two-spirit roles abhorrent. The children were taught they had to be Christians or they would burn in Hell forever.

Finally, the natives were placed on limited land with little space to hunt. They were forced to rely on the U.S. Government for their food. If parents didn't send their children to these schools, they were cut off from their food supply. They would have to either watch their children starve or run into the hills with their children to escape.

Native Americans turned to their ceremonies in trying times like these, but their ceremonies were outlawed. Whites were afraid they would lead to war. Ceremonies such as sun dances, ghost dances, pipe dances, sweats, potlatches, and those honoring two-spirits could come with severe punishments, including imprisonment. And when the children came back from boarding schools, they believed their own people were bad and unclean. In reality, many Native American ceremonies were outlawed until the American Indian Religious Freedom Act was passed in 1978.

My grandmother grew up on a reservation and went away to a boarding school. When she came back, she didn't know that her father had passed away while she was at school. My mother grew up on a reservation and went to boarding school. So did I and my siblings. There are still boarding schools—there is one outside of Salem, Oregon—but since 1978 the children are no longer forced to become Christian.

I have rediscovered my faith in native spirituality. My native religion is much like Christianity—we believe an entity created all things and we pray to our Creator, but we don't believe in Hell. If some people have something that they need to finish, there is reincarnation. Some tribes believe these people wait on the other side for a being coming into life—and as soon as it happens, they drop down into that being. Sometimes, though, they aren't patient and they drop into the opposite gender. They believe this is how two-spirit people come to be.

A lot of my native friends need our traditional knowledge and our history to be able to find their place in society. Our belief is that two-spirit people have a lot of power, and if they don't use their power in the right way, they will implode. They could self-destruct—using drugs, alcohol, or other destructive things. That's why I do a lot of talks in the native community, especially to those who are just coming out and just learning who they are as a two-spirit person.

I believe there is a part of our belief system that can be applied to everyone. Everyone has their rightful place. The Creator made all of us. We all belong. If an LGBTQ person is struggling with who they are, they should remember that they have gifts that we all need from them. They are important people. If they can feel that within themselves and know who they are, they can begin to understand that they are important to their families and to society. A two-spirit elder told me that all of our cultures have this within their histories prior to Christianity, and all of them said it is okay to be a two-spirit person.

I have a lot of relatives who are Christian, and I think a lot of parts of Christianity are good, but I am not a Christian myself. A long time ago, one of my relatives told me he felt badly for his preacher friend who felt there was only one way. His friend had been on that one path for so long that he didn't see any others. My relative was 100 years old at the time and had walked through the forest on many different paths. He knew there were many paths to the same place.

Toxic Faith
Pauline – Prairie Woman, 73
Seattle, Washington
April 2011

I have eight children. I am from the Blackfeet tribe of Montana. When my mother was pregnant with me, and when I was born, she lived on the prairie. My legal name is Pauline, but the name my mother gave me was Prairie Woman.

When my son, Raven, was growing up, I could tell that he was more feminine but I didn't think much more of it. I didn't notice it as much as in my other son, Hiram, who is four years older. As a born-again Christian, we don't condone a gay lifestyle. However, as a mother, I accept my boys. At first, we had some battles—especially with Hiram. He never told me he was gay, but I just knew it. I didn't have to be told.

I remember the first time I saw Hiram in drag. He was doing a show for a fundraiser put on every year by a local organization. Hiram's daughter came to the show, and she asked if it was all right for her dad to come say hello to me. I thought that it was strange that Hiram would ask permission to say hello to me, but soon he came walking around the corner in a beautiful dress. I was shocked, but it didn't bother me. I already knew that he was gay, but I had ever seen him in drag. When he got up to perform, I cried because he was so good.

When I recommitted my life to God, a battle inside me began. I did finally come to terms with my sons being gay, because I love my children unconditionally. I love who they are. I could never turn my back on them.

I think it was easier for me to accept because I have a brother, Steven, who is gay. My mother was also a Christian, and I don't remember her once having a battle with my brother over it. He would bring his partner to the house, and she would treat him just like he was her son. She never passed judgment on them in any way. I learned a lot from her. Steven is now in his 50s and whenever my boys go back to Montana, they always stay with him.

Now, I'm surrounded by a lot of gay people, and when they come here they never feel uncomfortable around me. Hiram has a friend, Bruce—he is so sweet and open, and I miss him when he doesn't come to see me. I feel the same way about Raven's partner. He came over a couple weeks ago and did some work on my computer for me. I told him that I had missed him. I couldn't see myself saying that to him before—when I first recommitted my life to God, I was so religious that I had toxic faith.

I was working at the church in the counseling department and we had this book on toxic faith—it was about judgmental religion. When I first became a Christian, women weren't allowed to wear makeup or jewelry and had to wear long dresses. That is toxic faith—being judgmental.

A lot of churches, even the church that I became ordained in, are against the gay lifestyle. My minister made a comment that, "God didn't make Adam and Steve, he made Adam and Eve," and after that Hiram quit going. For a while, both Hiram and Raven were trying to live a straight life. Raven gave me his journal to read, and I read where he had fought against his feelings. Sometimes I feel sad about that, but I know we serve a loving God who loves us unconditionally. That's where I find my comfort.

In 1990, I was very active in the church. I had a ministry in Chinatown, and I ministered in the King County Jail for five years and in the women's prison. I became the director of a transitional home and worked with girls on the street. I helped them get into school, if that's what they wanted, or to find jobs or their own apartment. During that time, I didn't really think about the fact that my sons were gay—I didn't condone it, but at the same time I accepted them.

Later, I was working on the reservation helping my brother at his church. A young gay man called my boss. He wanted to know who to talk to about telling his wife that he was gay, and my boss suggested that he talk to me. I wondered how he had kept it from his wife for so long, because even I could tell he was gay. I think she didn't know because she looked at him through different eyes. I told him to be truthful with her, and to tell her he loved her and needed her support in order to come out. I found out later that she felt deceived. It was hard, but they got divorced and he came out.

In the 1980s I was heavy into alcohol. I was addicted and homeless. I was even on heroin. My husband divorced me for a younger woman. I was so heartbroken that I left the reservation and moved to Seattle with my sister. By this time, my children were scattered all over the northwest, but they all hitchhiked to Seattle to be with me. There wasn't a place for all of us, so we ended up on the street. Sometime later, I finally got into public housing. I recommitted my life to God and got off alcohol and drugs. With Raven's encouragement, I went back to school and got my associates degree, and my two sons have gone to college.

My sons have taught me a lot. They aren't ashamed of who they are, and they don't try to hide things from me. They are both very open, and that helps me examine myself. It gave them the freedom to talk me about their lives and their significant others. They talk openly with me about the different things they do in the gay community—especially the two-spirit community—and I am very proud of them. I think my boys have helped me become a better Christian.

The funeral and miracles—Momma Traci

Last December, Daniel and I attended a funeral for the father of Daniel's high school friends, Anthony and Marisa. Daniel and I were ushered to the family section, with Daniel seated in the front row to take pictures of the service. I slipped into a pew behind him and was surprised to sit down next to Thomas. It was like finding a long-lost son.

So much had happened since the day Daniel asked me to help Anthony's parents through the ordeal of his coming out. Anthony's mom had been shocked but accepting, while his father had struggled with his religious beliefs. Then Marisa came out, and she and her father stopped speaking. He became sick. A darkness grew inside of him, and he and Rita split up. He moved in with his best friend, John, and was later diagnosed with cancer.

But then he began to change. He started to go to an all-accepting church. Marisa told me the cancer made her dad realize who was really important to him. He reconciled with his wife. Near the end, he asked for his children and their partners to be by his side.

As the funerary procession began, the minister was followed down the aisle by John, then Rita with her youngest daughter. Anthony walked alongside his partner, and Marisa with hers. I looked at Thomas, our eyes filled with tears at this miracle.

After the funeral, Thomas told me he was going forward with his dreams of acting and that he was involved in suicide prevention. He seemed to glow with self-confidence—the same boy we had feared would take his own life. Thomas's parents had apologized to him and had accepted him. It has been a long and difficult process, but his parents' hearts opened. Even though it was against their faith, they chose to accept their son because they realized they weren't a family without him. People can change and choose love.

The Rainbow — Momma Traci

This book has been an incredible journey. I have connected with so many wonderful people who shared their innermost stories.

Non-acceptance and guilt have caused too many gentle souls to deny themselves happiness and fulfillment. I've been forced to reflect on how I have judged others unfairly without walking in their shoes, and how my judgment has inflicted pain and guilt. Instead of really listening, it was easier to focus so intently on expressing my own opinion—an opinion I realize now was often tainted by my upbringing and unfounded fears.

I have had the honor of hearing many stories and of being the conduit for some to express their unspoken words. The journey to healing continues. After a rainstorm, the sun appears and paints a rainbow across the sky. My own journey through this book project has led me to appreciate each beautiful shade of color, and a feeling of hope washes over me. My wish is that this book does the same for you, the reader.

Thank you for journeying with me.

Momma Traci / Traci Leigh Taylor

Acknowledgements

This book would have never been written without the help and encouragement of all the people in my life, to whom I give my heartfelt thanks:

Daniel, who inspired me and gave me the push to get started.

My husband, Steve, for his love and patience always, but especially during the four years that my life was consumed by this book.

My daughter, Amanda, for her love and support.

Byron Beck, for telling me I had talent and needed to go forward. His Queer Window column about Daniel and me and about his coming to Portland with the first national tour of Oklahoma! ("Rose City Mama." Willamette Week 18 February 2004) and Byron's later coffee meeting with me gave me the courage I needed.

Dan DeWeese, my writing teacher at Portland Community College, who taught me how to write short stories by listening to the music of The Rolling Stones.

Pat Bingham, for his friendship and for the tedious job of editing these interviews after they were first transcribed.

Chelsea Bieker, for her editing, for our many meetings over coffee, and for helping me to understand the significance of these stories to my life.

Pamela Cowan, Tonya Macalino, Maggie Lynch and all my other friends at the Northwest Independent Writers Association (NIWA), for their encouragement and help along this unknown and scary path of publishing a book.

Michael Leleux, for his friendship, understanding of the message of my book, and designing the perfect book cover.

Jennifer Willis, for her final editing that helped my book become what I always wanted it to be.

And most of all, the wonderful people I have met along the way who have poured out their souls to me with the hope that this book will help to open hearts and minds.

RESOURCE LIST

<u>Books</u>

Bagemihl, Bruce.*Biological Exuberance: Animal Homosexuality and Natural Diversity*. New York: St. Martin's Press, 1999.

Chapman, Patrick M. *Thou Shall Not Love: What the Evangelicals Really Say to Gays*. New York; Haiduk Press, 1994.
Chellew-Hodge, Candace. *Bulletproof Faith: A Spiritual Survival Guide for Gay and Lesbian Christians*. San Francisco: Jossey-Bass, 2008.

Cole, Walter and Sharon Knorr. *Just Call Me Darcelle: A Memoir*. Portland: Independent Publishing, 2010.

Countryman,William L. *Dirt, Greed and Sex: Sexual Ethics in the New Testament and their Implications for Today*. Philadelphia: Fortress Press, 1988.

DeGeneres, Betty. *Love, Ellen: A Mother/Daughter Journey*. New York: It Books, 2000.

Dew, Robb Forman. *The Family Heart: A Memoir of When Our Son Came Out*. New York: Ballantine Books; Reprint, 1995.

Fairchild, Betty and Nancy Hayward. *Now That You Know: A Parent's Guide to Understanding Their Gay and Lesbian Children*. San Diego: Harcourt Brace International; 3rd Revised edition, 1998.

Glaser, Chris. *Uncommon Calling: A Gay Christian's Struggle to Serve the Church*. Louisville: Westminster John Knox Press, 1988.

Greenberg, Steven. *Wrestling With God & Man: Homosexuality in the Jewish Tradition*. Madison: University of Wisconsin Press, 2004.

Gross, Robert E., Mona West, ed. *Take Back the Word: A Queer Reading of the Bible*. Cleveland: The Pilgrim Press, 2000.

Helminiak, Daniel A. *What the Bible Really Says About Homosexuality*. San Francisco: Alamo Square Press, 1994.

Michaelson, Jay. *God vs. Gay? The Religious Case for Equality.* Boston: Beacon Press, 2011.

Miner, Jeff, and John Tyler Connoley. *The Children Are Free: Reexamining the Biblical Evidence on Same-sex Relationships.* Indianapolis: Jesus Metropolitan Community Church, 2002.

Plant, Richard. *The Pink Triangle: The Nazi war against Homosexuals.* New York: Holt Paperbacks; New edition, 1988.

Rodgers, Jack. *Jesus,The Bible and Homosexuality: Explode the Myths, Heal the Church.* Louisville: Westminster/John Knox Press, 2006.

Roscoe, Will, ed. *Living the Spirit: A Gay American Indian Anthology.* New York: Macmillan, 1988.

Shepard, Judy. *The meaning of Matthew: My son's murder in Laramie and a world Transformed.* New York: Plume, 2009.

Trachtenberg, Robert. *When I Knew.* New York: It Books; First edition, 2005.

Wilson, Nancy L. *Our Tribe: Queer Folks, God, Jesus and the Bible.* New York: HarperCollins, 1995.

Weekley, David. *In from the Wilderness,* Eugene: Whif and Stock Publishers, 2011.

On the Internet

AFC (The Ali Forney Center) a safe place for homeless LGBTQ youth in New York, *www.aliforneycenter.org*
Cascades Aids project. To prevent HIV infections, support and empower people affected and infected by HIV/AIDS, and eliminate HIV/AIDS-related stigma. http://cascadeaids.org/

FIERCE. A membership-based organization building the leadership and power of lesbian, gay, bisexual, transgender, and queer (LGBTQ) youth of color in New York City. http://www.fiercenyc.org

GLSEN (Gay, Lesbian & Straight Education Network). Organization for students, parents, and teachers that tries to affect positive change in schools. http://www.glsen.org/ *www.glsen.org*

Green Chimneys Organization. Providing residential, educational, clinical and recreational services that create and nurture connections to the community and the natural world. http://www.greenchimneys.org/

Love Yourself Project. To help you grow as a warm and welcoming human being. https://jaylesworthloveyours.wix.com/loveyourself

NSSR (The National Safe Schools Roundtable). A coalition of people and organizations from across the United States who are substantively involved, on a professional and/or volunteer basis, in making schools safe and welcoming for lesbian, gay, bisexual, transgender and queer (LGBTQ) youth. http://www.safeschoolsroundtable.org/

NWGA (Northwest Gender Alliance). A non-profit social, support and educational group, based in Portland,Oregon for trans individuals, historically for those who identify themselves as transgender (TG), transsexual (TS) or as crossdressers (CD). http://nwgenderalliance.org/

OGALLA (The LGBT Bar Association of Oregon). Promoting the fair and just treatment of all people under the law regardless of sexual orientation or gender identity. http://www.ogalla.org/

OSSCC (Oregon Safe Schools & Communities Coalition). Their belief is all youth deserve to feel safe and welcome in our schools and communities http://www.oregonsafeschools.org/

SSCP (Safe Schools and Training Institute Program). Providing an innovative framework to help schools realize the necessary steps needed to make their school a safer place. http://www.safeschoolcertification.org/

SMYRC (Sexual & Gender Minority Youth Resource Center). Creating safety and support for LGBTQQ youth in Oregon. http://www.pdxqcenter.org/programs/youth-programs/smyrc/

Tri-Ess (The Society for the Second Self). An international social support group for heterosexual crossdressers, their partners, the spouses of married crossdressers and their families. http://www.tri-ess.org/

TYFA (TransYouth Family Allies). Empowering children and families by partnering with educators, service providers and communities, to develop supportive environments in which gender may be expressed and respected. (http://www.imatyfa.org/)

The Trevor Project .Crisis intervention and suicide prevention services to lesbian, gay, bisexual, transgender and questioning (LGBTQ) young people ages 13-24. (http://www.thetrevorproject.org/)

TLPI (Transgender Law and Policy Institute). A non-profit organization dedicated
to engaging in effective advocacy for transgender people.(http://www.transgenderlaw.org/)

Write Around Portland. Changing lives through the power of writing. (http://www.writearound.org/index.html)

Films

Bent. Dir. Sean Mathias. DVD, MGM, 2003.

Birdcage. Dir. Mike Nichols. DVD, Fox Searchlight, 1997.

The Big Gay Musical. Dir. Casper Andreas and Fred M. Caruso. DVD, Bounty Films, 2010.

Fish Out of Water. Dir. Ky Dickens. DVD, First Run Features, 2010.

For The Bible Tells Me So. Dir. Daniel G. Karslake, DVD, First Run Features, 2008.
The Laramie Project. Dir. Moisés Kaufman. DVD, HBO, 2002.

The Matthew Shepard Story. Dir. Roger Spottiswoode. DVD, Echo Bridge Home Entertainment, 2010.

Prayers for Bobby. Dir. <u>A&E Television Networks</u>, DVD, A&E Home Video, 2013.

The Torch Song Trilogy. Dir.Paul Bogart. DVD, Warner Home Video, 2004.

Queen of Hearts: Community Therapist in Drag. Dir. Jan Haaken.DVD, Cinema Libra, 2008.

ABOUT THE AUTHOR

Traci Taylor lives in her home state of Oregon. She has four grown children and seven grandchildren, and she lives in the country with her husband, two dogs, and a cat. When she's not indulging her interests in gardening and photography, she enjoys feeding the wide range of birds that visit her home.

When her son, Daniel, came out in 1996 at the age of 15, Traci was thrust into a whole new world that she wanted to understand. Daniel was touring with his movie, *The Big Gay Musical,* when he announced in front of a Washington, D.C., audience that not only did his mom not mind that he was in a gay movie, she was writing an LGBTQ book.

Find Traci online at http://www.MommaTraci.com